EUROPEAN LOCAL-COLOR LITERATURE

D1281837

WORKS BY JOSEPHINE DONOVAN

Women and the Rise of the Novel, 1405–1726

Feminist Theory: The Intellectual Traditions

*After the Fall: The Demeter-Persephone Myth
in Wharton, Cather, and Glasgow*

New England Local Color Literature: A Women's Tradition

Sarah Orne Jewett

Uncle Tom's Cabin: Evil, Affliction, and Redemptive Love

*Gnosticism in Modern Literature: A Study of Selected
Works of Camus, Sartre, Hesse, and Kafka*

WORKS EDITED

*The Feminist Care Tradition in Animal Ethics:
A Reader* (Co-edited with Carol J. Adams)

*P. O. W. in the Pacific: Memoirs of an American
Doctor in World War II* by William N. Donovan

*Beyond Animal Rights: A Feminist Caring Ethic for the
Treatment of Animals* (Co-edited with Carol J. Adams)

*Animals and Women: Feminist Theoretical
Explorations* (Co-edited with Carol J. Adams)

Feminist Literary Criticism: Explorations in Theory

EUROPEAN LOCAL-COLOR LITERATURE

National Tales, Dorfgeschichten, Romans Champêtres

JOSEPHINE DONOVAN

continuum

The Continuum International Publishing Group Inc.
80 Maiden Lane, New York, NY 10038

The Continuum International Publishing Group Ltd
The Tower Building, 11 York Road, London SE1 7NX

www.continuumbooks.com

Library of Congress Cataloging-in-Publication Data
A catalog record for this book is available from the Library of Congress.

ISBN: 978-0-8264-2946-9 (hardback)
       978-1-4411-1900-1 (paperback)

Typeset by Pindar NZ, Auckland, New Zealand
Printed in the United States of America by Thomson-Shore, Inc.

Contents

Preface

This book has been a long time in the making. I first became interested in local-color literature over thirty years ago, when I began work that resulted in my books *Sarah Orne Jewett* (1980, rev. ed. 2001) and *New England Local Color Literature: A Women's Tradition* (1983), and various articles. At the time local color was considered a minor, fringe (and inferior) tradition, but since then scholars and critics have come to realize that it not only deserves a central place in the history of the cultural process of defining America but also that it produced numerous works of enduring value, masterpieces indeed.

While the focus up to now has been exclusively on the American tradition, this book will show that the local-color movement should be more broadly conceived and that the American school was but one branch of the stream.

When I first conceived of doing this book, I wondered whether the dialects used in the literature would prove to be so arcane and obscure as to prohibit the project. As it turned out, however, I soon realized that writers early understood that to reach a general literate audience they had to write in the standard language of their country and not in their regional dialect or *patois*, which would have been incomprehensible to the mainstream reader (and to me). Happily for me, and for the success of this project, then, these writers only used dialect sparingly or indicated it by modifying the standard language to reflect the regional accent, and they explained unfamiliar dialect terms in notes or parenthetically. Local-color literature thus is written in standard English, French, German, etc. This study therefore in its focus on the local-color genre excludes literatures written entirely in dialect or repressed languages, such as Irish, Gaelic, Breton, Occitan, Provençal, Basque, Friulian, Catalan, Yiddish, etc. A study of those literatures would be a very different book and one very difficult to accomplish, as it would require a reader conversant in many arcane ethnic languages.

The book traces the origins and early development of the local-color tradition, following a chain of influence from country to country. It focuses on the forgers of the tradition in each country or region — those who created and established the model that others followed. It does not dwell extensively on the genre's development after it was established, because, once the format was set, it changed little in succeeding renditions. The time frame for the emergence and early development of the European local-color tradition was roughly the first half of the nineteenth century. But the genre continued to flourish through the 1800s— its heyday in the United States was the latter third of the century. And, indeed, by 1900, there were literally hundreds of examples of the genre in all of the major Western countries.

My training in comparative literature at the University of Wisconsin-Madison under the tutelage of Fannie J. LeMoine, who directed my dissertation *Gnosticism in Modern Literature*, and, later, Robert O. Evans, prepared me for this undertaking. I will always be grateful for their early encouragement of my work.

I would also like to thank the staffs of the Interlibrary Loan departments at the Portsmouth Public Library, the University of Maine, and the University of New Hampshire for their Herculean efforts in tracking down obscure out-of-print titles, of which, in some cases, only one or two copies remain in existence. Thanks also to my editors at Continuum, especially Evander Lomke and Haaris Naqvi.

Unless otherwise indicated, all of the translations in this book are mine.

Portsmouth, New Hampshire
September 2009

Introduction

Local-color literature emerged in the early 1800s in Europe and flourished there and in the United States until the latter nineteenth century. It is characterized by a realistic focus upon a particular geographical locale, its native customs, its physical and cultural environment, and its regional dialect. The American tradition has received serious and sustained scholarly attention, especially in recent years, but the European tradition has attracted relatively little; to my knowledge no comprehensive comparative studies of the movement exist. In fact, the European tradition has yet to be clearly identified and analyzed as such. While a few studies exist of the provincial traditions in individual countries — such as Jürgen Hein, *Dorfgeschichte* (1976); Uwe Baur, *Dorfgeschichte: Zur Enstehen und gesellschaftlichen Funktion einer literarischen Gattung im Vormärz* (1978); Norbert Mecklenburg, *Erzählte Provinz: Regionalismus und Moderne im Roman* (1982); Paul Vernois, *Le Roman rustique de George Sand à Ramuz* (1962); or K. D. M. Snell, ed., *The Regional Novel in Britain and Ireland, 1800–1900* (1998) — there is only one major study of the movement as a whole: Rudolf Zellweger, *Les Débuts du roman rustique: Suisse-Allemagne-France, 1836–1856* (1941). The latter is very valuable, but it is obviously dated and doesn't include Irish and Scottish works. In addition, in Germany the genre has been neglected by critics because of its unfair association with Nazi *heimat* literature — an issue I explore in Chapters One and Four. As a comprehensive study of the development of the European local-color movement, this book will thus, I hope, fill a significant gap in the literary history of Western literature.

Some may be surprised at my expansive use of the term *local-color*. It is true the term is often used disparagingly — "mere local color" — to suggest lightweight, superficial use of local materials; however, I am hoping to expand its connotation to include the idea of validating local knowledges seen in counterposition to the abstract knowledges of modernity. The term *local* is therefore key and is why I choose to use "local color" instead of "regional" or "provincial" to designate the literary movement covered in this book. I thus subsume under the umbrella *local-color literature* the various terms used to designate regional literatures at the time: the "national tale" in Ireland and Scotland; the *Dorfgeschichte* (village tale) in German-speaking regions; *romans champêtres* (rural novels) in France.

Though still considered minor by critics,[1] local-color literature was a major literary movement in the nineteenth-century Western world, finding expression in Ireland, then migrating to Scotland; from there to Germany, Switzerland, various provinces of the Austro-Hungarian Empire, France, and the United States. Eventually, nearly every Western country, including Spain, Italy, Russia, Norway, Sweden, Canada, and several in Latin America participated.

This book focuses on the origins and early development of the movement, covering the Irish (national tale), Scottish, German (*Dorfgeschichte*), and French (*roman champêtre*) traditions in detail, with a chapter devoted to each. Chapter One lays out the theoretical lines pursued in the work; in particular, the construction of local-color literature as a reaction against the impositions of modernity upon the regions by the dominant metropolitan centers in the respective jurisdictions (London, Paris, Vienna, Boston-New York). This cultural colonization was resisted so as to preserve locally eccentric traditions and dialects in the face of metropolitan pressure to conform to imposed standards.

Among the major authors discussed are Maria Edgeworth (Irish); Sir Walter Scott (Scottish); Berthold Auerbach (German); Jeremias Gotthelf (Swiss); Alexandre Weill (Alsatian); Annette von Droste-Hülshoff (German); George Sand (French); and Sarah Orne Jewett (American). Other less well-known writers, such as Lady Morgan and William Carleton in Ireland; Elizabeth Hamilton, Mary Brunton, John Galt, and James Hogg in Scotland; Josef Rank, Adalbert Stifter, Leopold Kompert, and Karl Emil Franzos in Austria–Hungary; the realists of the Courbet circle, Ferdinand Fabre, Léon Cladel, Erckmann-Chatrian and Daniel Stauben in France are also treated in some detail. An Epilogue briefly details the expansion of the movement to other countries, including some notes on the European influence on the American local-colorists, an influence that has not been appreciated by Americanists or indeed studied at all.

The methodology employed in this work derives from the genealogical hermeneutic articulated by French theorist Michael Foucault. In the first of his lectures in *Power/Knowledge*, Foucault advocates searching for "subjugated knowledges" (80). "[I]t is through the re-appearance of . . . these local popular knowledges, these disqualified knowledges, that criticism performs its work" (82). The knowledge Foucault has in mind is "a particular, local, regional knowledge, a differential knowledge incapable of unanimity" (82); it is a "minor" knowledge (85). The critic's job, he suggests, is to "emancipate historical knowledges from [their] subjection" within "the hierarchical order of power associated with science" and to render these silenced knowledges "capable of opposition and of struggle against the coercion of a theoretical, unitary, formal and scientific discourse" (85). The location of "resistant practices," alternatives to "totalizing" disciplines, is thus a vital task for the literary historian (Dreyfus and Rabinow 202).

Local-color literature, I argue, harbors just such "subjugated knowledges." As an example of my approach I take the American local-color story "Miss Lucinda" (1861) by Rose Terry Cooke.[2] In this story I intervene in the work — going "beneath" the perspective of the author — to resurrect the silenced knowledge and perspective of the character. For Lucinda, like many of the characters in local-color literature, evinces a marginal, local, alternative knowledge that is cast in opposition to unifying translocal disciplines.

In "Miss Lucinda" the disciplinary process is effected by a French dancing master, Monsieur Jean Leclerc, whose name, "the clerk," suggests the bureaucratic functionary whose chief historical mission has been to impose rationalizing disciplines upon the regional populace. Leclerc enters Lucinda's world when he helps her recapture a pig who had gotten loose. Lucinda's relationship with her animals, Leclerc feels, is too undisciplined, a view the author shares. Indeed, her animals lived in her house on equal terms with her: "her cat had its own chair . . . her dog, a rug and basket" and her blind crow, a "special nest of flannel and cotton" (156). Lucinda does not believe in imposing a hierarchical disciplinary grid upon her creatures. She feels "that animals have feelings . . . and are of 'like passions'" with people and that they have souls (162–3). The author feels that Lucinda's undisciplinary practice is out of line (162–4).

Once Leclerc is installed in Lucinda's house (he had injured himself during the pig chase and is being nursed back to health by her), he begins disciplining her animals. He commences by "subduing" her German spaniel, Fun; the narrator cites (apparently nonironically) a legitimizing proverb: "'Women and spaniels,' the world knows, 'like kicking'" (168). Leclerc then takes on Lucinda's other dog, Toby. "[A] few well-timed slaps, administered with vigor, cured Toby of his worst tricks: though every blow made Miss Lucinda wince, and almost shook her good opinion of Monsieur Leclerc" (169). Leclerc also disposes of her pet pig when he becomes too unmanageable.

The taming process is not only applied to the animals but also to Lucinda herself. A crucial episode in the story concerns Lucinda's dancing lessons. Dancing here represents an alien discipline to which the rural woman tries awkwardly to conform. The other students laugh at the odd outfits she wears to the lessons, signifying her nonconformity; her "peculiar" practice of the steps is a further sign of her deviance (176). During this period her animals are neglected.

The denouement of the story is that she and Leclerc marry, and the final note is one of ridicule against Lucinda for her "sentimental" views of animals. In particular, Lucinda's willful ignorance of the fate of her pig, whom Leclerc had had slaughtered and sold as ham, is rightly seen as morally corrupt, but the author herself does not allow Lucinda to develop an alternative solution to the pig's rambunctiousness, which she might have done had she not been under the influence of Leclerc and his exchange-value ethic. In short, the story is about the erosion and elision of Lucinda's relationship/use-value ethic and its replacement through the imposition of an alien discipline, metonymically represented by the dancing; it is about the colonization of her and her world.

Lucinda's subdual reflects the fact that homogenizing institutions were gaining hegemony in the nineteenth-century Western world. Leclerc's French origin inadvertently highlights that the normalizing disciplines that were encroaching upon rural eccentricity by mid century were rooted in Cartesian Enlightenment rationalism. Much of Foucault's work was devoted to describing the process of this encroachment.

In *Discipline and Punish* Foucault identifies the prison as the model disciplinary grid to which other modern institutions such as hospitals, asylums, etc. conform. In the first volume of his *History of Sexuality*, he focuses upon the emergence of pseudoscientific disciplines such as sexology, which "entomologized" (*Histoire* 60) sexual life-styles into species and subspecies of deviance, thus ideologically colonizing people's life-world.

All these developments were part of what Edmund Husserl called the "mathematization" of the world effected by the imposition of the Cartesian/Newtonian paradigm, that material reality operates as a machine. Decades before Foucault, Marxist Frankfurt School theorists Max Horkheimer and Theodor Adorno saw the rationalizing process as a form of dominance. Transforming the world of nature "into mere objectivity," the Cartesian paradigm effects "the extirpation of animism" (5). Its practices, as seen in the scientific method, are dictatorial and manipulative (9). It requires the "subdual of difference, particularities" (22). In the impartiality of scientific knowledge, "that which is powerless has wholly lost any means of expression" (23).

Horkheimer and Adorno see the confrontation between the witch Circe and Odysseus in Homer's epic allegorically as a representation of this process. Circe turns Odysseus' men into pigs; the pig was a sacred animal to Demeter, which connects Circe to this ancient cult (71). "Miss Lucinda" may be seen as a reversal of this ancient story; it is not the Greek goddess who is triumphant in this story with her "insurrectionary" holistic knowledges but rather the representative of modern mathematizing, unitary discourse, the French dancing master.

The literature of the nineteenth-century local-color school records in one of its principal themes the clash between dominant, colonizing, mathematizing disciplines of modernity and the rural, eccentric culture Foucault saw as having counterhegemonic potential. Scores of stories and novels concern marginal communities peopled by deviant premoderns who live an "undisciplined" life-style. At times the authors seem to ally with the forces of "progress," as Cooke does in "Miss Lucinda," joining in the colonization of their characters. Much more often the authors are sympathetic to the characters whose lives were being erased by the encroaching powers. It is their world — their subjugated knowledges — that come to life in the literature of local color.

NOTES

1 See Renza and further discussion in Chapter One.
2 A fuller discussion appears in my article, "Breaking the Sentence."

resistance to the colonizing forces of capitalist modernity, identified with the middle and upper classes who more readily accommodated to and assimilated into the new order via education (74).

Successive European and American local-color writers followed the format laid out in the literature of their Irish and Scottish predecessors. In the earliest local-color stories in the United States, for example — those by Harriet Beecher Stowe and Rose Terry Cooke — the subjects are indigenous New Englanders who speak in authentic local dialect and are rooted in authentic locales. Often the narrator is more educated and views the "native" from an urban perspective, expressing the viewpoint of the metropole toward the province, with, however, the values of the premodern rural area receiving respectful attention.

In what is probably the first local-color story published in the U. S., Stowe's "A New England Sketch" (1834), we find the characteristic clash between an older, rooted, vernacular figure, Uncle Lot Griswold, and a young, educated, "modern" figure, James Benton. As schoolmaster, James is an outsider to Newbury, the "Yankee village," where Uncle Lot holds sway (33). James is also headed for college (he is 18), which further designates him a representative of modernity, and he speaks in standard English. Uncle Lot, by contrast, speaks in dialect and is educated largely in local knowledges or *mētis*: "He had the strong-grained practical sense, the calculating worldly wisdom of his class of people in New England" (36). As James is courting Uncle Lot's daughter, he has to overcome the older man's skepticism about his cocky confidence and claims to authority. In the process, however, ironically, it is James who comes to appreciate the accomplishments and wisdom of the native, Uncle Lot.

Similarly, in the writings of German, Swiss, French, and other European local-colorists the clash between the premodern local culture and the advent of modernity is a preeminent issue. The latter is often represented by an educated outsider, who speaks in the standard literary language of the nation or empire (*Hochdeutsch* or Parisian French), while the former is seen in the rural rustics who speak in dialect and exhibit particularized knowledge of local *mētis*.

In *No Place of Grace: Antimodernism and the Transformation of American Culture, 1880–1920*, Jackson Lears notes that in the last quarter of the nineteenth century the United States experienced a "second industrial revolution." Launched by the 1876 Centennial Exposition in Philadelphia, it saw the rise of not just technological innovations but also, more importantly, of "organized corporate capitalism" and a concomitant "rationalization of economic life," the imposition of Enlightenment modes of "technical 'rationality'" on much that had been unregulated theretofore (9). "The process of rationalization" ushered in by modernity "did more than transform the structure of economic life," Lear notes; "it also affected the structure of thought and feeling" (10). It was this ideological colonization that the local-colorists wrote against, affirming instead the value of nonstandardized, idiosyncratic, *local* tradition.

American local-colorist Sarah Orne Jewett's story "The Flight of Betsey Lane" (1893), an acknowledged locus classicus of her work, encapsulates the conflict between the modern and the premodern in nearly allegorical form. The eponymous protagonist is an elderly woman who lives in a "poor-house" in rural New England. She conceives a desire to visit the 1876 Centennial in Philadelphia and thanks to a financial windfall is able to make what is in effect a pilgrimage to the exposition. Betsey is enlightened and excited by the new inventions she sees there, but the author also points up the urban anomie that has accompanied modernity by remarking how an animated Betsey stood out against the "indifferent, stupid crowd that drifted along . . . seeing . . . nothing" (188). In the end, Betsey returns to her rural community — where "people knew each other well" (183) — to live out her life among her friends. The story affirms therefore the virtues of rural *Gemeinschaft* even while acknowledging the positive aspects of modernity; in particular, the liberties it afforded women, for, in making the trip by herself Betsey is, in effect, rehearsing her own "declaration of independence."

The "process of rationalization" and homogenization identified by Lears occurred, of course, not just in the United States but throughout the Western world as an accompaniment to the emergence of capitalist industrialism (as the dominant economic system) and modern science (as the dominant epistemology) — the twin pillars of modernity. First articulated in the philosophical systems of the Enlightenment, modernity found political expression in the formation of the modern nation-states and empires during the early modern period. These states were organized around major metropolitan centers (London, Paris, Vienna, Berlin, Boston/New York/Washington) where the bureaucratic apparatuses were located that enforced the governing standards, rules, tastes, norms of modernity upon regional locales, which had variant norms that were rooted in local tradition and lore.

To a great extent the imposition of metropolitan control on the provinces was a matter of the consolidation of power, as James C. Scott explains in *Seeing Like a State* (1998), an analysis of state formation as a project of modernity.

> The premodern state was, in many crucial aspects, partially blind; it knew precious little about its subjects, their wealth, their landholdings and yields, their location, their very identity . . . It lacked . . . a measure, a metric, that would allow it to "translate" what it

knew into a common standard necessary for a synoptic view . . . How did the state . . . get a handle on its subjects . . . ? Suddenly, processes as disparate as the creation of permanent last names, the standardization of weights and measures, . . . the standardization of language . . . seemed comprehensible as attempts at legibility and simplification. In each case officials took exceptionally complex, illegible, and local social practices . . . and created a standard grid whereby it could be centrally recorded and monitored. (2)

This centralization and standardization thus facilitated and consolidated metropolitan control over the regions. In France, for example, the imposition of the meter as a standard measure replaced particularistic measurement practices that varied widely from region to region. In the same way, a national language was established as the norm, relegating provincial dialects to the status of deviant and inferior. An early critic of the process in France, Benjamin Constant, saw the process as an imperialism: "The conquerors of our days . . . want their empire to possess a unified surface . . . The same code of law, the same measures, the same rules . . . The great slogan of the day is *uniformity*" (quoted in J. Scott 30).

In one of the most powerful critiques of modernity, *Reflections on the Revolution in France* (1790), Edmund Burke criticized the French imposition of geometrical order on the countryside in the aftermath of the Revolution: "the French builders, clearing away as mere rubbish whatever they found, and, like their ornamental gardens, forming every thing into an exact level." He deplores their practice of dividing France into equal departments, which are unnatural, he claims, unlike "the old divisions . . . [which were] various accidents at various times . . . not made on any fixed system" (285–6). Burke sees the imposition of such rational schemes as a colonial tyranny. "It is impossible not to observe that in the spirit of this geometrical distribution, and arithmetical arrangement, these pretended citizens treat France exactly like a country of conquest" (298).

And in a comment that heralds the emergence of the local-color movement, Burke notes, "It is boasted, that the geometrical policy has been adopted [in France], that all local ideas should be sunk, and that the people should no longer be Gascons, Picards, Bretons, Normans, but Frenchmen" (315). Resisting this territorial centralization and regional erasure, Edward Said notes, is "the imagination of anti-imperialism," which protests, "*our* space at home in the peripheries has been usurped and put to use by outsiders for *their* purpose" ("Yeats" 79). "Place is extremely important" in postcolonial literature, the writers of *The Empire Writes Back* note, "and epistemologies have developed which privilege space over time as the most important ordering concept of reality" (37). Such an emphasis on local space or place is a hallmark of local-color literature; it subverts the time of imperial history, "progress" toward modernity.

Establishing uniform standards was demanded by capitalists in the early modern period because they facilitated large-scale trade and exchange-value production. The gradual replacement of use-value production, the dominant economy in premodern societies (where production is largely by hand or with the help of domestic animals and for local consumption), by exchange-value production (where items are largely factory-made as commodities for sale) is a major aspect of the transformation of the premodern to the modern. Said indeed defines imperialism, seen as the culmination of capitalist development, as a movement that "achieves the domination, classification, and universal commodification of all space, under the aegis of the metropolitan center" ("Yeats" 78).

The modern state's identification of its citizenry (through the establishment of last names and censuses) also enabled the conscription of mass armies, first seen perhaps in the Napoleonic campaigns. Indeed, it was through the conquests of Napoleon that the institutions and ideologies of modernity were spread throughout Europe and it was partly in response to the French occupation that the earliest local-color literature was written in Germany (Berthold Auerbach) and in Switzerland (Jeremias Gotthelf). In the United States, while the earliest local-color literature appeared in the antebellum period, it was the Civil War which proved to be the American counterpart of the Napoleonic expansion in that it established that the nation-state took precedence over the regions whose deviancies from the national norm were either repressed militarily or relegated to the status of substandard, as national norms were established in the post–Civil War era. The heyday of local-color literature in the U. S. was the period of approximately 1870–1900, as writers resisted the pull of national and corporate homogenization, affirming instead the value of regional deviancy, *"local* color."

The enforcement of national social norms and standards was facilitated in part by the establishment of universal public education in state-sponsored schools, another project of modernity. One of the central figures in local-color literature is the schoolmaster, educated in the metropole, who comes to a rural locale to teach natives in the knowledges of modernity. His troubled relationship with the local population is the subject (often humorous) of numerous local-color stories in nearly every country but especially in the German-speaking world. Mass transportation and media systems which emerged during the nineteenth century, including perhaps most importantly the introduction of mass advertising, also facilitated the process of ideological colonization. The centralization of sources of information meant that nonmetropolitan sources rooted in regional traditions and often articulated in local dialects were muted or silenced.

James Scott remarks how "practical, local knowledge or 'mētis'" was derogated as the universal mathematical abstractions of modern scientific knowledge gained hegemony in the power centers of modernity, such as universities. Local knowledge or *mētis* is practical, craft-based knowledge rooted in the particulars of the local environment. It is transmitted orally or by manual practice, learning by doing, and through personal apprenticeships. "Mētis resists simplification into deductive principles which can successfully be transmitted through book learning," because it is context specific and cannot be generalized (316). An example of a practitioner of *mētis* would be a harbor pilot, who knows the vagaries of a particular harbor from practical navigational experience rather than from studying abstract generic navigational rules. Similarly, an herbalist (a figure who recurs in many local-color works), who knows the herbs of a particular region and how they may work on particular individuals, as opposed to a licensed medical doctor who learns generic rules about the application of certain drugs to relieve generic symptoms with minimal attention paid to the particular locale or circumstances of the patient. "The power of practical knowledge," Scott notes, "depends on an exceptionally close and astute observation of the environment" (324).

A celebrated study done by Russian theorist A. R. Luria in the 1930s helps to specify the nature of local knowledge or *mētis*. In asking a group of illiterate peasants (in rural Uzbekistan) to reflect upon a set of terms, such as *hammer, saw, log, hatchet,* Luria discovered that the illiterate, oral-based subject would not group them under a generic label, such as *tool* (excluding the log) — which would require deductive reasoning — but would envisage instead a practical operational narrative revolving around using the tools on the log. Luria concluded that those who were rooted in oral cultures and not trained in abstract, deductive thought-processes favored in modernity relied mainly on situational, pragmatic, and particularistic reasoning, which is contingent upon the given particulars of a particular situation and focused upon the outcome of a specific task or operation. Scott similarly notes that *mētis* is "partisan knowledge as opposed to generic knowledge," and is not based on statistical probability estimates but on working toward the successful outcome of a particular case (318).

As rationalist, deductive thought-processes are held to be superior in modernity, local knowledges or *mētis* are derogated as regressive and unsophisticated and are overruled by the referees of modernity as such whenever the two modes clash or interact. (In recent years postmodernist theory has moved toward revalidating narrative as an important form of knowledge but the dominant institutions of modernity — science, medicine, law — still relegate it to secondary, "anecdotal" status.) As a literature heavily infused with oral tradition, local-color fiction often affirms the validity of *mētis* or at least recognizes the significance of its clash with the knowledges of modernity. The standardization and normalizing processes that accompanied the establishment of modernity thus required the extirpation of, or at least minimization of, local deviancy, including *mētis*, and other oral traditions and customs.

Of particular importance was the standardization of language, the establishment and enforcement of an "official" vernacular, by the modern nation-state. In the United States, for example, the requirement that official standard English be taught in the schools became a national imperative in the post–Civil War period (see Nettels). The linguistic struggle between a metropolitan imperial center and the provinces has in fact been a continuing one in Western (and perhaps world) history, as various empires have attempted to impose a unifying cultural hegemony over conquered territories by, in particular, establishing a dominant language, as Latin was imposed, for example, on their provinces by the Romans. Mikhail Bakhtin has proposed that a kind of linguistic dialectic has been obtained throughout Western history between centripetal and centrifugal forces: the former pulling toward a unitary "Cartesian," "official" language; the latter toward diffused regional dialects and vernaculars, what he termed "heteroglossia" (*Dialogic Imagination* 271). Until the early modern period Latin remained the dominant "official" language in Western Europe; it was used in legal transactions, in universities, in serious written literature, as well as in the Church. Vernaculars remained "unofficial," largely oral languages that were used in rural and domestic environments. As the authority of Latin began to decline, however, and as vernaculars came into prominence, modern nation-states began decreeing a particular dialect of their country (usually that spoken in the metropole) as *the* official national language, which was then imposed upon the country's regions as the standard written language.

Labeling it "domestic colonization," whereby "various . . . provinces . . . are linguistically subdued and culturally subordinated," Scott argues that "of all state simplifications . . . the imposition of a single, official language may be the most powerful" (72). In his study of the process in France, Pierre Bourdieu similarly sees the repression of dialect by "official languages" as an example of "symbolic violence," reflecting in fact a kind of class struggle in that it is the lower classes who generally speak in regional dialects while the educated conform to the standard official language (36, 137). The authors of *The Empire Writes Back*, the study of postcolonial literature noted above, likewise identify language as a central feature of "imperial oppression": "The imperial education system installs a 'standard' version of the metropolitan language as the norm, and marginalizes all 'variants' as impurities" (7). Another critic notes, the process of repressing variant dialects reduced to "silence . . . those dispossessed of the official language . . . [L]acking the means of legitimate expression, they do not speak but are

8

spoken to" (Thompson 46). The local-colorists' use of dialect, therefore, may be seen as an attempt to give voice to these voiceless.

Since publishing sources were located in metropolitan centers, the standardized language of the metropole became the language used in printing. Spoken regional dialects or idiolects remained oral, not written languages (except in local-color literature where an attempt is made to replicate oral pronunciation with print approximations). Benedict Anderson in *Imagined Communities* (1983), a study of the origins of nationalism, suggests that the exigencies of print capitalism accelerated the formation of a standard print language. In "pre-print Europe," he writes, "the diversity of spoken languages . . . was . . . so immense . . . that had print-capitalism sought to exploit each potential oral vernacular market, it would have remained a capitalism of petty proportions." Instead, driven, as always, to expand its market, capitalism encouraged the development of a unified print-language which all readers within a national linguistic boundary could understand. "Nothing served to 'assemble' related vernaculars more than capitalism, which . . . created mechanically-reproduced print languages, capable of dissemination through the market . . . [P]rint capitalism gave a new fixity to language" (46–7).

The process of standardization and normalization imposed by the advocates of modernity was rooted in the philosophical premises of Cartesian rationalism, themselves reflective of the adoption of the Newtonian scientific paradigm in the seventeenth century, which effected the "mathematization of the world" noted in the Introduction. The reduction of reality — including biotic life-forms and the social life-world — to its quantitative properties rendered it machine-like; elided in the process were qualitative, subjective properties, such as color, taste, and emotion. Transforming nature "into mere objectivity," Cartesian/Newtonian epistemology occasioned "the disenchantment of the world" (Max Weber's term) along with the "extirpation of animism," according to Frankfurt School critics Max Horkheimer and Theodor Adorno (5), who viewed the Enlightenment paradigm as a dominative model imposed upon the manifold forms of social and biotic life. Necessarily, all that did not fit into the quantitative normalizing grid of the scientific model was marginalized; that is, rendered anomalous or invisible, which meant, in the case of deviant humans, voiceless. As Sandra Harding observes, "it is the scientific subject's voice that speaks with general and abstract authority; the objects of inquiry 'speak' only in response to what scientists ask them, and they speak in the *particular voice* of their *historically specific conditions and locations*" (124, emphasis added).

Marshall Berman, a prominent contemporary analyst of modernity, notes in *All That Is Solid Melts into Air* (1982) that early critics of modernity, such as Karl Marx, prominently lamented the *"desanctification"* effected by the secular world-view (157). Marx condemned the increasing commodification of life, in particular the objectification (*Verdinglichkeit*) of human beings and human relations effected in capitalist industrial labor relations. *The Communist Manifesto* laments not only the alienation of the worker, however, but the fact that the capitalist "has resolved personal worth into exchange value . . . [and] has reduced the family into a mere money relation . . . All that is holy is profaned" (Marx and Engels 11–12).

As the perspective of science sees only what can be objectified, it sees only dead matter and therefore an inanimate, lifeless, spiritless, profane world. Any imputation of, for example, animism to biotic forms is dismissed as chimera from the scientific point of view. If one thus sees the world entirely from a scientific perspective, the sacred, energized reality that is the subject of religion and myth (the numinous or the holy) is declared nonexistent and/or inaccessible.

> [R]educing Nature to her mathematical elements [the new scientific worldview] substituted a mechanical for a genial or animistic conception of the universe. The world was emptied, first of her indwelling spirits, then of her occult sympathies and antipathies, finally of her colours, smells, and tastes . . . Man with his new powers became rich like Midas but all that he touched has gone dead and cold.
>
> (C. S. Lewis 3–4)

Many of the most strident critics of modernity — Martin Heidegger, for example — formulated a kind of neo-Gnostic response, in which they deplore such desanctification (Heidegger's famous announcement that "the gods have fled," for example ["Hölderlin" 40]), and sought instead sources of resanctification: "Being has concealed itself from technological humanity. Thus deprived of a relationship with the originary ontological source, humanity can experience only entities" (Zimmerman 221). The banishment of the sacred effected by technological modernity has resulted, Heidegger claimed, in such social disorders as alienation and homelessness. Antimodernists like Heidegger therefore denigrated the metropolitan centers that were the seats of modernity, seeing them as seedbeds of the modern pathologies of homelessness and alienation (the Germans termed this anti-urban attitude *Grossstadtfeindlichkeit*), advocating instead a return to the provinces for sources of ontological revitalization and authenticity (what was termed a *Heimatkehr*, a "turn toward home").

At its worst, regional literature (mainly in Germany) degenerated into a kind of regionalist chauvinism, seen in the *Heimatroman* (the "home novel") around the turn of the nineteenth century, which mystified provincial roots and land ("*Blut und Boden*," "blood and soil") into the fascistic nationalism seen in the Nazi ideology espoused by Heidegger, where groups considered avatars of modernity, such as Jews, homosexuals, and feminists, among others, were scapegoated. At its best, however, regional or local-color literature (in Germany as well as in the U. S. and elsewhere) simply explored the clash between modern and pre- or antimodern without overly romanticizing or mystifying rural life and without falling into the *"völkische"* (racist) endorsements of *Heimatkunst* ("home art"). This distinction is extremely important in order to avoid unfairly tarring all regional/local-color literature with fascist association (see further exploration of this issue in Chapter Four).

Finally, on the social level the transition from the premodern to the modern entailed a shift from a fixed kinship/status identity to that of citizen whose relations are made by choice or contract. It is in the debates about this transformation that the situation of women became a prominent issue. In a life-world governed by kinship rules, individuals are identified principally by their relationship within a kin system and/or by class status. One had little choice about that identity or status; one generally was born into a condition that was strictly predetermined and rigidly maintained. With the advent of the concept of "personhood" or citizenship — both creations of Enlightenment political theory — one's social identity shifted to a universal generic category that in theory at least elided one's social/kin status. Citizens moreover could negotiate equally (again, in theory) with other citizens, forming contracts that were mutually agreed upon. Thus the freely chosen marriage contract replaced arranged marriages where the woman was little more than an object for exchange between father and husband. This issue is a central one in certain European local-color writings, notably by Sir Walter Scott, Alexandre Weill, Marie von Ebner-Eschenbach, Leopold Kompert, and George Sand. At the same time, most of these writers depict surprisingly strong — in some cases, even Amazonian — women characters in premodern habitats, suggesting that women had considerable power under premodern social arrangements in European peasant cultures. Ernst Bloch has indeed characterized these societies as matriarchal (327–8). As Jeremias Gotthelf, a Swiss local-colorist, asserted, "in the peasant home it is the woman who leads and makes the rules" ["in Bauernhaus ist es die Bäuerin, welche der führt und die Regel macht" (*Geld und Geist* 169)].

For women, the shift from a premodern kinship identity to the modern one of citizen or person has, nevertheless, been a hotly contested and often blocked process. Women have become bones of contention in colonial struggles because in opposing Western imperialism many anti-colonialists have also rejected Western liberal feminism as a project of modernity, insisting that the authentic course for colonized societies is to revert to premodern traditions, which generally meant keeping within traditionally

11

patriarchal kinship systems. In upholding the virtues of *Gemeinschaft* or close-knit community, which women have historically sustained, and in rejecting the evils of *Gesellschaft* (modern commercial society) — its anomie and alienation — the antimoderns worry that any change in women's status will mean a loss of the former and capitulation to the latter.

Women writers of the nineteenth century — by virtue of the fact that, on the one hand, most had achieved some measure of independence from traditional kinship roles and were educated enough to be conversant in some of the main ideas of modernity, including feminism. But, on the other, knew that women's predominant place remained within traditional premodern kinship systems, to which they themselves often remained emotionally attached — were positioned so as to appreciate both sides of the issue. The earliest local-color writers — those in Ireland, Maria Edgeworth, Lady Morgan, and Mary Leadbeater — all gave evidence in their writings of familiarity with the work of Mary Wollstonecraft whose *A Vindication of the Rights of Woman* (1792) was the first major modern feminist treatise.

In addition, because colonies or regions were deemed subordinate to the dominant metropolitan power, they easily correlated to the female in the male–female dyad under patriarchal rule: powerless, "relegated to the position of 'Other,' [and] marginalized" (Ashcroft et al. 174). A dominant theme in local-color literature is the exploration of this "feminine" otherness — this different way of doing things — often affirming it in opposition to standard (masculine) ways of thinking and behaving, which under modernity meant the abstract universalizing modes of Enlightenment rationalism. In Irish regional literature, for example, the natives are often portrayed (defensively) as irrational, emotional, erratic, and deviant, if not devious — traits traditionally associated with women-as-other to the masculinist modernist paradigm. It is "no accident," Marilyn Butler observes, "that women writers," such as Edgeworth, Morgan, Leadbeater, and S. C. [Anna Maria] Hall in Ireland and Elizabeth Hamilton, Jane Porter, Mary Brunton, and Susan Ferrier in Scotland, "authored the first handful of 'national tales' in the early 1800s. The imagined community and the empowered women tend to appear in symbiotic relation, each needing the other as a condition of existence" (Introduction to *Castle Rackrent and Ennui* 50). Women writers continued to dominate the genre in France and the United States but to a lesser extent in German-speaking regions, though the question of women's liberation from traditional roles remained an issue there as well.

An example of the classic local-colorist response to the forces of modernity may be made of the American writer Sarah Orne Jewett.[1] The nineteenth-century colonization of the premodern world of rural Maine, her home locale, by the powers and institutions of modernity was both literal and figurative: corporate industrial development and expanding communication and transportation systems were by the latter 1800s making incursions into rural territory — a form of creeping economic imperialism — but the domination was of the mind as well. An ideological colonization also occurred during this period through the growing imposition of normative standards in language, behavior, and culture by Enlightenment disciplines, such as science, pseudoscience, and social science. Numerous theorists have recognized that regional and local-color literature in the U. S. must be understood in terms of the post–Civil War effort at national unification (Louis Renza's work is especially perceptive in this regard), but the local-versus-national dialectic must also be understood within this larger global transformation — the transition from premodern to the modern.

Like her Scottish and Irish predecessors, Jewett articulated the standpoint of the premodern peasant, in her case in nineteenth-century rural Maine. But also like her predecessors, she often also mediated that standpoint through an upper-class, literate figure who, though herself a native, is conversant with the colonizer by virtue of class and education and writes in part to apprise said colonizer of the realities of the colonized. Jewett similarly comprehends the colonization process in terms of the clash between the premodern and the modern. Much of her work may be seen as an affirmation of instances of premodern "cultural resistance" she found in her rural locality. At the same time a decided ambivalence toward premodern "backwaters" is registered throughout her work, usually through the mediating narrator (as seen in her best-known work, *The Country of the Pointed Firs* [1896]) who has herself been urbanized and modernized to the point of being almost a stranger in the rural world of folk *Gemeinschaft* and yet who longs on a certain level to rejoin it.

This attitude is particularly evident in her story "A Guest at Home" (1882) and in her novels *A Marsh Island* (1885) and *A Country Doctor* (1884) where a young professional returns to a rural area after having been "modernized" in a metropolitan center. In each case the characters resolve the ambivalence by figuring out a way to integrate modern and premodern in their work (the first two protagonists are artists who like Jewett herself chose to focus on the rural area in their art in order to give voice to its inhabitants, to present them, so to speak, to the outsider denizens of the metropole who are their "audience"; in the latter case the protagonist is a doctor who uses her modern knowledge — medicine — to help rural folks).

As I discuss in a chapter entitled "Demeter's Garden Destroyed" in *After the Fall* (1989), upper-class literate women in the latter nineteenth century found themselves in a unique historical moment, one in which "harsh generational conflict" had broken out between mothers and daughters over the status of modern women (Smith-Rosenberg 33). Unlike their male counterparts who at least since the early modern period had been able to leave the premodern — the rural — for the city where they had access to the power/knowledges of Enlightenment modernity, most women in the Western world were confined to the largely illiterate, oral culture of the premodern until Jewett's generation. It was only in her day that universities and the professions — sites of modernity — began opening up to women and even in her day it was still considered highly deviant for a woman to leave the premodern bower and engage in a "professional" career. Her novel *A Country Doctor* in fact deals centrally with this issue, the "country doctor" being a woman.

While there was much that was attractive to a woman of Jewett's position in the power/knowledges of modernity — in particular, the rights, freedoms, and opportunities envisaged for women in liberal feminism, as well as the comforts and easements offered by modern inventions — there was also much that was threatening to the rural "female world of love and ritual" to which Jewett belonged emotionally. Like many women in her generation Jewett was genuinely torn between the two worlds, which were represented geographically in her life by Boston and rural Maine — the one the world of the "daughters"; the other of the "mothers." Those women who were educated in the discourses of modernity, the younger generation, necessarily became alienated from the premodern worlds of their mothers. Such education served, as Carroll Smith-Rosenberg remarks, "to draw young women out of their mothers' and grandmothers' domestic mindset"; they learned instead "to think and feel 'as a man'" (252–3).

Thinking "as a man" meant adopting the abstract, universalizing modes of Enlightenment secular rationalism, seen especially in the epistemology of the modern sciences and social sciences. The classificatory hermeneutic of modern science and modern medicine, as well as pseudosciences such as sexology — particularly important in Jewett's case — require that the individual "case" be fit into broad identificatory schemes in order to be recognized. In this way, anomalous and eccentric facts and individuals are either ignored and relegated to silence or branded deviant. These disciplines therefore established normalizing ideological standards that by the latter nineteenth century were effectively colonizing everyday life-worlds even in rural areas remote from the metropole where the professional experts and bureaucrats conversant in the disciplines and practices of modernity lived.

Sarah Orne Jewett's work reflects the author's complex negotiation between the colonized territory to which she belonged — that was home to her but from which she was in a sense exiled by virtue of class, education, travel, and metropolitan connections — and the increasingly hegemonic world of modernity to which she was in some ways attracted but by which in many ways repulsed. Her work engaged in this dialectic on several fronts.

First and most obvious is her articulation of the regional voices and idioms that are threatened with erasure by the nationalizing project of federalism. Second, in several works she establishes the claims of the sociologically deviant as against the imposition of pseudoscientific norms of behavior; in a few of these works this takes the form of a resistance to modern medicine. Finally, and perhaps most importantly, Jewett voices a refusal to accommodate to capitalist development, especially of the natural world. In this she was a proto-ecologist.

On the first point her and other local-colorists' use of dialect established a "deterritorialized" standpoint, a "point of under-development," a "*patois*," a "third world" from which to resist colonization from without — terms used to describe "minor literature" by French theorists Gilles Deleuze and Félix Guattari (33). In applying the Deleuze/Guattari theory to Jewett, Louis Renza notes how in, for example, her story "A White Heron," Jewett represents "'points of nonculture and underdevelopment, the zones of a linguistic third world' intent on sabotaging the major language of American patriarchal culture" (35). Jewett's and the other local-colorists' use of dialect throughout their work defiantly affirms the solidity and reality of this colonized linguistic realm — notwithstanding the fact that Jewett's frame narratives are in standard English (while she herself probably spoke with a Maine accent if not in a Maine dialect).[2] The frames in Jewett's work do not dominate, however, or erase the embedded dialects; they rather serve to accentuate them, even to elevate them much as a picture frame highlights the picture it encases or a setting enhances a gem. Such a frame says: "different but valuable." It affirms — indeed, emphasizes — the ontological presence of the items scored. The embedded dialect also often serves to ironize the frame language rendering it less authoritative, less "normal," much as the narrator's "modern" viewpoint in *The Country of the Pointed Firs* and other works is undercut as authoritatively dominant by indigenous premodern views.

Other practices, customs, and characters of premodern rural culture are similarly rendered ontologically present in Jewett's treatment. A work like *Pointed Firs* is a veritable catalog, for example, of use-value production practices — from Mrs. Todd's herbal preparations to the fisherman Elijah Tilley's knitting. Dunnet Landing is not a world of capitalist entrepreneurs engaged in economic imperialism. Mrs. Todd does charge for her herbs and presumably also charges rent of her tenant, but the relationship between the two quickly eclipses economic roles operating finally in terms of kinship relation. Dunnet Landing is in fact largely a subsistence economy, close in fact to being an exemplar of the premodern gift economy, governed as it is by kinship ties and codes of hospitality. Most of the economic exchange in the work is through gifts, and most of the products exchanged are hand-crafted. The increasing dominance of factory-made goods is lamented by another Jewett character, a tailoress, the title character in "Miss Debby's Neighbors" (1883), who complains of how people are now buying "cheap, ready-made clothes," which has the effect of making everyone look alike. "She always insisted . . . that the railroads were making everybody look and act of a piece, and that young folks were more alike than people of her own day" (191). Miss Debby is speaking of the ontic depletion effected by the commodity form.

In the same story the urban narrator, expressing the viewpoint of modernity with its emphasis on unifying hypotaxis, offers a complaint that the indigenous speaker's method "of going around Robin Hood's barn between the beginning of her story and its end can hardly be followed at all" (191). The indigenous narrator is uneducated and her narrative style reflects the oral mentality A. R. Luria identified in illiterate peasants, noted above, who resisted organizing material into deductive or hypotactic patterns (Ong 49–57). In his study of oral culture, *Orality and Literacy* (1982), Walter J. Ong lays out several features that characterize oral thought and expression, among them that it is "additive rather than subordinative," "aggregative rather than analytic," "redundant or 'copious,'" "empathetic and participatory rather than objectively distanced," and "situational rather than abstract" (36–49). All of these features readily describe the narrative technique not just of Miss Debby but of the numerous indigenous Jewett characters who narrate tales within her stories. In this way aspects of oral culture are embedded or transcribed in print in Jewett's and other local-colorists' work — another instance of the author serving as mediator between two cultures — oral and print, premodern and modern.

In the *Poetics* Aristotle distinguishes between a complex *propter hoc* [because of which] plot and a simple *post hoc* [after which] plot (10.20, 1465). The former is generally termed a hypotactic structure and the latter paratactic. Historically, illiterate and uneducated persons have used parataxis, a string of clauses connected by "ands" with little use of explanatory connectives ("since," "because," "wherefore"). Many, if not all, of Jewett's embedded narrators similarly speak in the fashion Ong describes, using primarily parataxis, and at the extreme (as in "Miss Debby's Neighbors") losing the unifying hypotactic thread of the narration. Significantly, in this story it is the modern author — urban, literate, and educated — who criticizes this round-about narrative tendency, looking vainly for some sort of deductive climax.

Like her European predecessors in the local-color movement, who used variations of this technique, Jewett constructed many of her stories in layers of narration where an outsider narrator from the metropole comes to a rural region, encounters an insider who tells her tale paratactically in vernacular idiom. This technique is used most famously perhaps in *Pointed Firs* but may also be seen in such masterful stories as "The Courting of Sister Wisby" (1887) and "An Autumn Holiday" (1881).

In "Sister Wisby," for example, the urban narrator, wandering in the country (the first few pages read indeed like a nature essay), encounters an herbalist, Mrs. Goodsoe, who is in the process of gathering "mulleins," an herb. The two engage in a meandering gossipy conversation in which the herbalist reveals herself to harbor typically antimodern attitudes. Her grasp of local knowledge or *mētis* is immediately apparent: when the urban narrator (who speaks in standard English, as opposed to Mrs. Goodsoe's dialect) asks whether the herbalist plans to gather the herb pennyroyal, she is immediately put down: "'Pennyr'yal!' repeated the dear little old woman, with an air of compassion for inferior knowledge; "tain't the right time, darlin'. Pennyr'yal's too rank now. But for mulleins this day is prime'" (57). When the narrator offers to help her cut the mullein, Mrs. Goodsoe tells her how: "'Now be keerful, dear heart . . . choose 'em well. There's odds in mulleins same's ther is in angels'" (57). The narrator "listened respectfully" (57), while Mrs. Goodsoe rambles on anecdotally, finally (two-thirds of the way through the story) reaching the main story about "Sister Wisby," which is sparked by a discussion of another herb, "Goldthread."

"An Autumn Holiday" similarly starts out as a nature essay, with the narrator wandering the countryside with her dog. Eventually (four pages into the story) she comes upon a house where she finds two women spinning wool. They stop and chat with the visitor and after several shorter anecdotes the main tale emerges (more than halfway through the story), which concerns a transvestite or transgendered man, "Miss Daniel Gunn" (Jewett's original title of the story, which was evidently transmuted to the tamer "An Autumn Holiday" by her Boston editor — an example of censorial flattening out of regional eccentricity by metropole norms).

Gunn is a retired militia captain in a nearby village who "got sun-struck" and came to believe he is his dead sister (153). He began wearing her clothes, adopting feminine mannerisms, and engaging in traditionally female activities such as sewing bees. What is significant about this story is that, uneducated in modern pseudosciences like sexology, the townspeople do not classify him under some deductive category; rather they adopt a pragmatic operational approach to his situation, as is characteristic of *mētis*. Since his sister's clothes don't fit properly, the townswomen sew him larger women's clothes that fit, thus allowing him to continue his eccentric behavior while retaining his personal identity, unstigmatized by the classificatory systems of modernity.

As a lesbian, Jewett may also have experienced personally the increasing "morbidification of female friendship" (as termed by Lillian Faderman) being effected by the colonizing ideology of sexology at the end of the nineteenth century. That her own "life-world" was being branded "unnatural," deviant, and pathological according to the new categories of sexual normality being established by sexologists like Richard von Krafft-Ebing necessarily evoked a critical response. Michel Foucault in fact singled out sexology as a signal instance of the categorizing mind-set endemic to modernist disciplines, "entomologiz[ing]," as it did, sexual life-styles into species and sub-species of deviancy (*Histoire* 60).

Jewett's most overt repudiation of these theories may be found in her novel *A Country Doctor*, but much of Jewett's work is devoted to a defense of eccentricity and deviancy. In *The Country of the Pointed Firs*, Mrs. Todd repeatedly sticks up for the community's "strayaways": "I never want to hear Joanna laughed about" (103), she warns when the eccentric hermit Joanna's story is broached. Significantly, her comments follow upon a discussion lamenting the increasing conformity, standardization, and homogenization in American life. Mrs. Fosdick observes: "What a lot o' queer folks there used to be about here, anyway, when we was young, Almiry. Everybody's just like everybody else now" (101). Mrs Todd agrees:

> Yes . . . there was certain a good many curiosities of human natur' in this neighborhood years ago. There was more energy then, and in some the energy took a singular turn. In these days the young folks is all copy-cats, 'fraid to death they won't be all just alike; as for the old folks, they pray for the advantage o' bein' a little different. (102)

Here again a note is sounded of ontological depletion — "there was more energy then"; ontic energy is being drained in the rush to assimilate and conform.

Jewett also has various characters who repudiate the claims of modern medicine, affirming instead the virtues of the ancient feminine practice of herbology. Mrs. Todd is one example; although she has an amicable relationship with the local doctor, it is likely that he — like Doctor Leslie in *A Country Doctor* — is an "irregular" physician on the order of Jewett's father who respects herbal lore and is himself skeptical of the scientific bent in modern medicine. Even more explicit in her rejection of modern disciplines — especially modern medicine — is the herbalist in "The Courting of Sister Wisby," Mrs. Goodsoe, who like many other Jewett characters laments the erasure of local eccentricity in the homogenization being effected by mass transportation and communication systems: "[I]n old times . . . [people] stood in their lot an' place, and were n't all just alike, either, same as pine-spills" (59). Modern doctors may be "bilin' over with book-larnin' [but they're] . . . truly ignorant of what to do for the sick . . . Book-fools I call 'em" (57). Mrs. Goodsoe espouses in effect a theory of bio-regionalism: illness should be treated with regionally grown remedies: "[F]olks was meant to be doctored with the stuff that grew right about 'em; 't was sufficient and so ordered" (59). As in *Pointed Firs*, Mrs. Goodsoe's position is mediated through a more modern narrator who challenges and occasionally demurs from her views. But, as in *Pointed Firs*, the narrative frame by no means dominates the rural perspective. Indeed, one senses, as in *Pointed Firs*, a kind of self-irony occurring: the limitations of the narrator's "modern" view are also being ironized as circumscribed and limited; she concludes by lamenting the modern "world [which is] foolish enough to sometimes undervalue medicinal herbs" (68).

A final aspect of Jewett's treatment of the resistance of the colonized to imperial impositions is found in her works that deal with nature, another issue that is prominent in local-color literature (on this aspect of the American/New England local-color school see Sylvia Mayer, *Naturethik und Neuengland-Regionalliteratur* [2004]). Jewett's resistance to capitalist and industrial development of the natural world is clearly stated in a number of letters. Perhaps her most poignant and moving statement of this position comes in an 1892 letter to Annie Fields: "The other day quite out of the clear sky a man came to Mary [Jewett's sister] with a plan for a syndicate to cut up and sell the river bank all in lots . . . Sometimes I get such a hunted feeling like the last wild thing that is left in the fields" (Fields 90). In a much earlier letter (1877) Jewett similarly remarks, "Berwick . . . is growing and flourishing in a way that breaks my heart" (Cary 36).

In several stories Jewett expressed intense empathy with the natural world even to the point of explicitly endorsing an animistic theory of nature; see especially "An October Ride," "A Winter Drive," and "River Driftwood," which were collected in *Country By-Ways* (1881). But Jewett's most powerful story of "cultural resistance" to colonization is her justly famous "A White Heron" (1886), which concerns a confrontation between the rural premodern world of Sylvia, a young girl who lives with her grandmother in an isolated woodland, and the world of modernity represented by an urban scientist, an ornithologist, who invades her peaceful green sanctuary looking for a rare white heron he hopes to kill and stuff for his collection. That the ornithologist has a scientific, classificatory, "entomologizing" purpose (to reprise Foucault's term) highlights his status within the text as an avatar of modernity. His perspective is that of the quantifying, objectifying gaze of modern science. He sees the bird as an object to be scrutinized and colonized within the scientific paradigm of species and subspecies of *avis*.

The girl, on the other hand, is preliterate and uneducated in the perspectives of modernity; she has an animist view of nature. Its creatures are alive to her as presences, as "persons." "There ain't a foot o' ground she don't know her way over," her grandmother explains, "and the wild creatur's counts her one o' themselves . . . Last winter she got the jay-birds to bangeing here" (165). (*Bangeing* is a good example of a Maine dialect term; still in use, it means "hanging around.") That Jewett grants equal ontological status to the creatures of the natural world may be seen in several other works in which she evinces a desire to give voice, to articulate the "language" of the nonhuman. In "River Driftwood," for example, the narrator meditates:

> Who is going to be the linguist who learns the first word of an old crow's warning to his mate . . . ? [H]ow long we shall have to go to school when people are expected to talk to the trees, and birds, and beasts in their own language! . . . Is it science that will give us back the gift, or shall we owe it to the successors of those friendly old saints who talked with the birds and fishes? (4–5)

Jewett's antimodern answer is clear: it is not science. Her resistance to its dominative colonizing claims is manifest as she continues,

> It is not necessary to tame [creatures] before they can be familiar and responsive; *we can meet them on their own ground* . . . Taming is only forcing them to learn some of our customs; we should be wise if we let them tame us to make use of some of theirs. (5, emphasis added)

Jewett proceeds to envisage a day of "universal suffrage . . . when the meaning of every living thing is understood, and is given its rights and accorded its true value" (6).

In "A White Heron" Sylvia, though inarticulate, has a similar viewpoint, and although she is attracted initially to the ornithologist and interested in his knowledges, and he stimulates her to expand her horizons (literally: she climbs a tree looking for the bird and sees the ocean in the distance, something she had never done before), she nevertheless is distressed by his willingness to destroy the natural world in order to learn more about it. She "would have liked him vastly better without his gun; she could not understand why he killed the very birds he seemed to like so much" (166). Also disturbing is the way in which the ornithologist is willing to exploit the girl's knowledge of the birds for his own purposes. The corruptness of his instrumental treatment of Sylvia is further emphasized when he offers her money, in a sense bribing her, to reveal the location of the white heron. The unholy alliance between modern science and capitalism is tacitly acknowledged in this moment.

In the end Sylvia takes a stand and refuses to reveal the bird's location to the ornithologist, thus saving the bird's life and upholding the claims of the premodern, animist, *local* world of rural Maine as against the modernist imperative.

No, she must keep silence. What is it that suddenly forbids her and makes her dumb? . . . The murmur of the pine's green branches is in her ears, she remembers how the white heron came flying through the golden air and how they watched the sea and the morning together, and Sylvia cannot speak; she cannot tell the heron's secret and give its life away. (171)

Sylvia cannot speak but her author does, giving voice to the inarticulate people — human and nonhuman — of rural Maine, telling their story, that it not be erased, that its claim to ontological status be upheld against the colonizing, extirpating forces of modernity.

NOTES

1 An earlier version of this section appeared in my article, "Local-Color Literature and Modernity: The Example of Jewett," *Tamkang Review* 38, no. 1 (December 2007):7–25.
2 On the question of Jewett's use of Maine dialect, see Cutler.

CHAPTER 2

The Irish National Tale

The "national tale" — the term used for regional or local-color literature in nineteenth-century Ireland — emerged during a period of identity crisis precipitated by a "double defeat" — the 1798 Rebellion and the *Act of Union of 1801*. Under the terms of the latter Ireland became part of Britain but forfeited its own political identity in losing its independent parliament. As a result, "the idea of a separate Irish identity was, perhaps, never more obviously in jeopardy, for the English aim was to limit Irish independence and to reduce a troublesome colony to a state of respectful duty and obligation" (Sloan 1).

As a colonial state, Ireland had undergone "earlier than any other colony, a process of hegemonic domination . . . Successive imperial measures to discipline and control this recalcitrant colony" established "state apparatuses later adopted . . . throughout the Empire" (Lloyd ix). As the "imperial model of identity" required the "homogenization of its subject peoples" (Lloyd x), resistance on the part of the Irish to imperial domination took the form of affirmation of cultural difference. The "national tale," which affirmed Irish differentness, arose as part of that resistance. Its authors — the Irish local-colorists — were in effect "plead[ing] the case of [a] racial or cultural minorit[y]" (Flanagan 133). Concern about the loss of a separate Irish identity is expressed, for example, in the Preface and Conclusion to Maria Edgeworth's *Castle Rackrent* (x, 70), which was published at the very time the *Act of Union* was passed (1800).

Local-color literature indeed only emerged in countries or regions whose culture was being threatened with erasure by a dominant imperial or metropolitan authority. "The national tale," Ina Ferris notes, "is a genre . . . of small European nations that stand in a certain relation of hostility to a larger and oppressive nation with whose fortunes their own are intertwined" (49). Thus, while *War and Peace* and *Persuasion* concern national issues, they are not per se national tales (Ferris 50). As Thomas Flanagan notes, "Jane Austen wrote English novels . . . but not novels 'about England.' Only a culture which felt urgently and consciously a need for definition could have produced the novels of Edgeworth or Scott" (101). Terry Eagleton similarly explains, "Not to brood obsessively about one's identity is the privilege of the victor," which is why "there is no great English novel about England" (*Heathcliff* 126).

Nearly every preface to Irish literature written in the early 1800s — including especially those in works by Edgeworth, Lady Morgan, Michael Whitty, John and Michael Banim, and William Carleton — contains a pledge to render Irish characters and manners accurately and realistically so as to counter demeaning stereotypes of the Irish then in common circulation. Implicit is a plea to the imperial reader not to look down on the Irish, to treat them with dignity as equal, if different, human beings.

In her "Essay on Irish Bulls" (1802), for example, a defense of Irish verbal idiosyncrasies and malapropisms, Maria Edgeworth notes, "Many foreign pictures of Irishmen are as grotesque and absurd as the Chinese pictures of lions: having never seen that animal" (194). She cites as an example of objectionable racist attitudes toward the Irish Voltaire's comment (in *The Age of Louis XIV*): "Some nations always had to be subject to others. The English have always had over the Irish the superiority of genius, wealth, and arms. *The superiority which the whites have* over the Negroes" (194, emphasis in original).

In his Preface to his *Tales of Irish Life* (1824), Michael Whitty states that for the English

> less is actually known . . . of the REAL STATE OF IRELAND than of the regions beyond the Ganges and Mississippi. Native writers from a false patriotism, have exaggerated and distorted facts [probably a reference to Lady Morgan], while foreigners, from prejudice and ignorance, have dealt largely in misrepresentations. (1:ii)

Noting an early instance of what Edward Said has called "orientalism" — where Europeans project exotic Otherness on non-European regions, Whitty complains that "English readers . . . are only pleased with representations of Irish life . . . where things are done and said which are as foreign to Ireland as . . . to Hindostan" (1:ii). In one of his "tales," "Poor Mary," Whitty further notes English misconceptions: "An Irishman is a Papist; *ergo*, a superstitious fool: an Irishman eats potatoes; *ergo*, he is starved; *ergo*, he must be unhappy" (2:3). These are false conclusions.

In her Epilogue to *Castle Rackrent* (1800) Maria Edgeworth similarly notes "the domestic habits of no nation in Europe were less known to the English than those of her sister country" and acknowledges a central motive in writing the novel was to present "the English reader . . . a specimen of manners and characters which are perhaps unknown in England" (69). Some years later, in the 1840s, William Carleton explains that his *Traits and Stories of the Irish Peasantry* (1843) were designed to "aid in removing many absurd prejudices which had existed for time immemorial against his countrymen," especially the English "gross and overcharged caricature of the Irish" (*Traits* 1:i).

As early as 1705, in her novel *The Fugitive* (later revised as *The Merry Wanderer* in 1725), Irish writer Mary Davys complained about English racist preconceptions about Ireland, "a place very much despis'd by those that know it not" (*Fugitive* 2). In *The Merry Wanderer* she laments that as an Irish author she must deflect anticipated disparagement of her work: "To tell the Reader I was born in Ireland is to bespeak a general Dislike to all I write, and he will, likely, be surprized, if every paragraph does not end with a Bull" (*Works* 1:161). (A "bull" was an Irish malapropism.)

The first episode of *The Fugitive* relates a comical charade in which the narrator, traveling in England, puts on an Englishman who is eager to see "some of the wild *Irish*" he'd heard were staying at a local inn. He offers a shilling to a servant to let him see them: "the Wench, who happen'd to have a little more Wit than he, came in with the jest, to see how far we would encourage it" (3). The narrator proposes playing along with his expectations: "For my part I was mightily pleas'd at the fancy . . . Now, said I, does this Fellow think that we have Horns and Hoofs . . . ? Pray let us humour his opinion . . . I am resolved to do all I can to confirm him in it" (4).

The humorous encounter proceeds:

> By this time he came staring in with Eyes, Ears and Mouth open . . . Come Friend, said I, you have a mind, I hear, to see some of the wild *Irish*. *Yes, Forsooth, said he, an yo pleasen, but pray yo where are thay*; why, said I, I am one of them; *Noa, noa, said he, forsooth yo looken laik one of us; but those Foke that I mean are Foke we long Tails, that have no cloaths on, but are cover' laik my brown Caw a whome, with their own Hair.* Come, said I, sit you down, and I'll tell you all . . . when I was three years old I was just such a Creature as you speak of, and one day . . . I went a little farther than I should have done, and was taeen in a Net with some other Vermin, which the *English* had spread on purpose for us, and when they had me, they cut off my Tail, and scalded off my Hair, and ever since I have been like one of you. (4–5)

He then asks her if she could speak before she was captured. She says, "Speak . . . no, I could make a Gapeing inarticulate Noise, as the rest of my fellow Beasts did, and went upon my Hands as well as Feet, in imitation of them; but for any other Knowledge, I had it not till I got into *English* hands" (5). He replies, wonderingly, "*yo may bless the day that ever yo met with that same Net b'r Lady. I have often heard of the waild* Irish *but I never saw any of them before*" (5). She tells him to go and tell his neighbors what he has seen. "Thus this poor Soul went away full of Wonder, to spread the Lye all over the Country, and left us full of Mirth, as he was of Folly" (6).

That these prejudices persisted for yet another century is repeatedly stated as a major motivation for their writing by the early nineteenth-century Irish local-colorists. Lady Morgan (Sydney Owenson) says in her *Patriotic Sketches of Ireland* (1809) that she wrote *The Wild Irish Girl* (1806) to counter "the falsity" and "ungracious information" she found circulating in England (ix). "[A]rmed with a pebble and a sling," she proceeded "against a host of gigantic prejudices" "to compose a national defense" (x). In *Florence Macarthy* (1818) Morgan notes that in a "series of [national] tales . . . the author has . . . endeavoured to sketch the brilliant aspect of a people struggling with adversity . . . to excite sympathy, and awaken justice" (1:vi). But in *The O'Briens and the O'Flahertys*, subtitled *A National Tale*, Morgan issues a more defiant warning to the English, wishing to "remind the party in England . . . 'we won't be bullied'" (1:139n).

The hope of eliciting sympathy in the oppressors is a note sounded in John Banim's explanation for the motivation behind his (and his brother Michael's) *Tales of the O'Hara Family* (1825): "They were inspired simply by a devoted love of country, and by an indignant wish to convince her slanderers, and in some slight degree to soften the hearts of her oppressors" (as quoted in MacCarthy, "Irish Regional Novelists," July–Sept. 1946, 28). An early Irish critic of the Irish local-color movement, writing in the *Dublin Review* in 1838, notes that the "national novels" are "vehicles for exciting interest and sympathy in the minds of those to whom the nation in question would otherwise have been a name and nothing more" (quoted in Ferris 57).

It is clear therefore that these writers saw themselves engaged in what today is called "cultural work" — changing attitudes and challenging oppressive ideologies. That Maria Edgeworth saw fiction thus as a political tool is apparent in an observation she made in an 1828 letter: commenting on the positive depiction of an African character in James Fennimore Cooper's novel *Red Rover*, she notes that such representation "does more for the Negro race than any act of Parliament can do. The one affects opinion, far above law in its range of power" (MacDonald, ed., *Education of the Heart* 154).

Her own novels may be seen in this light. *Castle Rackrent* (1800), the best known and most discussed by critics, concerns the generational history of an Irish landlord family narrated in dialect with comic irony by a long-term family steward, Thady Quirk. That history records the transition from the premodern undisciplined feudal regime of the idiosyncratic Rackrents to a modern administrative estate represented by Jason Quirk, Thady's son and an unscrupulous lawyer.

Maria Edgeworth (1768–1849) herself was well educated in the perspectives of the Enlightenment through the influence of her father Richard Lovell Edgeworth who was part of an intellectual circle that included Erasmus Darwin, Josiah Wedgwood, and James Watt, the leading liberal thinkers of the day, rationalist and pro-science. The Edgeworths, although of the Anglo-Irish Protestant Ascendancy, were long-term residents of Ireland, the family having settled there in the 1500s. In an 1802 essay Maria notes that she was "neither *born nor bred* in Ireland" (she was born and received her early education in England), but is "attached to the country . . . for its merits" ("Irish Bulls" 194). While thus a member of the ruling class, as a woman Edgeworth suffered the restrictions typically accorded women of the day. A family friend, for example, Thomas Day, disapproved of female authorship and persuaded her father to forbid the publication of Maria's first work, a translation of Madame de Genlis's *Adèle et Théodore: ou lettres sur l'éducation*. In response Maria wrote *Letters for Literary Ladies* (1795), which defended women's right to write and promoted the cause of higher education for women, emphasizing the importance of women developing their rational faculties — a point stressed by Mary Wollstonecraft, also a rationalist, in her 1792 feminist treatise.

Edgeworth's own subjugated status as a woman may thus have enabled her to appreciate the subjugated condition of the Irish vis-à-vis the English. One senses therefore that, as Marilyn Butler suggests, of all Edgeworth's characters, Thady is, along with Ellinor in the novel *Ennui*, "closest to the tone and value-system of [his] creator" (Introduction to *Castle Rackrent and Ennui* 49).

Thady is illiterate and the narrative purports to be an oral recitation "related to the editor" "several years ago" (Preface ix). It is told in "his vernacular idiom" and while the editor "had it once in contemplation to translate the language of Thady into plain English . . . Thady's idiom [proved] incapable of translation" (ix). So "for the information of the *ignorant* English reader, a few notes have been subjoined by the editor" (ix). The editor/author thus stands between the local oral culture and the literate imperial reader, translating in effect the former for the latter.

The Preface also offers a defense of the novel's focus on the "history" of "domestic lives" (vii). Unlike traditional histories where "the heroes . . . are so decked out by the fine fancy of the professed historian; they talk in such measured prose" that they are not credible. Instead Edgeworth intends to provide a "behind the scenes" look at little people, "a plain unvarnished tale," told in a direct simple style, unlike the currently fashionable "literary manufacture" of Ciceronian rhetoric where "much is often sacrificed to the rounding of a period, or the pointing of an antithesis" (viii). Rather, in the interests of authenticity, the author favors the kind of nonanalytical style identified by Luria in the thinking of illiterate peasants (see Chapter One), one that is reflective of "those who . . . without enlargement of mind to draw any conclusions from the facts they related, simply pour forth anecdotes . . . with all the minute prolixity of a gossip in a country town" (ix). This feminine, gossipy, *post hoc* divagating style, characteristic of many local-color narratives, is the rhetorical medium used by Thady in *Castle Rackrent*.

> My real name is Thady Quirk, though in the family I have always been known by no other than "Honest Thady" . . ., and now I've come to "Poor Thady"; for I wear a long greatcoat winter and summer, which is very handy, as I never put my arms into the sleeves; they are as good as new, though come Holantide next I've had it these seven years: it holds on by a single button round my neck, cloak fashion. (1–2)

Here we have a classic example of oral preliterate associative thinking: Thady ruminates upon his coat, examining it in terms that recall the thought patterns of Luria's Uzbekistan peasants, focusing on the practical operation of wearing the coat, rather than on the rhetorical point of the passage, which is that he looks poverty-stricken even though, as he eventually remarks, he is the father of a high-status individual, "Attorney Quirk" (2).

Thady's recounting of the annals of the Rackrent family is nearly always tinged with comic irony. Indeed, Thady plays the classical comical figure, the *eiron*, to the pretensions of the Rackrent patriarchs. In extolling Sir Patrick, the founder of the house, for example, he exclaims:

> The whole country rang with his praises! — Long life to him! I'm sure I love to look upon his picture, now opposite to me; though I never saw him, he must have been a portly gentleman . . . and remarkable for the largest pimple on his nose . . . He is said also to be the inventor of raspberry whiskey. (3)

Thus, Thady immediately undercuts rapturous hyperbolic praise of a heroic figure with decidedly unheroic aspects, the pimple and the raspberry whiskey.

Barry Sloan notes, Irish peasants' "conversation . . . [is often] a species of subversive warfare, often disguised as flattery or fawning, and always conducted from a defensive position" (18). In their analysis of postcolonial literature, Ashcroft et al. note how "women, like post-colonial peoples, have had to construct a language of their own when their only available 'tools' are those of the 'colonizer'" (175), forced to "pursue guerilla warfare against imperial domination" (174). Thady's subversively ironical treatment of his masters is an example of this kind of rhetorical strategy: ostensible praise which is continually undercut by controverting details.

Each of the successive patriarchs is subtly critiqued through negative details that Thady reports tongue-in-cheek as if in passing. When Sir Patrick dies, his body is seized for debt by creditors and his heir, Sir Murtagh, realizes he can claim this as an affront to his honor and use it as a pretext for refusing to pay the debts. "It was whispered (but none but the enemies of the family believe it) that this was all a sham seizure to get quit of the debts" (5). Sir Murtagh marries into the Skinflint family for money (many of the names in the novel are satirically allegorical) and is a hard-driver of his tenants: "in all our leases there were strict clauses heavy with penalties, which Sir Murtagh knew well how to enforce . . . he taught 'em all . . . to know the law of landlord and tenant" (7). And "my lady . . . often took money [bribes] from the tenants . . . to speak for them to Sir Murtagh about abatements and renewals" (9). Once her husband dies, "she had a fine jointure . . . and took herself away, to the great joy of the tenantry" (9).

The next-in-line Sir Kit is a rake and a gambler ("but that was the only fault he had, God bless him!" [20]) and imprisons his Jewish wife in her room for seven years for refusing to eat pork (18); she is only released after he is killed in a duel. Sir Conolly, the last of the Rackrents, "was ever [Thady's] great favourite . . . the most universally beloved man I had ever seen" (23). He also marries for money Isabella Moneygawls, who is unfortunately disinherited by her father for marrying a Rackrent. Sir Conolly decides to run for office in order to make money and escape creditors. When served with "a writ . . . a wine merchant had marked against my poor master for some hundreds of an old debt," Thady retorts, "put it in your pocket . . . and think no more of it . . . he's a member of Parliament now, praised be God, and such as you can't touch him" (38). However, Sir Conolly goes bankrupt and the property is seized by the new-era bureaucrat, Thady's son, Jason.

Despite the criticism embedded in his satirical treatment of the Rackrent patriarchs, Thady is emotionally tied to the family and remains loyal to them to the end, reflecting the ethic of a kinship culture. His son Jason, however, operates in terms of the ruthless calculative ethic of the new commercial culture where emotional kinship bonds — loyalty — count for little. "I could not bear to hear Jason giving out . . . against the family," Thady remarks, after Jason turns against Sir Conolly by serving him up a bill of debts (42). Jason, he notes, now

> looked down . . . upon poor old Thady, and was grown quite a gentleman, and had none of his relations near him; no wonder he was no kinder to poor Sir Condy than to his own kith and kin . . . [I]t was hard to be talking ill of my own, and I could not but grieve for my poor master's fine estate, all torn by these vultures of the law. (42)

Eventually the Rackrent estate has to be sold to pay off the debts with Jason the buyer.

> The execution came down, and everything at Castle Rackrent was seized by the gripers, and my son Jason, to his shame be it spoken, amongst them. I wondered, for the life of

me, how he could harden himself to do it; but then he had been studying the law, and had made himself Attorney Quirk. (49)

Jason has been transmogrified by a paramount institution of modernity into one who "thinks like a man," operating in terms of rationalist calculation which ignores particularized emotional appeal. When, during the final transaction, Thady offers his master some whiskey punch "for I saw his honour was tired out of his life, but Jason, very short and cruel, cuts me off with — 'Don't be talking of punch yet awhile; it's not time for punch yet a bit — units, tens, hundreds' goes he on, counting over the master's shoulder," enumerating the debt accounts (51). Thady finally confronts his son, saying, how can you do this, how can you betray the ancient bonds of loyalty; Jason replies in commercial terms, saying if Sir Conolly can find "a better purchaser, I'm content," but he's been given a good deal. "I have never . . . charged more than sixpence in the pound, receiver's fees" (53). Thady, "crying like a child," cannot watch when the deed is signed (54). And the local peasants, also loyal to the end, wail and rail against the sale (55). The clash between Thady and his son Jason reflects the transition from premodern to modern values. As Terry Eagleton notes, with Jason's ascension "we witness . . . the triumph of a new, ruthlessly utilitarian order over . . . a colorful if corrupt traditionalism" (*Heathcliff* 163).

In his study of early modern Irish literature Seamus Deane proposes that Burke's *Reflections on the Revolution in France* be seen as "the first of Ireland's national narratives" (25), reflecting as it does a "crisis in the relationship between two modes of civilization" (3), two opposing "languages": a cultural "language of sensibility" and an economic "language of calculation" (4). In the works of Maria Edgeworth, as in Burke, one finds similarly, Deane notes, "a tremulous accommodation between [the] two discourses . . . the language of sensibility, feudalized and given to nostalgia for a vanished past — and the other . . . the language of calculation (. . . rents, debts, interest, loans, mortgages, etc.)" (47).

As opposed to "its lack of historical sense, its refusal of habitual practices, its disabling tendency to abstraction, its aesthetic of distance, and its global pretensions" — all negative aspects of modernity — Burke offers an "aesthetic of the actual . . . that remains immersed in the local, the folklorish . . . [and] refuses the theoretical" (19). Both perspectives — the distancing perspective of modernity and the particularized focus of the premodern — are found in *Castle Rackrent*: the latter provided by Thady Quirk; the former by the editor. The tension between the premodern and the modern may thus be seen in the structure of the novel.

For Thady's narrative is framed and interlarded by comments made by an "editor" who is trained in the disciplines of Enlightenment modernity and who purports to translate Thady for an educated (largely English) readership. Where Thady includes reference to an Irish folk custom or superstition, such as "fairy-mounts" (he warns Sir Conolly against destroying one [8]) or "the Banshee," the editor includes a supercilious explanatory footnote; to wit, that it was believed "the vengeance to the fairies would fall upon the head of the presumptuous mortal" who disturbed them (8 n.1). Or: "The Banshee is a species of aristocratic fairy, who, in the shape of a little hideous old woman . . . [sings] in a mournful supernatural voice . . . to warn the family that some of them are soon to die" (8 n.2). The novel also includes a Glossary, another Enlightenment device that further explains Irish customs and dialect terms, such as *whillaluh*, a "lamentation over the dead," which the editor amplifies with passages from Virgil and Ovid (71). Fairies are further explained: "The country people in Ireland certainly *had* great admiration mixed with reverence, if not dread, of fairies. They believed that beneath these fairy-mounts were spacious subterranean palaces, inhabited by *the good people*, who must not on any account be disturbed" (77).

The novel thus has two diverging authoritative voices, Thady's and the editor's. Butler suggests that this divergence reflects "the split cultural personality of the colonizer" — the one voice "warmly and humorously Irish. The other . . . coolly and rationally English," setting up "the schizophrenic quality of the narration" (Introduction to *Castle Rackrent and Ennui* 16). The one voice expressed in "the 'feminine' gossip of an elderly Irish male narrator" and the other "the 'masculine' commentary of an equally fictional male editor" (18). Both voices are, of course, creations of Maria Edgeworth who, as noted, had a foot, so to speak, in both worlds — one in the feminized premodern colony and the other in the masculine imperial world of the modern metropole.

While the dialect used by Thady in *Castle Rackrent* is not markedly different in its vocabulary and pronunciation from standard English (he uses a few Irish terms, such as *childer* for "children"; *cratur* for "creature" or "person"; *kilt* for "injured"), in her next major work, "Essay on Irish Bulls," Edgeworth offers a sympathetic defense of the Irish vernacular, arguing indeed that in certain respects "the Irish speak *better English* than is commonly spoken by the natives of England" (160). The Irish share a verbal dexterity ("A well-dipped Irishman . . . can move, speak, think, like Demosthenes" [135]) and "in daily conversation . . . employ a superfluity of wit and metaphor which would be astonishing and unintelligible to the majority of the respectable body of English yeomen" (151).

Although the essay for the most part recounts comical episodes, the gruesome aspects of Irish subjugation are also reflected. One anecdote recounts the story of an Irish schoolboy, Dominick, who is beaten and tormented by English schoolmates for speaking in "brogue" (116): "his schoolfellows . . .

consider[ed] him as a being, if not of a different species, at least of a different *caste* from themselves" (117). Another example concerns the trial of a man who knifed an occupying English soldier because the soldier "looked upon me as dirt under his feet, because I was an Irishman; and at every word would say 'That's an Irish bull!' or 'Do you hear Paddy's brogue?'" (146).

The author hopes that the essay will help to change English racist attitudes by "diffusing a more just and enlarged idea of the Irish," urging that since the *Act of Union* it is no longer in England's interest "to deprecate the talents or ridicule the language of the Hibernians" (195).

Ennui (1809) is along with Lady Morgan's *Wild Irish Girl* (1806), discussed below, the first of the local-color novels of *Heimkehr*, homecoming, reflecting what Seamus Deane called "an ideology of . . . *Heimatlichkeit*" (23) (in reference to Burke's *Reflections*) — a German term loosely translated as "at-home-ness" or "rootedness." Edgeworth's novel concerns an English lord's return to Ireland and reconnection with his Irish roots. The novel also charts the protagonist's transformation from a feudal-era aristocrat to a modern meritocrat, thereby enacting allegorically the transition from the premodern to the modern.

Glenthorn is an absentee landlord — a much reviled figure in Irish literature — who at 25 is prone to idleness, various dissipations, and hence ennui. The serendipitous arrival of his childhood Irish nurse, Ellinor, at his estate in England, precipitates his rediscovery of Ireland — cast as a romantic exciting emotional *Other* to the rational, disciplined English world that engenders ennui. "Ellinor is," as Marilyn Butler notes, "Mother Ireland" (Introduction to *Castle Rackrent and Ennui* 46). Although illiterate, she speaks in brogue, and transmits oral history and folklore to Glenthorn, recounting tales of "fairies and *shadowless* witches, and *banshees*" (160). His interest thus reawakened, he returns to his estate, which is in "one of the wildest parts of Ireland" (176). "As I contemplated the scene, my imagination was seized with the idea of remoteness from civilized society" (179). The novel is saved, however, from becoming a romantic allegory (like *The Wild Irish Girl*) by Edgeworth's satire, which is directed both at Glenthorn for his supercilious vanities and at his Irish tenants. When he arrives at his estate, he is greeted by the latter in obsequiously manipulative terms that recall Thady's double-edged praise of his masters. "*Long may you live to reign over us!*" they cry moments before presenting him with a list of demands:

half a hundred more came with legends of traditionary *promises from . . . my lordship's father that was*; and for hours I was forced to listen to long stories *out of the face*, in which there was such a perplexing mixture of truth and fiction, involved in language so figurative . . . that . . . I could comprehend but a very small portion. (182)

Glenthorn thus assumes his colonial role, acting as a kind of enlightened despot on his estate, exercising "a feudal power" "over tenants who were almost vassals" (160). Traditionally, the lord of the manor dispensed benefices to vassals as he saw fit. They thus received in accordance with their ability to persuade him of their need. Glenthorn soon suspects, of the "Crowds of eloquent beggars who . . . surrounded me: many who had been resolutely struggling with their difficulties, slackened their exertions, and left their labour for the easier trade of imposing upon my credulity" (190).

Determining, however, that "the method of doing good, which seemed to require the least exertion, and which I, therefore, most willingly practised, was giving away money" (189), he proceeds to dispense his largesse. But, while enjoying his "feeling of benevolence," he becomes irritated at the Irish "dilatory habits": "the delays, and difficulties, and blunders, in the execution of my orders, provoked me beyond measure" (188). Glenthorn's Scottish agent Mr. M'Loud proposes the practices of capitalist modernity as an alternative to Glenthorn's benevolent but inefficient feudalism, citing that bible of modernity, Adam Smith's *Wealth of Nations* (1776), to cement his points (191). M'Loud favors a more stringent, if heartless, management style, arguing for lower wages, discouragement of large families, free trade beyond the region, which will encourage competition, and division of labor for more efficient manufacture of goods (191) — all hallmarks of Smith's capitalist theory. M'Loud also believes that better education is the key to bettering tenants' lives because it will teach them "to see clearly, and to follow steadily, their real interests" (193). M'Loud thus in effect envisages a revolutionary shift to capitalist democracy, whereby the colonized vassals are empowered to take control of their own lives economically and politically.

Glenthorn is otherwise disinherited by external events — notably the 1798 Rebellion and complex plot developments — so that the implications of M'Loud's theory are not further explored in the novel. For it turns out that Ellinor is Glenthorn's real mother, having exchanged him at birth for the real Earl of Glenthorn whom she raised as her own son Christy O'Donoghue. Upon learning this, Glenthorn abdicates in favor of Christy and, now himself a member of the lower-middle class, moves to Dublin, determined to become a lawyer. No longer defined by feudal status, he is told he has the *"abilities to be anything he pleased"*(304) — the creed of liberal individualism and democratic egalitarianism. The novel also promotes the Enlightenment's Lockean idea that it is environment rather than innate state that promotes or retards one's progress and success. For Christy O'Donoghue, though of aristocratic blood, fails in his management of the Glenthorn properties, while Glenthorn of humble parentage succeeds in becoming a lawyer. As in *Castle Rackrent*, therefore, we see in Glenthorn the rise of a new meritocratic class and downfall of the old feudal order (although Glenthorn, through twists of plot, ends up as owner again of his old estate). Ellinor also, like Thady representative of the old vernacular pre-modern culture, dies, signaling the eclipse of her ethnic world. Glenthorn has, however, through her reconnected with his Irish roots and has come to appreciate "an affectionate and generous people" (291).

That appreciation is also effected by his short-lived infatuation with a spirited upper-class Irish woman, Lady Geraldine, who lives on a neighboring estate. While she speaks standard English, as befitting her class, it has "certain Hibernian inflections . . . something . . . more interrogative, exclamatory . . . perhaps more rhetorical than the common language of English ladies" (203) with "more of the raciness of Irish wit, and the oddity of Irish humour" (205). As her language, so the woman herself: strong and outspoken. She ridicules a stiff contemptuous English traveler who is writing a guidebook to Ireland. "Imagine," she exclaims, "a set of sober English readers studying [his book] and swallowing all the nonsense it will contain!" (212). Rejecting faux imitation of English ways, she says the Irish should be proud of their cultural identity. "Let us dare to be ourselves!" (225). It is a message Glenthorn takes to heart; at the same time, the novel implies that, while emotionally engaging, the old Irish identity must absorb some of the new liberal ideology if it is to survive.

The Absentee (1812), a kind of cross between a novel of manners and a national tale, also concerns a *Heimkehr*, the return of another absentee landlord, Lord Colambre, to his Irish estate and his reconnection with his Irish roots. More so than in *Ennui*, however, this novel realistically exposes the abject living conditions of the Irish peasant even while extolling Ireland and the Irish as sites of authenticity and vitality, contrasted against the vapid social climbing and dissipated life-styles of the upper-crust English — to which Colambre's mother, Lady Clonbrony, vainly aspires to belong.

The opening sections of the novel provide a social satire of that upper-class London milieu. Lady Clonbrony is a victim of what today we might call internalized racism, as she desperately tries to suppress her Irish self so as to appear acceptably English, habitually "deprecat[ing] and abus[ing] every thing Irish" (56). Her English counterparts see through her sham English accent, however, and ridicule her thus: "you *cawnt* conceive the *peens* she *teekes* to talk of the *teebles* and *cheers* . . . and with so much *teest* to speak pure English" (2).

In her attempt to be accepted in the English upper classes she and her husband spend extravagantly, deriving their income from their Irish holdings. As part of his realization of the injustice of the colonial system, Colambre deplores the depletion of Irish natural resources to fund his parents' extravagant life-style. In particular, he decries the wasteful destruction of a forest on his father's land: "a great part of [the] timber, the growth of a century — swallowed in the entertainments of one winter in London! Our hills to be bare for another half century to come!" (193; see also 137, 161). A similar proto-ecological concern about the destruction of forests may be seen especially in the German local-color works (discussed in Chapter Four).

In order to discover for himself how the family Irish estate is being managed, Colambre returns to Ireland (for the first time as an adult) and visits incognito the towns owned by his father and managed by agents. His first eye-opener occurs when an innkeeper comments on his father's status as an absentee landlord. Lord Clonbrony, he says, "might as well be a West India planter and we negroes, for . . . he . . . has no more care, nor thought about us, than if he were in Jamaica . . . Shame for him!" (125). Despite Clonbrony's negligence, this particular town is well managed, thanks to its responsible agent, Burke. The next town Colambre visits (using the assumed name Evans) is not so fortunate. It "consisted of one row of miserable huts . . . no chimneys, the smoke making its way through a hole in the roof . . . dunghills before the doors, and green standing puddles, squalid children, with scarcely rags to cover them" (140). The agent, Garraghty, cheats the inhabitants, while himself living in luxury in Dublin (82–3). Colambre boards with the Widow O'Neil, a figure who like Ellinor in *Ennui* might be called "Mother Ireland," an honorable, humble peasant forced to live in dire poverty and threatened with eviction by the unscrupulous agent. Once he realizes the situation, Colambre reveals himself, saving the woman from eviction and promising to punish the agent. In its social and economic realism *The Absentee* provides the sharpest critique yet seen in literature of the English colonial exploitation of Ireland.

Ormond (1817), Edgeworth's next novel, one of her least-known works, draws a nearly allegorical contrast between two worlds: one, the Black Islands in western Ireland, a remote, primitive area untouched by modernity; the other, the corrupt Machiavellian world of capitalism and the modern bureaucratic state. Ruling over the former realm is "King" Cornelius (Corny) O'Shane and representing the latter is the Anglo-Irish landlord Sir Ulick O'Shane. The passage from — or indeed escape from — Sir Ulick's estate to King Condy's land by 18-year-old Harry Ormond is the principal plot of the novel, which may be seen as another instance of the *Heimkehr*, a return or rediscovery of one's authentic roots.

King Corny's world is, economically, that of subsistence and use-value production where individuals make what is necessary for their own survival, where there is little outside trade, little division of labor, and virtually no mass manufacture. It is a picture of a precapitalist, preindustrial economy. Corny, for example, is "his own shoemaker, hatter, and tailor" and makes his own violin. Harry (reflecting the influence of Adam Smith) wonders "whether it were not better managed in society where these things were performed by different tradesmen" (44). The violin, for example, is likely of inferior quality, he thinks. As an herbalist healer, Corny is also the unofficial doctor for the region. In tending to a wounded man, "he set to work compounding plasters and embrocations, preparing all sorts of decoctions of roots and leaves, famous *through the country*" (41). The narrator, as always reflecting a more modern point of view, is skeptical, however, about herbal medicine, noting that the injured man "got quite well . . . even with the assistance of the black hellebore of the ancients" (42). In addition to practicing medicine and other crafts, Corny explains, "I have no lawyers here, thank Heaven! . . . I am forced to be legislator, and lawyer, and ploughman, and all . . . the best I can for myself" (51).

Like Ellinor and the Widow O'Neil, Corny is honest, sincere, and authentic, as are the other inhabitants of the region. Sheelah, Corny's servant, tells Harry he can go "to fifty continents . . . you'll not find hearts warmer than those at the Black Islands" (151, 181). Corny extends his warmheartedness to other creatures, being kind in his treatment of animals (though he does hunt and fish), rejecting, for example, a cruel plowing practice: "that is against humanity to brute *bastes*" (51).

Sir Ulick, on the other hand, is a conniving politician, a "jobber" — that is, one who uses public money for private advancement (52) — a practice the narrator considers "shameful" (181). "A thorough-going friend of the powers that be," he is a "hack of the administration" (182). His wife, an Englishwoman, looks down on the Irish: "she dreaded Irish disturbances . . . and Irish dirt more; . . . nothing could be right, good, or genteel that was not English" (6). Sir Ulick's son Marcus, who manages their estate, treats the peasant tenants shabbily: "he vented his ill-humour on the poor Irish peasants — the *natives*, as he termed them in derision. He spoke to them as if they were slaves — he considered them savages" (197). His practice and attitude are contrasted to that of a more benevolent landlord who "governed neither by threats, punishments, abuse, nor tyranny; nor yet . . . by promises nor bribery, *favour* and *protection*, like Sir Ulick . . . He treated them neither as slaves . . . nor as dupes . . . [but] as reasonable beings, and as his fellow-creatures whom he wished to improve" (204).

In the end Sir Ulick dies bankrupt and in disgrace, having invested in various "schemes" that failed (290). "The cunning of his head spoiled the goodness of his heart" (290). Harry succeeds Corny as "king" of the Black Islands and vows to follow the model of benevolent management described above. It is recognized that the premodern *praxis* of King Corny is passing: Harry will introduce "improvements" — likely those embraced in *Wealth of Nations*. Moreover, Edgeworth conceives his mission in terms of "civilizing [i.e., modernizing] the people of the islands" (297), a colonial endeavor. A compromise is thus effected — the good qualities of the old ways will be preserved but new methods and ideas will be introduced.

In the fall of 1815 Maria Edgeworth received a letter from an American woman, Rachel Mordecai (later Lazarus), of Warrenton, North Carolina, complaining of the anti-Semitism in Edgeworth's work. "I would ask," Mordecai wrote, "how it could be that she, who on all other subjects shows such justice and liberality, should . . . appear biased by prejudice . . . whenever a *Jew* is introduced . . . ?" (Letter of 7 August 1815, in MacDonald, ed., *Education* 6). It was indeed true that Jewish stereotypes had appeared in Edgeworth's work. In *Castle Rackrent* Thady Quirk expresses prejudicial attitudes toward Jessica, Sir Kit's wife, who is Jewish. More seriously, Mr. Mordecai, a Jewish coach-maker in *The Absentee*, is an anti-Semitic stereotype, the ruthless money-grubber.

Remarkably, Edgeworth seems to have taken Mordecai's criticism to heart, writing her next novel *Harrington* (1817), which deals centrally with anti-Semitism, as an attempt to make amends. Indeed, the Jews supplant the Irish in this novel as the colonized people whose cause the author embraces — with the two groups seen as being linked in kindred victimhood. During an anti-Jewish riot, which occurs in London circa 1780, where the central Jewish characters in the novel, the Monteneros, are threatened, an Irishwoman peddler, the widow Levy, comes to their rescue. She herself is a "papish" (Catholic) whom the mob would "tear to pieces . . . did they suspect the *like*" (155). (The mob had indeed originally been after papists but finding none had turned against Jews as a substitute.) The widow Levy, a coarse lower-class woman who smokes a pipe and speaks in brogue is herself treated with contempt by aristocratic Anglo women, who shrink back when she confronts them. Perhaps her own oppression as an Irish Catholic enables her sympathy for the Jewish plight. "We were all brothers and sisters once" (155), she explains, offering what is likely the philosophy of Edgeworth herself.

The plot concerns the gradual overcoming of anti-Jewish prejudice by the protagonist, Harrington, who learns it when as a child he is frightened by a nanny with "stories of Jews who had been known to steal poor children for the purpose of killing, crucifying, and sacrificing them at their secret feasts and midnight abominations" (10). Later in his reading Harrington realizes how "the Jews are [depicted] as . . . wicked as the bad fairies . . . or allegorical personifications of the devils . . . even in modern tales . . . they are invariably represented as . . . mean, avaricious, unprincipled, treacherous" (21) — perhaps a *mea culpa* on Edgeworth's part for her depiction of Mordecai in *The Absentee* in just these terms.

In school the boys pick on a Jewish peddler boy, Jacob, an episode that recalls the similar bullying of the Irish boy, Dominick, described in the

"Essay on Irish Bulls." Harrington intervenes, saying Jacob is after all "a fellow creature" (33). Harrington eventually falls in love with a Jewish girl, Berenice Montenero, but his father threatens to disinherit him if he marries a Jew. By a twist of the plot, however, it turns out that Berenice is actually Protestant (208), and so they are free to wed. The redoubtable Rachel Mordecai criticized this ending in a letter of 8 October 1817, saying it "disappointed" her that Edgeworth had thus denied Berenice's Jewish identity at the last moment, even though she appreciated the general message of the novel.

Although they never met, Maria Edgeworth and Sydney Owenson, Lady Morgan (1776–1859), clearly influenced each other. Morgan's first "national tale," *The Wild Irish Girl* (1806), followed *Castle Rackrent* in its use of Irish vernacular; its realistic focus on Irish manners and its use of an "editor" who provides explanatory notes; conversely, Edgeworth's *Ennui* (1809) is a reworking of the *Irish Girl's Heimkehr* plot. The net effect of the two novels is quite different, however, as Edgeworth remained in the end an Enlightenment rationalist, while Morgan, although often given to satire, was at heart a Rousseauistic romantic. Like Edgeworth, however, Morgan saw fiction doing "cultural work," having a moral and/or political purpose. In her Preface to her novel *O'Donnel: A National Tale* (1814) she noted: "A novel is specially adapted to enable the advocate of any cause to steal upon the public." Although she was educated in Dublin, Morgan's family roots lay in the west of Ireland, in Sligo and Connaught Province, where Edgeworth's were in County Longford.

Like *Ennui* and *The Absentee, The Wild Irish Girl* concerns the entry or reentry of an absentee English landlord into the remote western part of Ireland — always considered the least anglicized and most authentically Irish of the provinces. The protagonist is a young law student, Henry Mortimer, whose education not in law but in the richness of Irish culture forms the substance of the novel. It is recounted in a series of 30 letters sent to an English member of Parliament; they therefore exude a smug colonialist condescension — at least the early letters. As in *Castle Rackrent*, an "editor" provides a reflective commentary on the narrative, offering more detailed authenticating information about Irish customs or, on occasion, ironizing the text, as for example, when Mortimer describes Glorvina, the "wild Irish girl" of the title, in hyperbolically romantic terms, the editor characterizes it in a note as "an overstrained bit of sentiment" (51 n.10; see also 61 n.1). It is in fact more in the notes that a realistic picture of Ireland emerges than in the tale itself, which devolves into a utopian fantasy.

In his first letter Mortimer acknowledges early "*confirmed prejudice*" of the Irish as being "close to barbarity" (1) and hopes in "Connaught," on the northwest coast, to "behold . . . the Irish character in its *primeval* ferocity" (4). He admits "I have always been taught to look upon the *inferior* Irish as beings forming a lower link than humanity, in the chain of creation" (173). Morgan's satirical treatment of Mortimer extends to his comically pompous Johnsonian rhetoric, which is interlarded with strained classical allusions. His assessment of Dublin, for example, thus:

> The wondrous extent of London excites our amazement; the compact uniformity of Dublin our admiration. But, as dispersion is less within the *coup d'œil* of observance, than aggregation, the harmonious architecture of Dublin at once arrests the eye, while the scattered splendours of London excite a less immediate and more progressive admiration. (3)

Mortimer's airy bombast is punctured by his first encounter with Irish poverty, which occurs shortly thereafter when, while reading Horace under a tree, he notices an impoverished Irish peasant struggling along the road, leading a "sorry lame cow" (11); "almost a skeleton, and scarcely able to crawl," she "seemed to share in the obvious poverty of her master" (12). Murtach O'Shaughnessy is himself a laborer whose family is ill and starving and who had hoped to sell the cow to feed the family. He speaks to the cow in Irish and explains to Mortimer, "One can better suffer themselves a thousand times over than see one's poor dumb baste want: it is, next, please your honour, to feeling one's child in want. God help him who has witnessed both!" (13). The editor adds a note: "neither . . . the character or story of Murtoch, partakes in the least degree of fiction" (12 n.9). Mortimer has the sense to realize that O'Shaughnessy belies the "intemperate, cruel, idle savage" stereotype of the Irish peasant, for here was "a heart . . . tenderly alive to the finest feelings of humanity" (14).

Mortimer gives O'Shaughnessy money, which he spends on hay for the cow, whiskey for himself, and wine and bacon — instead of medicine — for his wife. When Mortimer criticizes his drinking, Murtoch replies, whiskey "is mate, drink and clothes to us, for we forget we have but little of one and less of the other, when we get *the drop* within us. Och, long life to them that lightened the tax on whiskey" (14). He rejects medicine for his wife in favor of the folk remedy of wine and bacon because they were, he said, "Better than any thing the *physicians* could prescribe to keep the disorder *from the heart*" (15). An editorial note amplifies that the Irish peasant saw wine as "the elixir of life" (15 n.14) and that to keep "any disorder from the heart, is supposed . . . to be the secret of longevity" (15 n.15).

Mortimer proceeds on his journey, noting the beautiful plaintive songs the peasants sing while working the fields. The editors adds her own note: "The Editor can at this moment *hum* the air with which the women in Connaught call in their cow" (15 n.16).

Once he reaches the family estate in western Ireland, Mortimer discovers it to be run by a mean-spirited steward who has contempt for the Irish.

> He had now, he said been near five years among them, and had never met an individual of the lower order who did not deserve an halter at least: for his part, he kept a tight hand on them . . . And as for the labourers and workmen, a slave-driver was the only fit man to deal with them: they were all rebellious, idle, cruel, and treacherous. (20)

In an appended note the editor cites *An Enquiry into the Causes of Popular Discontents in Ireland, Etc. Etc.*:

> A horde of tyrants exists in Ireland . . . in the multitude of *agents of absentees* . . .; middlemen . . . who exercise the same insolence they receive from their superiors, on those unfortunate beings who are placed at the extremity of the scale of degradation — the Irish Peasantry! (21 n.1)

Morgan herself in fact wrote a tract, *Absenteeism*, deploring its evils (1825).

Like Colambre in *The Absentee*, Mortimer assumes an incognito identity — as an artist — to avoid in his case being stigmatized as the son of an absentee landlord. In this capacity he is taken into a castle inhabited by an ancient Irish noble, the Prince of Inismore, and his daughter Glorvina. At this point the novel becomes a utopian fantasy, for the inhabitants of this realm are unspoiled, naturally virtuous Rousseauesque innocents who operate in terms of a philosophy of "benevolence" (47). The narrator feels he has passed into "an age of primeval simplicity and primeval virtue" (117). Not surprisingly perhaps the narrator identifies Glorvina with books he is reading: Rousseau's *La Nouvelle Héloïse*, Bernardin de Saint Pierre's *Paul et Virginie*, Chateaubriand's *Atala*, and Goethe's *The Sorrows of Young Werther* (140) — all classics of European Romanticism.

Belying all stereotypes — and rendering the novel's title ironic, Glorvina is highly educated, speaking not in brogue, as one would expect, but the king's English. "Where can she have acquired this elegance of manner? — reared amidst rocks, and woods, and mountains" (60). "[S]he speaks in the language of the court, [while] she looks like the artless inhabitant of a cottage" (61). She thus overturns his common English prejudice of expecting the Irish to be uncouth: "What had I to expect from the Wild Irish Girl? Deprived of all those touching allurements which society only gives; reared in the wilds and solitude" (50).

At first Mortimer expresses a sexist skepticism about the worth of educating women. "How much must a woman lose, and how little can she gain, by that commutation which gives her own acquirements for her own graces! For my part, you know I have always kept clear of the *bas-bleus*" (56). Glorvina's educated status must be seen thus as a repudiation of Rousseau's sexist ideas about education, as expressed in *Émile,* and adopted by Mortimer. In *Émile, ou l'Éducation* (1762) Rousseau proposed a "natural" experiential education for boys (Émile) but for girls (Sophie) it was a matter of learning to become "a coquettish slave in order to render her a more alluring object of desire, a *sweeter* companion to man . . . What nonsense!" Mary Wollstonecraft exclaimed in *A Vindication of the Rights of Woman* (108). In *The Wild Irish Girl* Glorvina receives not the education of Sophie but of Émile.

Morgan indeed was herself a feminist (though the term was not yet in use), influenced by Wollstonecraft and other feminist thinkers of the day. In her Preface to the *Patriotic Sketches of Ireland,* Morgan acknowledges the temerity of a woman daring to write (*The Wild Irish Girl*) (ix), but says she proceeded, even though such audacity was "incompatible with my sex and years" (x). Some years later Morgan wrote a lengthy (two-volume) history of powerful women in antiquity, ironically entitled *Woman and Her Master* (1840), in which she denounces the contemporary practice of "educating women for the Harem" and espouses equal education for women, decrying the fact that

> [her] imputed inaptitude for the higher intellectual pursuits, and presumed incapacity for concentration, are still insisted upon; and while woman is permitted to cultivate the arts which merely please, and which frequently corrupt, she is denounced as a thing unsexed, a *lusus naturae,* if she directs her thoughts to pursuits which aspire to serve, and which never fail to elevate.

> ("Woman"154)

Despite the fact that women have been made the "Pariah of the species, [an] alien to law, [a] dupe of fictions and subject of force" ("Woman"155), they have managed to make their mark in history, which Morgan records in her study.

In *The Wild Irish Girl* Glorvina's tutor, Father John, declares her to be a genius (Rousseau maintained in *Émile* that women cannot have genius ["as for works of genius, they are beyond [women's] capacity" — as quoted in Wollstonecraft 124 n.1]. "I soon found that my interesting pupil possessed a genius that almost anticipated by the force of its own powers," Father John observes to Mortimer. Recognizing the power of "her ambitious mind," the tutor says he decided to leave "her mind free in the election of its studies" (a benefit accorded only to males in Rousseau's novel). While thoroughly familiar with Irish folk ways and history, Glorvina shows herself to be a child of the Enlightenment in her critical attitude toward superstitious aspects of traditional religion and her belief in progress and natural law. "The age in which religious error held her empire undisputed is gone by. The human mind, however slow, however opposed its progress, is still, by a divine and invariable law, propelled toward truth" (186). She also has the natural kindness and compassion seen in various rustic figures in Edgeworth's work, being sensitive to animal suffering and opposed to animal cruelty (85–6, 129). She thus synthesizes a modern intellectual view with premodern sensitivities.

Glorvina's apotheosis may be seen then as a repudiation not just of sexist ideas about women but also of racist ideas about the Irish, who were also thought, as we have seen, to be of a lower intellectual order than the English. Even more so perhaps than in Edgeworth, the cause of women and that of the Irish are seen in Morgan's view to merge. In the end Mortimer and Glorvina marry, a union that is offered in hope that "the distinctions of English and Irish, of Protestant and Catholic, [may] for ever [be] buried" (253). Mortimer is to succeed Glorvina's father as a benevolent landlord with Glorvina accorded equal status.

Morgan's *Florence Macarthy: An Irish Tale* followed in 1818. As a lengthy picaresque novel with numbers of characters and adventures, it is atypical of the local-color genre; nevertheless, because of its defensive focus on the condition, manners, and history of the Irish, it warrants inclusion in its ranks. The novel has two plots: one concerning the return to Ireland of a wrongfully disinherited landlord, Walter Fitzadelm; the other the story of the title character, who operates in disguise through much of the novel, living finally as a reclusive writer who composes "National Tales" (4:35) — thus a thinly disguised autobiographical persona.

As in Edgeworth's *Absentee* and *Ormond*, as well as *The Wild Irish Girl*, Ireland is seen to be under the rule of unscrupulous middlemen — in this case the Crawleys, who form "the BUREAUCRATIE, or office tyranny, by which Ireland has so long been governed" (2:35). "In that official class the acquisition of fortune . . . [was] accumulated by servile arts, political, and fraudulent intrigues" (2:14–15). As against this capitalist Machiavellianism are the little people of Ireland oppressed by "centuries of cruelty, and injustice of misrule, and military violence" (2:232).

Above these middlemen are the negligent upper classes who are depicted, as in *Absentee* and *Ennui*, as frivolous and callously indifferent to the Irish lower classes' suffering. When one Anglo landlady visits her tenants' homes, she can't stand the stench and squalor and has to leave. "If I stay a moment here, I shall catch a typhus fever or be suffocated by the stench" (2:244). The peasant woman who greeted her was "barefooted and bare-legged, her eyes bleared with smoke, her form attenuated by insufficient diet . . . her dress in shreds" (2:240).

As in much Irish local-color literature, Morgan critiques and satirizes false English notions about Ireland. An English traveler arrives reading Spenser's *State of Ireland*, which, we are told, views Ireland "through a smoked glass" (1:14). The real Ireland is promptly introduced in the form of an Irish stevedore: "miserably clad, disgustingly filthy, squalid, meagre, and famished" (1:22). In Dublin "the very air . . . was infected by noxious vapours . . . from piles of putrid matter. The houses . . . were in ruins . . . Here living wretchedness could scarcely find a shelter" (1:38–9). In the countryside "from a few mud-built huts . . . occasionally issued a child or, a pig, while the head of a squalid mistress appeared" (1:193). The English traveler laments "there is . . . no pastoral manners, no subjects for the Idyls of Theocritus, nor the Arcadia of Sannazaro" — references to pastorals of antiquity and the Renaissance, respectively.

Aside from the two protagonists, the most prominent figure in the novel — a counterpart to Thady Quirk and the Widow O'Neil — is Terence Oge O'Leary, a character Maria Edgeworth admired, though she didn't otherwise care for the novel. O'Leary is Fitzadelm's former schoolmaster, a local eccentric well versed in Irish history and lore, and fiercely anti-English. "They pound us in a mortar . . . they perish us with want, and burn us with fire, still the Irish spirit is to the fore" (4:118). O'Leary is writing a history of the Macarthy clan "in the Phœnician tongue, vulgo-vocato Irish, it being more precise and copious than the English" (1:263). He keeps a pet eagle, dusts the furniture with his wig (as Thady did), refers to the "good people . . . the fairies" (1:296), and is kind to animals (3:203). His "native tongue" is Irish (1:285).

Irish premodern customs are noted in passing by the narrator; as, for example, the lack of a standard measure of distance.

> In Ireland, it is extremely difficult, to learn either the way or the distance . . . In remote places, it may be literally said, that "the way lengthens as we go," since every one, of whom inquiries are made, adds a mile or two to the original distance. (1:244–5n)

A *fetch* is a "mysterious voice heard in lonely places [that] gives notice of approaching death" (1:258). The term "a *cuppan* of parliament" is explained as "a little cup [of] . . . *Parliament* whiskey, that is *licensed*" (1:163).

In an 1825 letter Maria Edgeworth noted the common denominators shared by diverse oppressed peoples, who

> have been so long degraded by slavery that they cannot exert themselves sufficiently to regain or deserve liberty. This is the greatest evil and injury done by tyranny. It induces the vices of falsehood and cunning [in] the miserable, the only arms of the weak against

the strong. In the Greeks, the West Indian slaves, the Irish "poor slave" . . . the same defects of character from the same causes appear. But we must not do the cruel injustice of supposing that these faults of character are *natural* and inherent and incurable.

(MacDonald, ed., *Education* 80)

Lady Morgan offers a similar idea in *Florence Macarthy*, drawing a tacit parallel between the oppressed Irish peasant and the colonized Indians of South America (where the protagonists Fitzadelm and Macarthy both had spent time fighting in liberation struggles). "Borne down . . . by long slavery and injustice, the native Indian submits to his vexatious existence, with an affected patience, a seeming apathy, which veils the cunning and ferocity of the enslaved and degraded in all countries" (3:136). An authorial note suggests why her Irish protagonists became engaged in foreign wars: "it is natural that the natives of an oppressed country should sympathize with the oppressed wherever they may exist" (3:289 n.1).

Nevertheless, Morgan like Edgeworth, does not embrace the idea of revolution. Her model, similar to her predecessor's, is that of enlightened landlordism. The protagonists wed and vow to be responsible and residential landlords on their estates. "Repeal the act which banishes our landlords [the *Act of Union*], and exhausts the country of its revenue and resources, and then disease [and poverty] will disappear" (4:80).

Morgan continued her championing of the Irish cause in her next (and last) "national tale," *The O'Briens and the O'Flahertys*, a lengthy (four-volume) adventure-filled historical romance, set in Connemara in the pre-Union era of the latter 1700s. Once again Morgan prefaces her work with a feminist apologia: "I anticipate upon this, as upon similar occasions, that I shall be accused of unfeminine presumption in 'meddling with politics'" (1:vi), noting how *Florence Macarthy* had enraged "half the *Bureaucratie* of Ireland" (1:xi).

One might well argue that this novel takes us even farther from the classic local-color work with its narrow focus on the everyday small-scale details and issues of rural life rather than with sweeping tides of historical events. However, *The O'Briens and the O'Flahertys* continues to provide realistically revealing canvases of the premodern world of nineteenth-century Ireland. The *Heimkehr* plot, which covers the return to Ireland of the native Murrogh O'Brien to reclaim his patrimony in rural Connemara and his marriage to Beavoin O'Flaherty, an Irish patriot, need not concern us.

Instead let us note in passing the intensity of the lament that echoes in the novel for a vanishing world. There is Murrogh's foster brother, Shane, for example, a (literally) wild Irish man, an insurrectionary who lives in the woods and speaks mainly Irish (while Murrogh, having lived abroad and been educated in Dublin, has lost much of his Irish, though he can still understand it). Shane speaks with affection about his rural habitat.

> Ay, and the cabin down by the cromleck, and the cow in the bawn, and St. Endeas' Cross, and the ating and dhrinking and the puffins, and the sunfish, and the uishge, and the mead . . . God is good . . . and there's berries in the bramble and cresses in the ditch, and wather in the ford; and is not that good enough for the wild Irish *giocah*? (2:303)

In *The Wild Irish Girl* Mortimer noted of another Irish speaker, "He seems not so much to speak the English language, as literally to translate the Irish; and he borrows so much and so happily, from the peculiar idiom of his vernacular tongue" (54). The same may be said of Shane with his use of Irish terms — *cromleck* (creek); *uishge* (whiskey); *giocah* (vagabond/outlaw) — as of O'Leary in *Florence Macarthy* and other Morgan characters. The authentic transcription of Irish dialect is one of the strengths of Morgan's novels, lending the sense of *"vraisemblance"* that she says in the Preface she aspired to (1:viii). In this she paved the way for later Irish writers such as the Banim brothers and William Carleton.

The O'Briens and the O'Flahertys, like her other national tales, deplores the miserable treatment and condition of the Irish peasantry who "appear morally and physically to be reduced to a state, to which, that of the beasts of the field is preferable" (1:24). Like Colambre in *The Absentee*, Murrogh decries the wanton destruction of Irish forests, another historical effect of modernity repeatedly lamented in local-color literature. First, "the axe of the stranger had . . . been early laid to the root of Irish forests." Later, "the noblest forest trees were consumed as fuel" (4:12) in the wars of rebellion.

Third in the quartet of women pioneers of Irish local-color literature in the early 1800s was Mary (Shakleton) Leadbeater (1758–1826). A Quaker influenced by Mary Wollstonecraft and William Godwin and born to a family of educators (her grandfather Abraham Shakleton ran a school attended by Edmund Burke, who remained a family friend), Leadbeater was thus endued into the political and social ideas of modernity but as a lifelong resident of Ballitore, a small town in County Kildare, she knew well the customs and manners of premodern rural Ireland. Her *Cottage Dialogues among the Irish Peasantry* (1811) followed Edgeworth's and Morgan's early work and was influenced by them, although she never met either of her predecessors. Edgeworth nevertheless wrote an enthusiastic Preface to the *Cottage Dialogues*, along with notes "to explain to the English reader the Hibernian idiom, and local customs" (vi). Those notes were deleted for the Irish language edition.

The *Cottage Dialogues* is a didactic work of 54 "dialogues," designed to educate peasants in modern ideas and methods. As such, it is tiresome as literature but interesting as an example of a colonial attempt to lift the natives out of "backward" ways of thinking and behaving. A servant woman, Nancy, for example, is held up as a model of "bad" behavior. She is resistant to modern ways, refusing to have her children inoculated with "cow pock" to prevent smallpox (227). Consequently, a son contracts the disease and dies; then her husband dies and she takes to drink and dies herself. Her "idleness" and inefficiency, along with her smoking and drinking are also excoriated.

Much more interesting and significant as a pioneering local-color work, because it includes myriad details about the actual practices of village life of the time, is Leadbeater's *The Annals of Ballitore*, a nonfictional anecdotal chronicle of her town during the period 1766–1824. Based on a journal she kept in those years, the *Annals* was assembled or written around 1824 but not published until 1862. The *Annals* distinguishes itself by its realism and lack of a political agenda. Unlike Edgeworth and Morgan, it seems Leadbeater in the *Annals* did not purport to be doing cultural work, but rather was simply recording a kind of family history of her village. In her accurate portrayals of village residents she pioneered one of the hallmarks of the classic local-color tale.

In the *Annals* we learn that Leadbeater herself was a colonial intermediary between an absentee landlord, Melisina Trench, and her Irish tenants. Leadbeater was enthusiastic about modern inventions such as smallpox vaccinations (which her mother resisted, leading Mary to have a mild case of the disease herself in 1766), and approved of such Enlightenment developments as liberal education methods, prison reform, and savings banks open to commoners. She speaks favorably of the instauration of a school for poor children based on the methods of Johan Heinrich Pestalozzi (1746–1827) (1:395), a Swiss educator who advocated a Rousseauistic approach emphasizing the development of each individual's talents through experiential knowledge. (Maria Edgeworth and her father wrote a treatise, *Practical Education* [1798], which reflected these views. In 1820 Edgeworth heard Pestalozzi lecture in Paris and visited him at his home in Switzerland.) Pestalozzi also wrote one of the first of the German *Dorfgeschichten* — village stories (*Lienhard und Gertrud, ein Buch für das Volk* [1781]) — a temperance tract that lacks, however, sufficient regional specificity to be characterized as a local-color work (see Zellweger 24). Nevertheless, in its missionary mission, and as it was translated into English in 1800, it likely influenced Leadbeater.

In an 1822 journal entry Leadbeater also notes approvingly the adoption of more humane prison management, "Goldsmith's plan of prison discipline, as described in the 'Vicar of Wakefield.' . . . Thus what has been looked on as impracticable and romantic may . . . in time prevail over long established error" (1:408). The system described by Goldsmith emphasized rehabilitation rather than cruel punishment, providing prisoners with training in crafts, and treating them as redeemable. "[I]nstead of converting correction into vengeance . . . We should . . . find that creatures, whose souls are held to be as dross, only wanted the hand of a refiner" (*Vicar* 238). "It is thus that reason speaks, and untutored nature says the same thing" (*Vicar* 237) — an echo of Rousseau. Goldsmith and Leadbeater reflect the influence of Enlightenment reformer Cesare Bonesana Beccaria's *Dei e delle pene delitti* (1764) [*On Crimes and Punishment*]. In England the Quakers were especially active in prison reform.

At the same time, despite her enthusiasm for some of the key reforms of modernity, Leadbeater, by her own admission had a "fondness for 'the days of other times'" (2:291), citing with approbation Burke's comment that "the advantage in trying [farming experiments] often consisted in proving that the old way was best" (1:120). In 1799 when "the trees of Ballitore" were advertised "to be sold by auction," she comments that the seller "had never sported in his youth beneath these shades, watched the successive budding of the beech, the ash, and the elm, and remarked their beautiful diversity of foliage" (1:269). When several are felled, "I dreamed of the devoted trees, and I wept for their downfall" (1:270). Still, she admits, there is "a freer circulation of air" afterward which prevents "those putrid fevers which [had] so often visited Ballitore" beforehand (1:271).

Her affectionate and detailed portrait of various village inhabitants is Leadbeater's most important contribution to the genre. Her Aunt Carleton prefigures the eccentric spinster character found in many a New England local-color work. She has the "gift of healing," maintains a large "assortment of drugs . . . [and] distilled simples," which she sells or gives away to the poor (1:60). She has two foster children (1:63), various pet animals, including a pig who can open a door latch (1:70), and hens who lay eggs on a cushion under her chair (1:70). Here again we get a glimpse of the "undisciplined" world of premodernity seen in Cooke's "Miss Lucinda" noted in the Introduction where boundaries (between species, between inner and outer space) remain much more fluid than today. Aunt Carleton is also a kind of village therapist/rescuer, saving, for example, a woman being brutalized by her husband (1:59).

Leadbeater describes the superstitions and customs seen in other Irish works, such as a belief in fairies, the Banshee, and the fetch. But her perspective is decidedly one of modern skepticism. "All the learning and piety in our village could not conquer the superstition of the age . . . [which] has made of dreams an instrument of torture to weak and susceptible minds" (entry of 1772, 1:87).

In her concern for realism Leadbeater contrasts her own work to William Wordsworth's (had she read Dorothy Wordsworth, she might have found a kindred soul), which she says she does not find "always *understandable*." Decrying the symbolic "metaphysical" dimension to Wordsworth's pedlar, she notes of her own pedlar character (in the novella *The Pedlars: A Tale* [1826]), "it would ill become me and my pedlar to be metaphysical" (2:397). "My pedlar is a plain, honest man, by no means metaphysical, and no more sentimental than are many of our poor countrymen" (2:395).

The Annals of Ballitore may be seen thus as one of the first literary attempts at unsentimental, unromantic, but respectful depiction of local provincial life. Its immediate successor was John Galt's similar (though fictional) annals in Scotland (see Chapter Three) but it created a format that echoed down in later works in the genre.

Mrs. [Anna Maria Fielding] S. C. Hall (1800–81) was undoubtedly familiar with Leadbeater's *Cottage Dialogues*, as well as with Edgeworth's and Morgan's work, when she wrote *Sketches of Irish Character* (1829). Set in Barrow, County Wexford, where she grew up, it contains 28 "sketches," most of which are poignant short stories about Irish peasants. A few, however, are didactic essays about Irish foibles, notably their alleged laziness, irresponsibility, and procrastination — perennial complaints about the colonized by the colonizer. In her teens Fielding moved to England with her widowed mother and later married an Englishman, S. C. Hall. The narrator of the sketches purports to be remembering incidents and characters known in her youth in Barrow. As the narrator, her father, and her dog Neptune recur in several of the sketches, one has the impression that many if not all of the anecdotes had a basis in reality.

More so perhaps than its predecessors, Hall's *Sketches* records eccentric marginals untouched by modern disciplines and resistant to them. There is, for example, a self-flagellating mendicant woman in "The Reparee" who has taken "a vow never to let the hood fall off her head . . . and never to lay aside on a bed for the next seven years. Oh! there's a power o' holiness about her, plaze your honour," a character exclaims. "The poor thing's heart aches for the sins o' the world and she wishes to ease 'em" (282). In "The Barrow Postman" the hermit Grey Lambert lives in an abandoned castle with his dog, Bag (89–90, 104). "Jack the Shrimp" (166–74) concerns a similar character, a shrimper whose loyal dog, Crab, saves his life but is then himself adopted by the narrator's dog after Jack is later killed in a fight with an English soldier. Other eccentrics include Peggy the Fisher in "Lilly O'Brien" (27–65); Nelly Clary in "Kelly the Piper" (258–74) and "The Reparee" (275–96); the title character in "Mabel O'Neil's Curse," a "sort of wild woman" (338), who hates the "cowardly red-coats" and wishes "they could ha' rid the country o' these beggarly Cromwellians" (340); "Old Frank," who "had a most confirmed belief in banshees, cluricawns, fairies, and mermaids . . . He could never be prevailed upon to root up large mushrooms (fairy tables) or to pull bullrushes (fairy horses), lest he might offend the good people" (380): "Oh, Miss, don't laugh . . . it's bad to disbelieve the fairies" (385).

Colonial attempts to impose modern methods are resisted. A young English bride's attempts "to improve Ireland" prove difficult (163), though her "exact neatness was a positive reproof to the slovenly habits of the uncultivated peasantry" (154). An Irish peasant woman protests, "I want to . . . put a stop to her *improvements,* as ye call 'em . . . bringin' foreign ways into the country" (160). "Peter the Prophet" (203–17), an eccentric Cassandra-like curmudgeon predicts doom will result from the reforms of modernity: "As if the people can't burn turf as their grandfathers did afore them" (203). In "Annie Leslie" (297–318), a story about tenant eviction, an itinerant fish hawker, Alick the Traveler, who wanders the countryside with his donkey, reproaches the tenant for adopting modern methods: "couldn't ye have been content to mind yer farm, and not be putting English plans of improvement into an Irish head, where it's so hard to make them fit?" (307). When the tenant finds his rent doubled, the narrator notes, "An Irish farmer must often play the spaniel to his landlord . . . hardly daring to believe himself a man . . . But the Mind, though it may be suppressed, cannot be destroyed; with the Irish peasant *cunning* frequently take the place of boldness; and he becomes dangerous to his oppressors" (309). In "Kelly the Piper" (258–74) we are given another example of peasants' insincere flattering of their landlord: "Every blessing in life on yer honour! — and proud are we all to see your honour looking so fresh and bravely fine this morning" (263).

Though herself, like Edgeworth, of the landlord class, Hall thus evinces considerable sympathy with — even identification with — the dominated peasants and remembers the Ireland of her youth with affection: "Barrow, in my remembrance, always seems like fairyland — its fields so green, its trees so beautiful" (380). And she notes how the natives also appreciate and love its natural beauty.

> The being who lives amid the beauties of nature, although he may not express, must feel the elevating, yet gentle influence of the herb, and flower, and tree. Many a time have I heard the ploughman suspend his whistle to listen to that of the melodious blackbird; and well do I remember the beautiful expression of a peasant neighbor watching the beauty of a sunset. (312)

Hall wrote a number of further works about Ireland, including *Lights and Shadows of Irish Life* (1838) and *Tales of the Irish Peasantry* (1840). She was very prolific with her complete oeuvre totaling more than 100 works.

Probably the least known of the Irish local-color writers (none of the relevant secondary works mention him) is Michael Whitty (1795–1873), who was born in Nicharee parish, Duncormick, in County Wexford, attended Maynooth, studying for the Roman Catholic priesthood, a pursuit he abandoned, later emigrating to England where he became a journalist. In 1824 he published his *Tales of Irish Life, Illustrative of the Manners, Customs, and Condition of the People*, a two-volume work comprising 15 short stories.

Although historical events form a backdrop in many Irish works of the day — in particular the 1798 Rebellion, which figures in *Ennui, Florence Macarthy, The O'Briens and the Flahertys* and in *The Annals of Ballitore*, where Leadbeater records successive occupations of the town by insurgents and government soldiers — none before Whitty focuses on the indigenous religious strife between Protestants and Catholics. Perhaps because of his training in the priesthood, Whitty seems especially sensitive to the profound religious prejudices that animated each side of this prolonged struggle. In "North and South; or Prejudice Removed" (2:23–46) we learn, "The Orangemen of the North and the Ribandmen of the South . . . equal one another in hatred, folly, and bigotry" (2:29). The story is a kind of morality tale about how a Catholic, Henry Fitzgerald, who takes a job in Ulster, is gradually accepted by his Protestant employers who "expected to see in Henry a kind of Popish monster" and are surprised to find him "a rational being" (2:36). Henry also overcomes his idea that all Protestants are damned and marries the employer's daughter (a Protestant), while the employer's Protestant son weds Henry's Catholic sister.

A grimmer view of the religious strife is seen in "Protestant Bill" (2:208–29). The protagonist is a Protestant who grows up in a Catholic area and as a kid is taunted by Catholics, whom he therefore grows up hating. As an adult he becomes a local constable and for sport shoots Catholics' dogs. In revenge for this and other offenses, the local insurgents — the White Boys — burn his house down; eventually he is discredited and defeated. A similar struggle is depicted in "Turncoat Watt; Or, Village Politics" (2:91–119) where Methodists attempt to set up a parish and a school but are eventually forced either to convert to Catholicism or leave town.

"The Witch of Scollough's Gap" (1:171–207) sees Catholics' rage at their unjust treatment as fomenting the Rebellion of 1798. Since Oliver Cromwell's "invasion" (in the seventeenth century) "the laws . . . confirmed the political robbery . . . [and] degraded . . . life by galling prohibitions, and enslaved . . . by disqualifying statutes" (1:172). The central characters belong to the rebel group — the United Irishmen. One of the most striking of these is Magg who inspires rebel troops on her "white steed" (1:198) and with her fiery oration. The "witch" of the title is Briedhe Kinsellah, who lives in an abandoned castle, brews medicinal herbs, and operates a kind of protection racket whereby local peasants pay her protection money (in gifts) to keep her from "inflicting diseases on men and cattle" (1:187). She wears a scarlet cloak and has "red and glaring" eyes (1:190). She is also a Cassandra, correctly predicting doom for the rebels. Briedhe is another example of the marginal uncivilized figure evidently prevalent enough in premodern societies as to be commonly found in numerous local-color works. Another such character is Nell, a servant woman in "The Robber" (1:122–70). "The snakes" on the Furies' heads weren't "half so repugnant as the uncombed locks of this infernal looking beldam" (1:141). In "The Common" (2:72–90), Whitty notes how uncouth personages of this type are a fading phenomenon as the modern forces of homogenization take hold.

> It is in societies not equalized by the progress of polished manners that original characters can only be found: The attrition caused by the freedom of well-regulated discourse veers off the acerbity of disposition, and forms a similarity of thinking. (2:73)

The transition from the premodern feudal system to the modern liberal state is treated in "The Last Chieftain of Erin" (2:120–71), which bears some resemblance to *Ormond* and *The Wild Irish Girl*, set as it is in the "remoter parts of Connaught" (2:121), concerning the downfall of a regional chief. The transition entails pacification and acceptance of English rule, but the narrator sees this as a progressive embracement of Enlightenment ideals. "Ancient customs . . . disappear but slowly before the light of reason and rational liberty, particularly when both are introduced by those who were looked upon as oppressors" (2:120).

Cormac O'Connor, the "last chieftain," is evicted from his Ballintobber Castle for failure to pay debt and exiled to Inniskea Island where he dreams of "expelling the strangers, as the English were called" (2:125). His son Fedlin returns from service with the Austrian military during the Napoleonic Wars, organizes a rebellion against the English occupier, but falls in love with his opponent's daughter. After various complications the two eventually wed and Fedlin swears allegiance to the English king, which betokens a recognition that "it was better to be a subject among freemen than a superior among slaves" (2:170) — Whitty clearly here enunciating the imperial point of view.

That point of view is also evident in the first story of the series, "Limping Mogue" (1:1–41), which concerns an Englishman, John Ellice, who tries to civilize the natives, so to speak, but eventually gives it up as a hopeless cause and returns to England. At first,

> he began to lay out his ground on an improved English plan, and commenced teaching [the peasants] the use of newly-invented implements of . . . husbandry . . . But the

> Irish . . . continued . . . ignorant because too vain to acquire knowledge . . . They have retarded improvement by ridicule. (1:4)

Finding the local judge partial and corrupt, Ellice realizes "there is no law, in Ireland, for an Englishman" (1:7). Nor are the laws respected by the Irish; in fact "they are detested, because they are every way violated" (1:12). An Irish neighbor explains that being powerless, the Irish have had to "oppos[e] artifice to power" (1:11), engaging in devious chicanery. "The Irish peasantry," Whitty notes in another story, "are made cunning by poverty, liars by necessity" (2:92).

While showing thus some sympathy with the imperial power, Whitty nevertheless like the other writers noted above excoriates the evils of the system, especially absentee landlordism, as seen in his story, "The Absentee" (1:87–121); unscrupulous agents and merciless evictions, as seen in "The Informer" (1:208–24), which deplores

> the short leases which landlords give . . . [leaving] the unfortunate tenant at the caprice of a merciless or mercenary agent . . . Thus do the inhumanity and bad policy of landlords and their agents bring ruin and consequent infamy on thousands of the Irish peasantry; and to these facts may be attributed the burnings and destruction of property which have disgraced that unfortunate country. (1:213)

The solution which Whitty offers is the same as that proposed by Edgeworth and the others — benevolent landlordism, as seen in his story "The Indulgent Landlord" (2:230–49).

Writing at the same time as Whitty were the brothers John (1798–1842) and Michael (1796–1874) Banim, of Kilkenny, whose multi-volume *Tales of the O'Hara Family* began appearing in 1825. Though the brothers collaborated on the works, John was the chief architect and dominant writer. Michael used the pseudonym "Barnes O'Hara" and John, "Abel." The "tales" are really novels, the best of which are *Crohoore of the Bill-Hook* and *The Nowlans*. Both provide expansive detailed scenes of Irish Catholic peasant life — perhaps the most realistic and insightful so far seen — yet the plots are driven by violent events and they devolve at times into gothic melodrama. In their emphasis on romantic adventure the Banims likely had as their model Sir Walter Scott whose novels by this time were being widely read in Ireland (see Chapter Three).

While Whitty took seriously the anger of the Irish revolutionaries, none of the writers discussed to this point register the evil brutality of the violence that accompanied the political activities of the day as the Banims did. The depth of the insurgents' ferocious hatred and bitterness comes alive in their pages. *Crohoore of the Bill-Hook*, thought to be mainly by Michael Banim, opens with a gruesome murder of Anthony Dooling, a farmer, and his entire family, a deed accomplished by a bill-hook, a kind of pruning sickle. A daughter, Alley, is kidnapped, and an adopted son, Crohoore, is suspected of the murder and the kidnapping. The plot concerns the tracking down of the real murderer, Jack Doran, a jilted suitor of Alley's, who is also a ruthless leader of the White Boys, the rebel band.

The world Banim describes is one rife with dark superstitions, numerous wild, uncivilized characters, dire poverty, lawlessness, and stark oppression. Many of the characters speak Irish, which is then translated in a footnote (for example, 1:15, 20–2, 40, 99, 138); or translated directly in the text (as when the narrator notes of a funeral wail — the *keenthechaun* — "the whole delivered in the Irish tongue . . . composed on the instant" [1:2]); or rendered in dialect.

The ritual of keening at Irish wakes and funerals, described in detail, evinces the mood of the novel. "The wild son was chaunted by a tall worn woman, with matted locks and a haggard face" (1:47). A mother keens her murdered insurgent son; "bursting into an irregular and dismal song, uttered in many an unequal dhass or verse, his keenthecaun":

> I nursed you at my breast; I baked your marriage cake; I sit at your head — Ullah! (1:242)

> But I weep for you now; you fell revenging yourself on our enemies; the blood of the traitors shall alone nourish the green grass on your grave. (1:254)

The distinguished Irish critic Bridget MacCarthy once commented on this passage: "Who will not say that this is the voice of Gaelic Ireland, not merely of Banim's time, but of the ageless Ireland of strong primeval memories?" ("Irish Regional Novelists," July–Sept. 1946, 31).

At a meeting of the White Boys, an eloquent oration by Terence Delany (later killed and mourned by the mother noted above) is translated, the narrator notes.

> The Irish peasant . . . poured out a speech in his native tongue, adopting it instinctively as the most ready and powerful medium of expressing his feelings; for one who boggles and stammers is ridiculous in English, becomes eloquent in Irish: we follow the speaker in translation, which will necessarily, shew none of the rude *patois* he must have betrayed had he attempted . . . to display his feelings in a language almost unknown to . . . him. (1:197)

Of Terence's dying words the narrator again apologizes for the improbability of such elegant diction coming from a peasant, insisting that it is but a literal translation of an eloquent language:

> if the language uttered by Terence Delany appear too refined for one of his situation in life, it is . . . in strict unison with the genius and idiom of the language in which he spoke, and from which we have literally translated; in the Irish there is nothing of . . . vulgarism; its construction even in the mouths of the peasantry, who to this day use it, has been and can be but little corrupted. (1:247–48)

Terence is a prime example of a peasant driven to violence by his own horrific treatment by a heartless government agent, Peery Clancy, a tithe-proctor (tax-collector). Clancy's modus operandi is to bewilder tenants with confusing bureaucratic instructions, forcing them to sell all they own in order to pay the tithes. At the White Boy meeting one of the members protests against "the rievin', plunderin', murtherin' rapperies o' tithe-proctors, the bitther foes iv ould Ireland's land . . . never heedin' the moans o' the poor neighbours, that are left to starve, or not like ould horses in the ditches" (1:192). When Terence's wife and children die of starvation, to mete revenge he joins the White Boys who then lynch Clancy, bury him to the neck, and cut off his ears (1:214, 218–19).

While many of the superstitions and folk beliefs seen in other works — such as fairies, banshees, fetches, Leprechauns — are also depicted in Banim's novel, they are not seen as quaint or amusing but rather dark, ominous, and nefarious. Crohoore, for example, is demonized by village gossips because of his alleged connection with the fairies and witch-like powers (1:42), as well as his odd looks. He had "fiery-red hair," a "knobby forehead," bushy brows, a large head, and a dwarf body (1:17–18), and is thus said to look "like the old bouchal [devil] himself" (1:19). It is largely because of these prejudicial beliefs that he is erroneously assumed to be the murderer. The woman who harbors him and is thought to be his mother is a toothless old crone whose face is "shrivelled up into innumerable wrinkles" (1:57). Her ex-husband Sheeum-na-Sheeog lives in "a wild hovel" (1:333), is thought to have lived with the fairy people for ten years and become a "fairy-man" (335), a "wizard" (337). (*Sheeog* means fairy offspring or changeling — one who has been turned into or replaced by a fairy.) Because of his magical powers he is fearfully consulted by locals as a seer.

Banim seems to be struggling more with the question of narrative structure than any of the earlier writers, tempted himself as narrator by the rambling associative logic of oral discourse (seen in Thady Quirk) but summoned by the requirements of hypotactic narrative coherence. After a lengthy digression that describes "Fair Day" in Kilkenny, Banim apologizes. "We regret that now, when we have not rehearsed the hundredth part of [the fair's] novelties, pleasures, and incidents, we are no longer free to indulge our teeming garrulity; but the story to which we have yoked ourselves requires immediate attention" (1:315). He excuses similar digressions on at least two other occasions (1:282, 295).

Banim thus seems more immersed in the folk world of the Irish peasant than previous writers who saw that world from without and from a perspective of modern liberalism. Banim understands and to an extent shares that viewpoint but at times loses himself in sympathetic identification with his subjects, presenting their world directly, uncritically, and probably more realistically.

The Nowlans by John Banim is framed by a letter from "Abel O'Hara" to "Barnes" saying the following story was gleaned while passing the night with the Nowlan family in Tipperary. (A similar frame introduces *The Fetches* [1825].) Taking the position of the educated outsider, Abel notes the narrowness of the Nowlan father's ideas, which are "bounded by the Slieve Bloom mountains" (6). The mother, brought up Protestant and a reluctant convert, still considers herself like many Protestants to be of a "superior caste . . . a race of beings as much above Irish papists, as white men above black" (16). The mother also for unknown reasons (perhaps her lack of education) speaks in a much stronger dialect — with Irish terms thrown in ("musha" [26]; "*a-chorra-ma-chree*" [28]) — than the other characters.

The central plot of the novel concerns the Nowlan son John who studies for the priesthood but falls in love with Letty Adams and elopes with her to Dublin, abandoning the priesthood, for which he is stigmatized by society. Impoverished and outcast, Letty soon dies. A parallel plot, however, between Letty's evil brother Frank and John's sister Peggy, degenerates into gothic melodrama. In its sense of dark foreboding and tragic destiny, and in the unity of its plot, *The Nowlans* prefigures Thomas Hardy. But in its emphasis on details of local color and in tangential discussions about the injustices of English rule, it may be classified as another "national tale." On numerous occasions indeed the Banims expressed as their motivation a desire "to insinuate through fiction . . . the causes of Irish discontent" (as cited by Yeats, Introduction to *Representative Irish Tales* 95). "The faults of the lower orders of the Irish are sufficiently well known; . . . it cannot . . . do any one harm to exhibit them in a favorable light to their British fellow-subjects" ("Stolen Sheep" in *Representative Irish Tales* 98). Late in his life John Banim worried, however, that he had dwelt too much on "the dark side of the Irish character" (as quoted in Flanagan 202).

The local-color tradition in Irish literature continued in the works of Charles Lever, Samuel Lover, Gerald Griffin, and Charles Kickham, but its culminating masterpiece was produced by an Ulsterman, William Carleton (1794–1869), termed by William Butler Yeats in 1889 "the greatest novelist of Ireland" (Appendix, *Representative Irish Tales* 363). That opinion is shared by many modern critics, including Bridget MacCarthy — "by far the greatest of the early Irish novelists" ("Irish Regional Novelists," July–Sept. 1946, 33) — and Terry Eagleton — "the finest nineteenth-century novelist" (*Heathcliff* 207). In Carleton's work, Thomas Flanagan notes, "the values of Gaelic Ireland and those of modern Europe clashed with explosive and tragic force" (258).

Carleton was born in the townland of Prillisk, Clogher Parish, County Tyrone, in the province of Ulster, which is now Northern Ireland. Like Whitty, he was raised a Catholic and planned at one point to become a priest and study at Maynooth. He ended up in Dublin, however, a Protestant convert and a writer, publishing the first series in his *Traits and Stories of the Irish Peasantry* in 1830, and the second series in 1832. A definitive combined edition appeared in 1842.

Carleton grew up in a peasant family of native Irish speakers; his father was bilingual but his mother, Mary Kelly, "was not so well acquainted with the English tongue," Carleton explained in his Introduction (1:ix). She was known and admired locally as a keener and singer of old Irish airs, of which she preferred the original Irish versions. Once when asked to give the English translation, she replied, "The English words and the air are like a quarrelling man and wife: *the Irish melts into the tune, but the English doesn't*" (1:x). Carleton is thus especially sensitive to the issue of Irish dialect, and laments how "the English tongue is gradually superceding the Irish. In my own native place, for instance, there is not by any means so much Irish spoken now, as there was twenty or five-and-twenty years ago." He claims that the false English stereotype of the "wild Irishman" developed from the fact that "in the early periods of communication between the countries" the Irish "expressed [themselves] with difficulty" in English, as it was not their native tongue, "and often impressed the idiom of [their] own language upon one with which [they] were not familiar" (1:ii).

As a youth Carleton heard numerous "old tales, legends, and historical anecdotes" from his father, whose "stock of them was inexhaustible" (1:x). More often than not these were in Irish, so that as an adult Carleton found himself translating them into English, "transfer[ring] the genius, the idiomatic peculiarity and conversational spirit of the one language into the other, precisely as the people do in their dialogue" (1:ix). The dialect Carleton transcribes in *Traits and Stories* is true to this spirit, being much thicker and peppered with Irish phrases (which are translated in footnotes) than that used in earlier works.

Thus immersed as a child in folk culture — he was, he said, "one of themselves" (1:viii) — Carleton nevertheless was well educated — in the Latin-based Catholic "hedge schools" — and well read. He was influenced by, among others, Mary Davys and acknowledged as his predecessors all the local-color writers treated above, noting especially the contribution of the women writers. "It would be difficult indeed, in any country, to name three women who have done more in setting right the character of Ireland and her people . . . than Miss Edgeworth, Lady Morgan, and Mrs. Hall," singling out the latter for especial praise (1:iv). Like them, as noted above, Carleton hoped to dispel negative stereotypes through his work but that purpose seems to have been lost in the telling of the tales, for they are by no means didactic or shaped toward any political point. Rather they are loosely and associatively organized in the manner of anecdotal oral history, and their oral origin remains deeply impressed in the narrative structure, to the point where Carleton created a unique genre — an amalgam of transcribed oral history and embedded tales.

The first section of the work (the first five stories) is structured in a framed-novelle format like Boccaccio's *Decameron* or Marguerite de Navarre's *Heptameron*. The setting is an Irish *ceili*, an evening gathering for gossip and tale-telling. Several residents of a village in Clogher parish sit around chatting "the long winter nights" in the cottage of Ned and Nancy M'Keown "in front of [a] kitchen-fire of blazing turf" (1:9); out of their gossip and banter the central story emerges with each villager to tell a story in turn. The fourth story begins, for example, "The succeeding evening found them all assembled about Ned's fireside in the usual manner; where M'Roarkin, after a wheezy fit of coughing and a draught of Nancy's porter, commenced to give them an account of LARRY M'FARLAND'S WAKE" (1:84). Carleton abandoned this format after the fifth story, but continued to have the embedded tales emerge out of conversations among characters. The amusing and witty banter among the characters is in fact one of the great charms of Carleton's book, often outweighing in length and interest the story's plots themselves. The first story, for example, consists largely in such banter, with a character sketch emerging of the hen-pecked title character, Ned M'Keown. Carleton admits in a note that he fashioned the hen-pecked aspect in revenge for the real Ned's having chastized him in his youth. When said Ned learned of this, he was "indignant and wrathful . . . [saying] 'there's that *young* Carleton has put me in a book, an made Nancy leather *me*!'" (1:50n).

Often, Carleton prefaces the story with a lengthy nonfictional essay. "Ned M'Keown" (1:22) opens the work with several pages pinpointing the locale of the M'Keown house, detailing its physical characteristics: it

was situated . . . in a delightful vale, which runs up, for twelve or fifteen miles, between two ranges of well-defined mountains . . . Through these meadows ran a smooth river, called the Mullin-burn, which wound its way through them with such tortuosity, that it was proverbial in the neighborhood to say of any man remarkable for dishonesty, "he's as crooked as the Mullin-burn". (1:1–2)

"The Hedge School" (1:271–324) is prefaced with a lengthy disquisition explaining the subject, with the story proper, "The Abduction of Mat Kavanagh, The Hedge Schoolmaster," only introduced after several pages (1:280). Similarly, "The Lough Derg Pilgrim" (1:236–70) opens with an autobiographical history of the composition of the story. The second series of *Traits and Stories* opens with a lengthy (12-page) essay on Irish oaths before the story proper is reached. Throughout, the work is heavily annotated with explanations of Irish terms and customs. The net effect of this combination of factual, autobiographical, historical, geographical material — i.e., nonfiction — with fictional anecdotes is to create a unique genre that remains very much rooted in oral narrative tradition.

Many of the tales are themselves trickster stories, a typical folklore genre, where characters perform con artistry or scams on one another. In "The Party Fight and Funeral" (1:180–236) the author/narrator hides behind a coffin one night and scares onlookers by pretending to be the voice of the dead man and making the coffin move. In "The Lough Derg Pilgrim" a central character is a gypsy con artist, Nell M'Collum, who fleeces pilgrims, including the narrator. "Phil Purcel: The Pig Driver" (1:407–27) operates a scam in England where he sells the same pig 24 times to different, unwitting English buyers. This story satirizes the English for thinking the Irish simpletons. "The degree of estimation in which these civilized English held Phil was so low . . . as if he had been an animal of an inferior species" (1:419). "Good heavens! What barbarous habits these Irish have . . . and how far they are removed from anything like civilization!" (1:421). Both Phil and his pig turn out to be cleverer than the English dupes.

Often the satire is directed at Catholic rituals and/or corruption. "The Station" (1:145–80) concerns a witty confrontation between Phaddy, a recalcitrant Catholic peasant, and Father Philemy, trying vainly to get money out of his parishioner. The story includes a comical description of the Catholic sacrament of Confession, where parishioners confess their sins, which the priest performed in itinerant fashion in country homes. (Catholics were required to confess once a year but were expected to do so more often.) Phaddy is skeptical, however, of the efficacy of sacraments, as seen in this exchange with his wife, Katty, who wishes he would perform his Confession duty more often.

"Phaddy . . . now take warnin' in time, and mend your life."

"Why, what do you see wrong in my life? am I a drunkard? am I lazy? did ever I neglect my business? was I ever bad to you or to the childher? . . ."

"That's true enough, but what signifies it all? When did ye cross a priest's foot to go to your duty? Not for the last five years, Phaddy . . . ."

"And what are you the betther of all yer confessions? Did they ever mend yer temper, avourneen? no, indeed, Katty, but you're ten times worse tempered coming back from the priest than before ye go to him." . . . Katty made no reply to him, but turned up her eyes, and crossed herself, at the wickedness of her unmanageable husband. (1:153)

The satire of Catholic rituals and superstitions is from a modern secular point of view. "The Lough Derg Pilgrim," which concerns pilgrimages to a religious shrine of St. Patrick, deplores the ritual as a vain and foolish relic of premodern times, "a dreary and degraded superstition, the enemy of mental cultivation, and destined to keep the human understanding in . . . [a] dark unproductive state" (1:238). By contrast stands the nearby modern "Protestant city of Enniskillin," a site of progressive industry and "reasonable worship" (1:238). Here, as elsewhere in Irish literature of the day, Catholic culture is seen to be regressive and premodern, while Protestantism is associated with modernity and capitalist entrepreneurialism.

"Phil Purcel: The Pig Driver" presents, however, a more affectionate view of premodern times, not unlike that espoused by Thady Quirk, arguing that despite the lack of Enlightenment theories people were better off under the old feudal system.

In Phil's time . . . pig-driving . . . had [not] . . . made such rapid advances as in modern times. It was then . . . unaccompanied by the improvements of poverty, sickness, and famine. Political economy had not then taught the people how to be poor upon the most scientific principles. Free trade had not shown the nation the most approved plan of reducing itself to the lowest possible state of distress; nor liberalism enabled the working classes to scoff at religion, and wisely stop at the very line between outrage and rebellion . . . The people, it is true, were somewhat attached to their landlords, but still they were burdened with the unnecessary appendages of good coats and stout shoes; . . . and had the mortification of being able to pay their rents, and feed in comfort. They were not, as . . . now . . . improved by the intellectual march of politics and poverty . . . [N]othing is more consolatory to a person acquainted with the public rights and constitutional privileges, than to understand those liberal principles upon which he fasts and goes naked. (1:408)

Even the pigs, the narrator contends, were better in the old days — leaner, longer-legged, able to outrun a greyhound. But "this breed is now a curiosity — few specimens . . . remaining except in the mountainous parts of the country, whither these lovers of liberty . . . have retired to avoid the encroachments of civilization, and exhibit their Irish antipathy" to being marketed in England (1:409). Moreover, in the premodern past the boundary line between the species was, as we noted previously, less sharply demarked. "Nothing could present a finer display of true friendship found upon a sense of equality, mutual interest, and good-will, than the Irishman and his pig . . . He and his family, and his pig, like the Arabian and his horse, all slept in the same bed" (1:410). Phil is especially attuned to his pigs, having had "from his infancy . . . an uncommon attachment [to them], and by a mind naturally shrewd and observing, made himself intimately acquainted with their habits and instincts" (1:413). (A lengthy footnote gives an "authentic account of a horse '*Whisperer*'" who had a similar way with horses [1:413n].)

One of the stranger stories in the collection for the modern reader is "The Lianhan Shee" (2:75–96). Replete with ancient superstitions, the world the story depicts is dark and ominous. The title character is a kind of Wandering Jew, a woman cursed until she can get someone to drink her "hellish draught" (2:85). (The term *Shee* [*sí*] means "fairy" in Irish.) She arrives one day at the cottage of Mary Sullivan and tempts her with the brew by promising that drinking it will yield her great riches, a Faustian bargain. It eventually turns out that the woman's downfall was due to a priest having seduced her, which she reveals when the priest tries to exorcize her. He then commits suicide by self-immolation. The story also reveals various folk superstitions held by Mary — a belief in fairies (2:76n) and in crickets and grasshoppers as intelligent creatures who understand human language and must be treated with respect or warded off with holy water lest they bear bad luck (2:77). The author implies that these superstitions, the Lianhan Shee, and Catholic rituals are all of a piece — relics of a dark, unenlightened age.

"Going to Maynooth" (2:97–187) presents the conflict between metropolitan education and rural tradition in terms of a generational divide. Young Denis O'Shaughnessy is a prodigy preparing to attend Maynooth to become a priest. In the process, proud of his new-found knowledge, he becomes arrogantly condescending toward his own family, speaking himself in artificially convoluted rhetoric. "Fadher, . . . I condimnate your as being a most ungrammatical ould man, an' not fit to argue wid any one that knows Murray's English Grammar . . . ; that is the cognition between the nominative case and the verb, the consanguinity between the substantive and the adjective" (2:99). His class status rises; he acquires the accessories of a gentleman, a saddle for his horse and that symbol of modernity, a watch. His attitude toward his family becomes increasingly arrogant; he asks his father to address him as "Sir" rather than Denis or "Dinny" (2:114), a request the father admits, "cuts me more than I'll say, to think that I must be callin' the boy that I'd spill the last dhrop of my blood for, afther the manner of a sthranger" (2:117). The author/narrator criticizes Denis for "substituting the cold forms of artificial life for the warmth of honest hearts like theirs" (2:117). Eventually, Denis repents, returns home emotionally and physically, cementing his tie to the homeland by marrying a local girl. While Denis' destination was the priesthood, the story lays out a classic local-color pattern — that of the young son (or later, daughter) leaving home for the metropole, becoming "educated" in Enlightenment disciplines, which makes him seem a stranger to his own people and they to him. Usually, he comes to appreciate the rural premodern world of the hearth and returns to it, another kind of *Heimkehr*. The pattern is especially strong in the German and American traditions (as noted in the discussion of Stowe's "A New England Sketch" in Chapter One).

Flanagan holds that Carleton's "truest instincts . . . were pantheistic and pagan" (292). A good example of the paganism may be seen in "Ned M'Keown" where the author/narrator writes favorably of a Catholic mass conducted in a natural setting that suggests a pagan influence. It is located on a "forth" —

> a small green, perfectly circular, and about twenty yards in diameter. Around it grew a row of overspreading hawthorns, whose branches formed a canopy that almost shaded it from sun and storm. Its area was encompassed by tiers of seats . . . covered with the flowery grass . . . At the extremity of this little circle was a plain altar of wood, covered with a thatched shed, under which the priest celebrated mass. (1:16)

Alas, Carleton laments in a note, "this very beautiful but simple place of worship does not now exist," having been replaced by a chapel (1:16n).

A character in "The Party Fight and Funeral" proposes that a correspondence exists between the natural and the moral world that is not simply metaphorical.

> [T]here is a mysterious connection between natural and moral things, which invests both nature and sentiment with a feeling that certainly would not come home to our hearts, if such a connection did not exist. A rose-tree beside a grave will lead us from sentiment to reflection. (1:211)

Flanagan, analyzing Carleton's description of two wells in "Tubber Derg; Or, the Red Well" (2:363–414) — one crystal and the other a "crimson" "Chalybeate *spa*" (2:364) — suggests not just a symbolic interpretation (that they represent the saintly and the violent sides of Irish character and history) but that Carleton's "comparison of his people to the moorlands and meadows on which they lived is something more than metaphor" (292).

The sense of a spiritual presence in nature (here reflecting a likely Wordsworthian influence) is apparent in the opening section of "The Party

Fight and Funeral." The narrator is returning to his native village after a 15-year absence (another *Heimkehr*). It is a moonlit night.

> The deep gloom of the valleys, the towering height of the dark hills, and the pale silvery light of a sleeping lake . . . gave me such a distinct notion of the sublime and beautiful . . . Sometimes I stopped for a few minutes . . . and contemplating the dark mountains as they stood out against the firmament, then kindled into magnificent grandeur by the myriads of stars that glowed in its expanse. There was perfect silence and solitude around me . . . A sublime sense of religious awe descended on me; my soul kindled into a glow of solemn and elevated devotion, which gave me a more intense perception of the presence of God than I had ever before experienced. (1:186–87)

While his emphasis is generally on the gayer side of Irish life, Carleton does not ignore the dark side — its violence, hatred, and poverty. "Wildgoose Lodge" (2:349–62) concerns a ruthless act of violence committed by a rebel group. "The Party Fight and Funeral" describes a chilling ritual where the family and friends of a murdered partisan take the coffin to the home of his alleged murderer with the dead man's widow screaming out curses at the house.

> Come out! . . . come out and look at the sight that's here before you! Come and view *your own work*! Lay but your hand upon the coffin, and the blood of him you murdhered will spout . . . in your guilty face . . . May our curse light upon you this day! . . . May you, and all belonging to you wither off of the 'airth. (1:226)

The injustices at the root of Irish violence are depicted in "The Poor Scholar" (2:257–348), a powerful story about a Catholic family, the M'Evoys, dispossessed of its land by a rackrent agent who gives it to his bastard son, an "Orangeman" (2:259). Young Jimmy M'Evoy resolves to leave home and get an education in order to obtain justice for his family. While he is away, a famine occurs, which is described in grim terms, and Jimmy nearly dies. "The number of interments that took place daily in the parish was awful; nothing could be seen but funerals attended by groups of ragged and emaciated creatures, from whose hollow eyes gleamed forth the wolfish fire of famine" (2:300). Eventually, Jimmy locates the absentee landlord who rectifies the injustice, restoring M'Evoy to his property and paying for Jimmy's education, resulting in a joyous return home.

"Tubber Derg" also concerns the evils of absentee landlordism where an honorable peasant (the M'Carthy) family is evicted by an unscrupulous agent and reduced to begging to survive. Eventually, family members obtain laboring jobs, save up enough capital to buy a farm near their old one, and thus also return home.

Staying or returning home thus remains the heart of local-color literature. The emphasis on the beloved details of familiar place is seen in story
after story. The home site that the M'Carthys are forced to leave is described
as a natural unit of which the inhabitants are an organic part.

> On the south side of a sloping tract . . . stood a white, moderate sized farm-house . . . a
> graceful object in the landscape of which it formed a part . . . On each side of the house
> stood a clump of old beeches, the only survivors of that species then remaining in the
> country . . . Above the mound on which it stood, rose two steep hills, overgrown with
> furze and fern, except on their tops, which were clothed with purple heath . . . Exactly
> between these hills the sun went down during the month of June. (2:364)

It is this sense of exactitude, knowing — having experienced — the precise
location of the setting summer sun, that exemplifies the sense of *local*
detail, which characterizes the genre. Carleton is certainly one of the greatest writers in its tradition.

CHAPTER 3

The Scottish National Tale

In his General Preface to the *Waverley* novels, written in 1829, Sir Walter Scott explained that his reasons for writing about his native land were similar to those expressed by Maria Edgeworth: to acquaint the English with their subjugated (in his case, Scottish) neighbors.

> I felt that something might be attempted for my own country of the same kind with that which Miss Edgeworth so fortunately achieved for Ireland — something which might introduce her natives to those of her sister kingdom in a more favorable light than they have been placed hitherto, and tend to procure sympathy for their virtues and indulgence for their foibles.

(*Waverley* 523)

While the Irish national tale may have provided the historical impetus, it is likely the Scottish national tale would have emerged on its own as the political and cultural situation of Scotland was propitious for its engenderment. As noted in the previous chapter, regional or local-color writing generally emerged in countries or regions colonized culturally or politically by a dominant alien metropolitan power. Although Scotland was not, like Ireland, a political colony of England, it was a subordinate appendage. As in Ireland, England was identified with modernity; the English language was valorized, superceding the native Gaelic, which was associated with premodern, precivilized ways of being. Scotland, too, had its *Act of Union* (in 1707, preceding the Irish Act by nearly 100 years) in which it merged politically and economically with England, its own parliament being assimilated into the English (a process reversed in recent years with the establishment of a separate Scottish parliament). But Scottish resistance to English domination remained a potent force, particularly in the Highlands, a resistance that culminated in the Jacobite uprising in 1745–46, which attempted to restore "Bonnie Prince Charlie," Charles Edward, the grandson of James II, a Stuart pretender, to the throne (of England and Scotland) — an event that forms the backdrop of Scott's *Waverley*. These rebellious forces were defeated in the Battle of Culloden in 1746, an event that resulted in the permanent relegation of Gaelic culture to the margins of the dominant Anglo empire. Shortly thereafter repressive cultural legislation was passed, banning, for example, the wearing of tartans and kilts — symbols then as now of the alternative culture of the Scottish Highlands — and proscribing the Gaelic language.

Although these bans were lifted in 1782, they reflected a clear desire on the part of the Anglo imperial authorities to wipe out "the culture of Gaeldom." "The Gaels with their distinct and 'alien' language and dress and social customs were [seen as] subhuman, they were vermin. Nowadays, it would be called [cultural] genocide" (Magnusson 623). Conditions in the Highlands continued to worsen as the result of the "Highland Clearances" during the latter quarter of the eighteenth and first part of the nineteenth centuries. The "Clearances" involved displacing thousands of Highlanders as part of a large-scale movement toward capitalist industrial-ized agriculture billed as a modernist improvement. Economic and social repression of the Highlands thus intensified through this process, as it disrupted the traditional semi-feudal clan system and forced the eviction and emigration of tens of thousands of small-scale landowners and tenants to make space for large-scale industrialized sheep-farming, which was promoted as a modern, more productive improvement over the older, less profitable system. Magnus Magnusson in his history of Scotland describes the "severities of the Highland Clearances" as "barbarous," "when thousands of impoverished clansmen were ejected from their homes to make way for large-scale sheep farming" (654). Another historian stresses the devastating effect of the Clearances; as a result of which "rural society [in Scotland] . . . was totally reconstructed" (633). "'Modernity' was born in Scotland in the late eighteenth century as a result of all these changes" (633).

The clash between the premodern and the modern was particularly weighty in Scotland because of the powerful intellectual influence of the writers of the Scottish Enlightenment in the late eighteenth century. Indeed, what we have come to know as "the Enlightenment" was in great measure formulated by Scottish (along with French) thinkers: Adam Smith and David Hume, for example.

The Highland Clearances were a project of Enlightenment modernity. "'Improvement' meant . . . draining bogs [, etc.] . . . but . . . also . . . new systems of land tenure, rents, and distribution to maximize production and profitability" (McNeil 4).

> [S]mall property owners and tenants . . . were least able to adapt to the new demands of agrarian capitalism . . . Improvement entailed not the preservation of traditional Highland ways, but their total negation . . . [T]he discourse of improvement was part

of an imperial epistemology that reordered the landscape . . . absorbing and erasing indigenous land and cultural practices around the globe.

(McNeil 5)

The project reflected a "desire to reshape the Highlands, to erase its difference . . . in the name of 'progress'" (McNeil 5).

Scottish writers of the early nineteenth century were thus faced with a situation of cultural, social, and economic colonization not unlike that of their Irish counterparts. A desire to record and preserve ancient local customs and knowledge in the face of English hegemony was likewise a primary motivation. But, also like the Irish writers, the Scottish authors were for the most part highly educated and themselves largely assimilated in English culture (an important exception here being James Hogg, the "Ettrick Shepherd"). Often they had roots in premodern culture but by virtue of education and assimilation were able to see it from an enlightened, modern perspective. Their works thus manifest a kind of "'cultural schizophrenia,' marked by tensions between a native organic language [and culture] of the hearth and [a] synthetic cosmopolitan one of polite society" (McNeil 4).

As in Ireland, language use was a key site of the struggle between archaic local culture and Anglo modernity. By the time of the local-color movement — the early 1800s — the native language of Gaelic was spoken only in the Highlands; the rest of the country spoke English but in a dialect called "Scots."

Another Enlightenment project of standardization and "improvement" emerged in the late eighteenth century in the call to repress Scots, which was considered lower class and uncultured, and to replace it with the king's English as the standard conversational language. (Standard English was already the norm in written communication but Scots dialect was commonly used in conversation even by such educated Scots as David Hume and Sir Walter Scott.) John Sinclair, for example, declared in 1782 that "Scotticisms" were "uncouth" and "unintelligible" (D. Craig 57). Adam Smith urged that Scot "vulgarisms" be eliminated from common usage (D. Craig 53). "Anglicisation" was seen as part of "the great work of self-improvement" (56) required by "the Union with "the 'more mature' England" (54). The "'coarseness' and 'vulgarity' of 'provincial dialect'" were deplored (55).

Scottish local-color writers, like local-colorists elsewhere, used dialect in their fiction, thereby affirming its validity and implicitly resisting the Enlightenment call for a standardized anglicized norm. But the dialect was mainly in the dialogue between rural people, while the frame narrative remained in standard English — a characteristic format adopted by local-colorists so as to reach a metropolitan audience. The Scottish writers also characteristically wrote with sympathetic detail about the repressed Highland culture, thus helping to keep it alive as a cultural, if not a political, reality.

Yet, while their work by definition was antagonistic to Enlightenment universalism and homogenization, it was, however, fostered ironically by a strain of Scottish Enlightenment thought that provided a theoretical basis for local-color art. That strain evolved out of Hume's aesthetic theory, which derived from Locke's "principle of association." According to Hume, the "aesthetic experience" is "a train of associative connections" triggered by the work of art (C. Craig 241). "The power of art [was seen to lie] in its capacity to stimulate associations" (241). Objects that evoke memories were held to be the most potent sources of the aesthetic experience — thus local objects known from childhood were primary. Archibald Alison in *Essays on the Native and Principles of Taste* (1790) wrote, "there is no man, who has not some interesting association with particular scene . . . and who does not feel [its] beauty or sublimity enhanced to him, by such connection [such as] the view of the house where one was born" (quoted in C. Craig 242). Cairns Craig notes, "the purely local [thus] becomes the most powerful of associative influences . . . By this means, neo-classic universalism is reversed into the most detailed particularism" (242).

Unlike the Romantic theory of the transcendent imagination, which yields universal truths through Wordsworthian "spots of time," this associative aesthetic theory considers art to yield particular knowledge of a secular world threatened by "time's erasure" (C. Craig 246). The local-colorists, whether or not consciously aware of this theory, operated in consonance with it, seeking to transmit eccentric particularized local knowledge in defiance of the homogenizing sweep of the projects of modernity.

As in Ireland, the earliest Scottish local-color writers were women — perhaps emboldened to write because of their historic connection to and knowledge of the minute details of local life or perhaps, as suggested in the previous chapter, because of a certain identification with oppressed peoples on account of their own subjugated condition.

Scott began writing *Waverley*, the first of his Scottish novels, in 1805, but he did not complete it until 1814. Meanwhile, several other writers had put forth works that focused centrally on Scottish culture and history, especially that of the northwestern section of the country — the Highlands, which played a role in the Scottish literary imagination similar to that played by the west of Ireland in the Irish — an uncivilized, premodern Other. In his Postscript to the first edition of *Waverley* (1814), Scott acknowledged not only the influence of Edgeworth whose "admirable Irish portraits" he says he hoped "to emulate" (493), but also that of "Mrs. Hamilton's Glenburnie and the late account of Highland Superstitions" (494) — references to

Elizabeth Hamilton's *Cottagers of Glenburnie* (1808), which Scott praised for the "striking and impressive fidelity" of its "picture" of the "rural habits of Scotland" (494); and to Anne MacVicar Grant's *Essays on the Superstitions of the Highlanders of Scotland* (1811), a nonfiction description of Highland culture that depicted it from the condescending viewpoint of an educated "civilized" outsider (though Grant lived in the Highlands for 30 years) as "barbaric." The *Essays* was preceded by Grant's similarly focused *Letters from the Mountains* (1806). Elsewhere Scott is said to have credited Jane Porter's *The Scottish Chiefs* (1810), a highly popular historical romance, as being "the parent . . . of the Waverley novels" (Anderson and Riddell 183). Writing contemporaneously with Scott were three other women writers who wrote fictional works that focused wholly or to a significant degree on Scotland: Mary (Balfour) Brunton (1778–1818), Christian Isobel Johnstone (1781–1857), and Susan Ferrier (1782–1854).

The Cottagers of Glenburnie: A Tale for the Farmer's Inglenook (1808) by Elizabeth Hamilton (1758–1816) must be considered the pioneer work of the Scottish local-color tradition. Though Hamilton was born in Belfast to an Irish mother, she was brought up in Scotland and identified more with the heritage of her Scottish father. The *Cottagers* most resembles Mary Leadbeater's *Cottage Dialogues among the Irish Peasantry* (1811), though if influences passed between them it would have to have been that the former influenced the latter. Like the Irish *Cottage Dialogues*, the Scottish *Cottagers* is a didactic work of, one might say, attempted cultural colonization. The main character, Mrs. Mason, is imbued with Enlightenment ideas of "improvement" and the central plot concerns her attempts to persuade a recalcitrant "backward" Scottish family — the MacClartys (who speak in Scots dialect while she uses standard English) — to adopt modern ways. As with Nancy, the model of backward behavior in Leadbeater's work, Mrs. MacClarty is shiftless, disorganized, inefficient, and resistant to modern ideas.

Her garden, for example, is unweeded (148–9) and unproductive. Mrs. Mason says she should raise peas and other nutritious vegetables instead of just kale, leeks, and cabbage (then, as now, primary components of ethnic Scottish cuisine). But Mrs. MacClarty refuses. "[G]reen kail's gude enough for us" (149).

On matters of health and medicine Mrs. MacClarty is similarly recalcitrant. When told she should wash her hands before eating, she says, "I see nae gude o' sic nicety" (159). When Mr. MacClarty becomes ill a local quack bleeds him and applies a "poultice of herbs" (206). "Poor Mrs. Mason was greatly shocked" to see him "thus sported with, by an ignorant and presuming blockhead: but found that her opinions were looked upon with . . . prejudice" (206). A regular doctor is finally called in but the family's failure to follow his advice leads to the man's death and "the contagion's spread"

(207), which "the local folk" accept fatalistically saying it's "the wull o' God that he's to dee" (208). But Mrs. Mason argues that it is God's will that we "make use of the reason he has bestowed upon us" (208) to enact improvements. A local interlocutor identifies her theory as the doctrine of "works" (208) — reprising the theological debate between salvation by works versus salvation by grace or faith — the latter the Calvinist Presbyterian position held by the majority of rural Scots at the time; the former the more liberal "social gospel" position favored in urban educated circles.

While the villagers continue to disapprove of the changes Mrs. Mason has managed to effect at the MacClartys', a servant, Grizzel, remarks how the new methods are yielding greater profits for less work: "*we* never got sae muckle [much] for *our* butter, nor our cheese . . . as I got the day . . . I cou'd ha sold twice as muckle at the same price" (239). Moreover, "I never . . . got thro' my work sae easy in my life; — for you see Mrs. Mason has just a set time for ilka [every] turn; so that folk are never running in ane anothers gait [way]" (239). Organizing time according to a clock and establishing a set work routine is one of the hallmarks of capitalist mechanized labor, which Mrs. Mason, as an apostle of modernity, has introduced.

Eventually, the cottagers of Glenburnie come around; there's a "change of sentiment" even "in the most sturdy stickler for the *gude auld gaits*, [which] foreboded the improvements that were speedily to take place in the village" (352).

Stemming from a very different novelistic tradition, yet reshaping it into a national tale with a local-color focus, are the writers Mary Brunton and Susan Ferrier. Both wrote novels of manners — probably under the influence of Maria Edgeworth (especially *The Absentee*) — but both turned their novels away from a high-society drawing-room setting toward the provincial world of the Scottish Highlands — offering a countervailing site of authenticity and virtue.

Mary Brunton's *Discipline* (1814) charts the downward course of a wealthy, spoiled, frivolous young woman, Ellen Percy, who is forced to support herself when her father dies and she loses her fortune. She does so by moving to Scotland from England, finding work as a nanny in an upper-crust Edinburgh family, the Boswells. Mrs. Boswell is an evil-stepmother type, who poisons Ellen's dog Fido (who had accompanied her to Scotland) and then has Ellen imprisoned in an insane asylum. Thus far the novel has all the earmarks of a sentimentalist novel — then in vogue — which charts the miseries and abuses suffered by an innocent victim. Ellen, however, links up with a destitute Highlander, Cecil Graham, whom she helps financially despite her own poverty. Cecil repays her by connecting Ellen with Cecil's Highland clan, another representative of which — Charlotte — operates as a kind of *dea ex machina*, restoring to Ellen her lost fortune and inviting her to her clan headquarters, Castle Eredine, in the Highlands, where she marries Charlotte's brother Henry and thus becomes part of the clan. Ellen had known Henry in England under the name Maitland (which he used because it had a more Anglo mercantile ring than Graham, suggesting the subterfuges required of a colonial subject).

Charlotte and other clan members are bilingual, speaking both Gaelic and English, and Ellen learns Gaelic. Highland customs and superstitions — held mainly by Cecil — are explained in detailed footnotes, adding the ethnographic interest also found in many of the Irish local-color works. The author notes, "the Highland scenes . . . are all borrowed from fact" (362n). However, Brunton apparently gleaned some information from Anne Grant's *Essays on the Superstitions of the Highlanders of Scotland*; it is given, for example, as the source of details about a funeral rite (266n).

The novel is set in 1793, at the height of the Highland Clearances, which are criticized as an unacceptably drastic attempt to modernize the region. By contrast, the author endorses the clan system of benevolent despotism where the patriarch Graham rules paternalistically and effects change gradually and piecemeal. "Though . . . his commands were not always consonant to English ideas of liberty, they were uniformly dictated by the spirit of disinterested justice and humanity; and Graham, in exercising the control of an absolute prince, was guided by the feelings of a father" (338).

Unlike Enlightenment schemes of improvement, like the Highland Clearances,

> there was nothing theatrical in his plans for [his people's] interest or improvement. They were minute and practicable, rather than magnificent. *No whole communities were to be hurried into civilisation, nor districts depopulated by way of improvement.* (338, emphasis added)

Rather, his "humble plans" are particularized according to the needs of individual families. One might indeed draw a parallel between Graham's "minute" and specific projects and local-color literature itself, with its "minute" focus on local knowledge.

Ellen rapidly integrates into her new environment. "In less than a week, I was as much at home as if I had been born in Glen Eredine" (349). Thus her saga may be seen as a kind of *Heimkehr*, a rediscovery of and arrival at her true home, the false mercantile world of London left far behind.

Susan Ferrier's *Marriage: A Novel* (1818) similarly contrasts the vain, foppish, superficial world of the English upper class with the authentic rootedness of the Scottish Highlander. It is a sentimentalist novel of manners with a Cinderella plot, but the Cinderella is Mary Douglas, born (of a Scottish father and English mother) and raised in Scotland. At the age of 18 she is sent to her mother in England to be civilized. Her mother, revealing her anti-Scot prejudices, despairs of the task:

> What can I do with a girl who has been educated in Scotland? She must be vulgar — all Scotchwomen are so. They have red hands and rough voices; they yawn and blow their noses . . . Then, to hear the Scotch brogue — oh heavens! . . . [N]obody can live in that odious country without being infected with its *patois*. (189)

The mother, Lady Juliana, had earlier lived in Scotland but hated it. Noting the setting of her husband's ancestral home — "a small sullen-looking lake was in front . . . a thick drizzling rain . . . dark and troubled waters" — she remarks, "Good God, what a scene! how I pity the unhappy wretches . . . doomed to dwell in such a place" (9). She mimics the local dialect, which she can't understand; despises Scotch broth — "leeks, greens, and grease" (16); and can't stand the "hideous sounds" of the bagpipe (26). Unable to appreciate the local color, "the demon of *ennui* again took possession of her vacant mind; and she relapsed into all her capricious humours and childish impertinences" (98).

Contrasted to Lady Juliana, who is a stock sentimentalist figure, are a number of realistically particularized local characters, all of whom speak in Scots dialect and are rooted in a close-knit community with close ties to nature and subsistence living. Mary's uncle is seen, for example, "following the primitive occupation of the plough, his face glowing with health, and lighted up with good humour and happiness" (96). Mary herself has a special sensitivity to nature; she "could descry beauty in the form of a wave, and elegance in the weeping birch" (198). And she feels a spiritual presence in nature, "I own I love to believe in things supernatural; it seems to connect us with another world" (208). "The soul rises up from nature to nature's God" (209).

Yet the modern world is encroaching upon this idyllic, unspoiled realm. Mrs. Macshake, another local character, an elderly Edinburgh eccentric, remarks, "But fowk are naither born, nor kirsened [christened], nor do they wad [wed] or dee [die] as they used to du — aw [all] thing's changed" (214). She reminisces, "What I used to sit an' luck [look] oot at bonny green parks and see the coos [cows] milket . . . what see I noo [now], but stane [stone] an' lime, an' stoor an' dirt . . . Improvements indeed!" (215). She pauses to take a "pinch of snuff" (216), and we are informed that Mrs. Macshake is an "indigenous plant . . . born at a time when Scotland was very different from what it is now . . . The ladies of those days possess[ed] *raciness*" (221).

More consciously than the other writers in the genre, Ferrier relies upon the Locke–Hume association theory described above (although the Irish writer Lady Morgan also used the theory explicitly. In *Patriotic Sketches* she stated, "The mind, by an association of its ideas, discloses a 'spell of attraction' in everything which carries . . . the character of ages gone by" or which is novel or rare [69]). When Mary's father, Douglas, returned as an adult to Scotland (he had left at age eight), "the wild but august scenery . . . associated with . . . boyish exploits . . . still served to endear them to his heart" (8). Thus early childhood associative memory is seen to play an important part in the *Heimkehr*. Once in London Mary nostalgically recalls "the bare-footed Highland girl bounding over trackless heath-covered hills . . . So much do early associations tincture all our future ideas" (254). On seeing her old aunt Grizzy again, "Lochmarlie flashed on her fancy, at again hearing its native accents . . . Association and affection still retained their magic influence" (372). The perhaps predictable denouement is that Mary meets and marries a Scot, Col. Charles Lennox, and returns to live in Scotland. "The hills, the air, the waters, the people, even the *peat-stacks*, had a charm that touched her heart, and brought tears . . . But her feelings arose to rapture when Lochmarlie burst upon her view" (466).

Far different from the works of her sister writers Brunton, Ferrier, or indeed Hamilton is *Clan-Albin* (1815), by Christian Isobel Johnstone, the first Scottish novel to be subtitled *A National Tale*. A lengthy romantic epic not unlike those by Lady Morgan, the novel opens in 1780 in the Highlands where the main focus remains. While the novel includes many ethnographic footnotes — by now characteristic of the genre — suggesting a metropolitan audience, it is told from a point of view embedded within — that is, sympathetic to, knowledgeable about, and defensive of — Highland culture, which is seen as threatened with erasure by capitalist industrialism and modern reconstructions such as the Highland Clearances then in progress. Glen-Albin, "a solitary and remote valley in the Western Highlands" (1:5) is the site of Dunalbin, "a Highland bhalie [village]" (1:35), which includes about 30 families, all linked to the Albin clan, "all living together as one great family," self-sufficient "before the introduction of sheep-farming" (1:35) — an explicit repudiation of the Highland Clearances. A central character deplores the developing "dark lanes of manufacturing town," asserting that "the present generation of Highlanders could never be made manufacturers . . . her generous heart revolted at the idea of her high-spirited countrymen sinking into the abject condition of hewers of wood and drawers of water to a people they had hitherto shunned and despised" (91) — i.e., the English.

Unlike the monotonous repetition of a single task characteristic of industrialized labor, the inhabitants of Glen-Albin engage in the multi-faceted practices characteristic of premodern production. A central character, Ronald MacAlpin, for example, is "a blacksmith, farmer, distiller, and drover" (1:5) all in one. Moome, the village herbalist/doctor ("Moome" means "Nurse, or second mother" [1:13n]), has a cow and a flock of sheep that run freely in the hills; she herself makes cheese and spins the wool from the sheep to make garments for the needy (1:36).

When Norman, the protagonist, journeys away from the Highlands for the first time, he deplores "the numerous smoky manufactures" he discovers, with "every stream polluted by . . . some dye-vat or fulling mill" (2:82). He "recalled all he had heard of the 'division of labour,' and the 'Wealth of Nations,' with . . . asperity" (2:83). The Highlands is thus set up as a premodern and preferable alternative to Adam Smith's capitalist modernity.

One of the most interesting characters in the novel is the aforementioned Moome, who could well be called "Mother Scotland." She exemplifies the unspoiled premodern world, being a store of local lore. She speaks in Gaelic and has a knowledge of traditional herbal medicine; she "had a thousand *charms* against every disease . . . [and] possessed the power of . . . counteracting the baneful effects of the *evil eye*" (1:60). Like others of her ilk, she believes in fairies and other superstitions, and has "second sight" (1:21) — a uniquely Scottish belief in the ability to foresee the future. She is also a repository and composer of local oral history and literature — poems and tales (1:60). For, "in a Highland glen, every rock, every bush is storied" (1:74) — a view shared by the most famous of the Scottish local-colorists, Sir Walter Scott (1771–1832).

Scott's view of the Highlands is, however, more ambivalent than that of his female predecessors and contemporaries. Especially in the novels that deal with Highlander military violence and brutality, namely *Waverley* (1814) and *Rob Roy* (1817), a less attractive side of Highlander mentality is revealed. At the same time, in these and especially in his other Scottish novels, notably *Guy Mannering* (1815) and *The Antiquary* (1816), Scott provides a rich and sympathetic portrait of the Scottish rural world of the late eighteenth century and its inhabitants. Along with Maria Edgeworth, because of his enormous popularity and influence, Scott must be considered a monumental figure in the growth of the local-color tradition.

Himself an anglicized Lowland Scot, Scott spent time as a youth in the Highlands, listening to tales and oral histories told by inhabitants, many of which provided a basis for his treatment of Highlander culture in his fiction (many incidents or descriptions of customs and rituals are footnoted as having been told personally to the author). Intellectually, Scott was a disciple of the Enlightenment and he recognized the economic advantages the *1707 Union Act* had brought to Scotland. At the same time, he found commercial machinations and enterprise distasteful (as seen in the attitudes of various protagonists), preferring the forthright originality and authenticity of premodern, precommercial ways of being, which he feared were being erased by capitalist modernity. Like other local-colorists Scott came then to see the rural regional world as an "alternative to modernity," and in his fiction he sought to "dramatise . . . [the] values . . . lost in the process of modernisation" (C. Craig 253).

> Deep in Scott . . . lay the uneasiness of the anglicised Scot, the contradiction of Jacobite [Highlander] sympathies and Hanoverian [English] loyalties, the paradox of the realist who recognizes the economic advantages of union with England, and the nationalist whose whole being cries out in shame at the betrayal of his traditions and culture.

> (Reed 51)

After giving a speech about the importance of preserving certain Scottish legal traditions, Scott is said to have tearfully lamented, "little by little . . . you will destroy and undermine, until nothing of what makes Scotland Scotland shall remain" (Reed 51).

Scott's view of regional life stressed its temporal and geographical uniqueness and his interest and sympathy are most at play when describing eccentric marginalized local characters — those who didn't fit into modern commercial culture. George Sand, herself an author of French regional novels (to be treated in Chapter Five below), is alleged to have remarked of Scott: "He is the poet of the peasant, soldier, outlaw and artisan" (Lukács 52).

But these characters are not transcending romantic figures; instead they are very much rooted in, and outgrowths of, their particular local place and historical time. The Hungarian critic Georg Lukács noted how Scott's personages are individualized in such a way that their "traits of character . . . are brought into a very complex, very live relationship with the age in which they live" (Lukács 50), deriving "the[ir] individuality . . . from the historical peculiarity of their age" (Lukács 15) — and one might add, place. But by "historical particularity" Lukács does not necessarily mean past history set in an earlier period but rather real political, economic events set in time. "What in Scott has been called . . . 'authenticity of local colour' is in fact this artistic demonstration of historical reality" (Lukács 45). And thus while Scott is thought of as the author of historical novels, it would be more accurate, at least in the case of his Scottish novels, to qualify the concept by noting that they are rooted in historically realistic events — many of which were, however, nearly contemporary to him. "The events portrayed are . . . near enough [historically] . . . for him to have associated in childhood with those who saw them happen . . . [It was] living history" (Reed 50).

"Tradition," Scott once remarked, "depends on locality" (Reed 10). The local landscape was in Scott's view imbued for its inhabitants with personal and historical significance. His concern, one critic notes, is with the relationship between "humanity and history" rather than with "humanity and God," and that history, played out in a particular terrain, is "precisely *regional*" because of its unique historical and personal associations (C. Craig 245). Samuel Taylor Coleridge, the Romantic poet, once noted the difference between his and Scott's view of natural place settings: "Scott and myself were exact but harmonious opposites in this — that every old ruin, hill, river or tree called up in his mind a host of historical or geographical associations"; whereas he (Coleridge) admitted to being oblivious to such (as cited in C. Craig 245).

Scott completed *Waverley*, the first of his Scottish novels, in 1813 and published it anonymously the following year. In his Preface to the third edition (1814) Scott explains his purpose as to provide "a sketch of ancient Scottish manners" (*Waverley* 563). While the lengthy, adventure-filled novel is certainly more than a sketch, it does manage to convey much information about Highlander culture. *Manners* was a term then in use, David Craig explains, to mean "the ways of a people now distant from one, whether in time or socially, interesting because picturesque . . . part . . . of a way of life, now melting away" (151). It became a standard descriptor of local-color fiction, often appearing in subtitles to novels or stories. In his "postscript" to the first edition Scott similarly noted his "purpose of preserving some idea of the ancient manners of which I have witnessed the almost total extinction" (493). Consciously following Maria Edgeworth in repudiating stereotypical depictions of his compatriots, Scott further notes,

> It has been my object to describe these persons, not by a caricatured and exaggerated use of the national dialect, but by their habits, manners, and feelings; so as in some distant degree to emulate the admirable Irish portraits drawn by Miss Edgeworth. (493)

(Scott and Edgeworth shared a mutual admiration, developed a strong literary friendship, exchanging many letters and visiting each other's homes in Abbotsford, Scotland, and Edgeworthtown, Ireland, respectively.)

Waverley's subtitle, *Or, 'Tis Sixty Years Since*, highlights the historical setting, the 1745 uprising. The plot concerns a somewhat hapless young Englishman, Edward Waverley, of a romantic and "bookish" (56) disposition, who gets caught up rather inadvertently in the Jacobite rebellion, which is fueled mainly by the anti-Union Highlanders, the goal of which is to restore the Stuarts (in the person of Prince Charles Edward, a character in the novel) to the throne. Waverley enters Scotland as a member of the English army, commissioned to serve in a regiment of dragoons. His real introduction to the country comes on a visit to a family friend, the baron Bradwardine, who lives on an estate in the Scottish Lowlands. The hamlet where the estate is located is wracked by "miserable" poverty and Scott's description of it recalls Edgeworth's similar portrayal of Irish villages in *The Absentee*.

[The houses] stood, without any respect for regularity, one each side of a straggling kind of unpaved street, where children, almost in a primitive state of nakedness, lay sprawling . . . The whole scene was depressing; for it argued . . . at least a stagnation of industry, and perhaps of intellect. (74–5)

Scott quickly blames the apparent degeneracy of the peasants on their social conditions. Though the peoples' "features" were "rough," they were "remarkably intelligent; grave, but the very reverse of stupid" (75). "It seemed . . . as if poverty, and indolence, its too frequent companion, were combining to depress the natural genius and acquired information of a hardy, intelligent, and reflecting peasantry" (76).

The Bradwardine family, which includes Rose, whom Edward in the end marries (signifying Anglo-Scot union), are anglicized, educated upper-class Lowlanders who speak standard English. In their entourage are lower-class eccentrics who speak in Scots dialect, notably Davie Gellatley, the village idiot, and his mother, Janet, once tried as a witch "on the infallible grounds that she was very old, very ugly, very poor" (114). Though the charges are dropped, she continues to have that reputation in the village (458). In a note the author observes, "The accounts of the trials for witchcraft form one of the most deplorable chapters in Scottish story" (115n). Janet later helps rescue Edward who is by then wanted by the English for treason. As her mother was a Highlander, she knows Gaelic, though she speaks mainly in Scots dialect.

The Bradwardine estate is thus a kind of intermediary between civilized England and the Highland wilds, to which Waverley soon proceeds, where he meets the central Highland characters — Fergus Mac-Ivor, a clan leader, and his sister Flora. Scott's ambivalence about Highland culture becomes apparent in his treatment of these figures, who while powerful and forthrightly ferocious, representing a warrior ethic — as opposed to the bland negotiative spirit of a commercial culture — are nevertheless in the end unattractive characters. Fergus, for example, who has a "manly appearance" (254), is portrayed as an ambitious Machiavellian operator, who runs a protectionist racket on the Lowland gentry (extorting protection money from them to keep him from stealing their cattle). Fergus believes, as he tells Waverley, "a man must use every fair means to enhance his importance" (301). Waverley comes to realize that "Fergus's brain was a perpetual workshop of scheme and intrigue of every possible kind and description" (368); his "military spirit . . . was so much warped and blended with his plans and political views, that it was less that of a soldier than of a petty sovereign" (365). He "regarded his patriarchal influence too much as a means of accomplishing his own aggrandizement" (170). Moreover, Fergus is cold-blooded and cruel. Edward "had now been more than once shocked at the small degree of sympathy which Fergus exhibited for the feelings of even those he loved" (354). And he is appalled when Fergus bashes the head of a young subordinate with a pistol butt (397, 408). Flora, though less physically violent, is similarly ruthless in her partisan fanaticism.

Because of his dallying in the Highlands away from his unit, Edward is declared AWOL and, persuaded by the prince, he joins the rebel band with whose cause he has some sympathy. But his disillusionment with Fergus, his distaste for battle, and his feeling himself alien among the Highlanders leads him to regret his decision. Looking around at the "wild dress and appearance of his Highland associates . . . their . . . uncouth and unknown language," Waverley wonders, "am I then a traitor to my country . . . and a foe . . . to my native England?" (339).

Set up as a more admirable counter to Fergus is the English officer Colonel Talbot, another old friend of the family, whom Waverley encounters as a prisoner. Talbot chides Edward for joining the rebels and urges him to return to the English side, promising to arrange a pardon if he does so. While Talbot is an honorable figure, he has nothing but colonial contempt for the Scots, who speak, he says, in "gibberish . . . even the Lowlanders talk a kind of English little better than the negroes in Jamaica" (387). Nevertheless, Edward arranges for his release and in turn, after the defeat of the Highlanders, Talbot arranges Waverley's pardon, as promised. Returning to England, his "native country," Waverley accomplishes a *Heimkehr* of sorts (unusual in that it involves a return to the imperial seat); he "began to experience that pleasure which almost all feel who return to a verdant, populous, and highly-cultivated country, from scenes of waste desolation" (478). He soon goes back to Scotland, however, to wed Rose. Talbot meanwhile buys the ruined Bradalbine estate, fixes it up, and returns it to the baron (482–5) — thus enacting a colonial improvement upon a subject locale.

One would be tempted to see the novel as an affirmation of Scotland's union with — and subjugation to — England, given the plot denouements (Fergus is executed and Flora remorsefully joins a convent, thus effectively disempowering the Highland cause), were it not for the various lower-echelon Scots who are portrayed sympathetically. One example of admirable self-sufficiency is an upscale cottager who hospitably takes Waverley in after he's been injured in a hunt. We learn he

> had prepared for [Waverley] every accommodation which the simple habits of living, then universal in the Highlands, put in his power. In this person, an old man about seventy, Edward admired a relic of primitive simplicity. He wore no dress but what his estate afforded. The cloth was the fleece of his own sheep, woven by his own servants, and stained into tartan by the dyes produced from the herbs and lichens of the hills

around him. His linen was spun by his daughters and maid-servants, from his own flax, nor did his table . . . offer an article but what was of native produce. (193)

Even Flora is at first depicted in positive, romanticized terms as a kind of "wild Scottish girl" close to nature, beautiful, a harpist, and bardic singer of Gaelic airs (175–80).

But while enchanted by her and by Highland culture in general, Waverley remains a modern. He is skeptical of the traditional doctoring he receives after his hunting injuries. "The surgeon . . . appeared to unite the characters of a leech and a conjuror. He was an old smoke-dried Highlander, wearing a venerable grey beard, and . . . [wearing] a tartan frock, the skirts of which descended to the knee" (190). Before treating Edward he makes a ritualistic tour around the patient, moving three times "from east to west according to the course of the sun" (190). This blessing ritual, the *deasil*, is still performed by old Highlanders, the author informs us in a note (190n). The surgeon next bleeds him with a cupping-glass and mixes up an herbal concoction all the while murmuring incantatory words — some in Gaelic, some in "gibberish" (190). The herbs had been gathered under a full moon while the herbalist recited this charm:

> Hail to thee, thou holy herb,
> That sprang on holy ground . . . (190)

On another occasion Edward gets into an argument with Fergus over the existence of a ghost, the "Bodach Glas," the "Grey Spectre," whom the clansman claims to have seen. "How can you, my dear Fergus, tell such nonsense with a grave face?" Edward retorts (406). As a secular modern, he "had little doubt that this phantom was the operation of an exhausted frame and depressed spirits, working on the belief common to all Highlanders in such superstitions" (408). (The Bodach Glas was an ancestral spirit who figures in a Gaelic folk tale [Parsons 75].)

While *Waverley* thus seems in the end to tilt toward Anglo modernity, *Guy Mannering; Or, the Astrologer* (1815), Scott's next novel, remains solidly anchored in rural Scotland, implicitly critiquing modernity and affirming the value of unassimilated marginal folk, such as Meg Merrilies, a gypsy, and Dinmont, a Scottish peasant. The central plot follows the by now established pattern of the *Heimkehr*, in this case of a young Scot, Harry Bertram, who is kidnapped in Scotland as a five-year-old child, raised abroad, ends up in India, then returns to Scotland under the name of Brown, unaware of his true identity.

Meanwhile, shortly after the kidnapping, Harry's father, Godfrey Bertram, owner of Ellangowan, the ancestral estate, is elected judicial commissioner in a new progressive administration, bent on imposing various modern reforms and "improvements" on the local populace. As with the Highland Clearances, which Scott likely had in mind, these drastic changes cause much turmoil in peoples' daily lives.

> The zeal of our worthy friend [Bertram] now involved in great distress sundry personages . . . The 'long-remembered beggar,' who for twenty years had made his regular round within the neighborhood, received rather as a humble friend than an object of charity, was sent to the neighborhood workhouse. The decrepid [sic] dame, who traveled round the parish upon a hand-barrow . . . shared the same disastrous fate. The 'daft Jock,' who, half knave, half idiot, had been the sport of . . . village children . . . was remitted to the country bridewell, where, secluded from free air and sunshine, the only advantages he was capable of enjoying, he pined and died in . . . six months. The old sailor, who had so long rejoiced the smoke rafters of every kitchen . . . was banished from the county for no better reason, than that he was supposed to speak with a strong Irish accent. (33)

The local people are not happy with these changes. "We are not made of stone or wood, and the things which connect themselves with our hearts and habits cannot, like bark or lichen, be rent away without our missing them," the author notes (34) — a clear assertion of the contextual, associative nature of human identity, the importance of local customs, and an implicit repudiation of the Enlightenment concept of the "person" as one stripped of all local, contingent qualities.

The worst of Bertram's "improvements" is his removal of a colony of gypsies from his own estate — a "clearance" that parallels that done in the Highlands. The gypsies had lived in a glen on the estate for generations, almost as feudal tenants, serving under the laird in wartime and providing various services and products in time of peace (37). As Bertram watches the pathetic gypsy caravan leave the property, he feels pangs of guilt at having "thus summarily dismissed them from their ancient place of refuge . . . ought the circumstance of his becoming a magistrate to have made at once such a change [?] . . . sending seven families at once upon the wide world" (43).

The most powerful of the gypsies — and the moral centrum of the novel — is Meg Merrilies, a woman of "masculine stature" and "witch-like" appearance; with "raven," later "grizzled . . . locks" (123), given to wearing a long, red cloak, and often depicted smoking a tobacco pipe. She has the ability to foresee and foretell the future, and predicts the crises in Harry's life when he is an infant (20). She retains a strong attachment to Ellangowan, the Bertram estate, and some years after the gypsy clearance asks a traveler about it.

"Did ye ever see a place they ca' Dercleugh, about a mile frae the Place of Ellangowan?

"I wot weel have I, gudewife, — a wild-looking den it is . . . "

"It was a blithe bit [happy place] ance!" said Meg, speaking to herself — "Did ye notice if there was an auld saugh [willow] tree that's maist blawn down, but yet its roots are in the earth . . . many a day hae I . . . sat . . . under that saugh." (122)

Like the old willow's, Meg's spiritual roots, though dislodged, have remained emotionally anchored in her old locale. She is distressed when she learns that an upstart ne'er-do-well, Glossin, has taken over the estate in the wake of Bertram's bankruptcy and death, and determines, once she's aware of young Harry's return, to help restore him to ownership of the estate. Thus, though treated shabbily by Bertram senior, she retains a kind of kinship loyalty to the family, reflecting a precapitalist ethic contrasted to that of commercial connivers like Glossin.

Another ethical touchstone in the novel is the peasant Dinmont whom Harry meets soon after arriving in Scotland with his terrier dog, Wasp, on his *Heimkehr* journey. Dinmont is a simple, honest yeoman who lives happily with his family on a modest farm. Scott details this rural habitat beyond what is necessary to the plot, taking the opportunity to describe "manners . . . [which] have either altogether disappeared, or are greatly modified . . . during the last thirty years." Because of the advent of "progressive improvement," the "habits of life" of the new generation are now "regulated so as better to keep pace with those of the civilised world" (128). At the time of Harry's visit "all was rough and neglected in the neighborhood of the house; — a paltry garden, no pains taken to make the vicinity dry or comfortable, and all those little neatnesses which give the eye so much pleasure in looking at an English farmhouse totally wanting" (132) — criticisms that recall those made in Elizabeth Hamilton's *Cottagers of Glenburnie*. Yet, despite the disorderliness, the animals are healthy and well cared for, the children scamper around merrily, and the domestic household is a cheery, loving and tightly knit unit. (Indeed, Scott's description of the Dinmont hearth strikingly anticipates Harriet Beecher Stowe's cheery domestic scenes among the slaves in *Uncle Tom's Cabin* before Tom is sold down river. Stowe was heavily influenced by Scott. See Epilogue.) After many adventures, Harry is restored to the family estate and thus to his Scottish heritage, thanks in part to the efforts of Meg and Dinmont.

Edie Ochiltree, an itinerant beggar in Scott's next novel, *The Antiquary* (1816), plays a role similar to Meg Merrilies in *Guy Mannering*: the marginalized dialect-speaking outsider whose wisdom and knowledge supercedes in moral authority that of the more educated, anglicized characters. In a

Preface Scott explained that in these two novels he "sought [his] principal characters in [those] who are the last to feel the influence of that general polish which assimilates . . . the manners of different nations" (3) — in other words, in those who have not yet been touched by or who resist modern global homogenization. He further notes that in *The Antiquary* he had "been more solicitous to describe manners minutely, than to arrange . . . an artificial . . . narration" (3); indeed, the novel is of much greater interest for its portrait of rural Scottish culture and denizens than for its highly "artificial narration."

Despite its numerous twists and turns, the underlying plot, like that of the preceding novel, concerns the roundabout *Heimkehr* of a disinherited Scottish earl, Lovel, who had been kidnapped in infancy. Much of the novel is devoted to the various personages Lovel meets in the course of his patrimonial return, who in effect introduce him (and the reader) to Scottish culture. The most important of these are Jonathan Oldbuck, the antiquarian; Edie Ochiltree; and Elsbeth o' the Craigburnfoot. The novel is set in 1794, thus during the height of the French Revolution, which Oldbuck for one thinks has gone too far, though he supports its "whiggish doctrines" (277). Despite the epithet applied to his name, Oldbuck actually (as seen in this opinion) represents the more modern Enlightenment point of view in the novel. He is a Hanoverian, disbelieves in ghosts, and uses critical empirical methods to discern the veracity of information. For example, he questions the authenticity of James Macpherson's *Ossian* poems, then popular, which purported to be translations of ancient Gaelic verse still circulating orally in the Highlands; these were eventually determined to have been written at least in part by Macpherson himself and not original to Ossian. Oldbuck also reflects a modern temperament in his criticism of his sister's divagating narrative style (71) — a characteristic, as we have seen, of paratactic oral storytelling. The sister, uneducated, speaks in heavy dialect, unlike Oldbuck who speaks Johnsonian English.

Edie Ochiltree is one of those characters seen throughout local-color literature who remain untouched by modernity. He is a "Blue-gown," named for the outfit itinerant beggars wore in Scotland at the time. He had "a long white beard . . . a right brick-dust complexion" and wore "a slouched hat of huge dimensions," along with the gown to which were attached "a pewter badge" and "two or three wallets" (30).

> [A] contemner of all ordinary rules of hours and times, . . . when he is hungry he eats; when thirsty he drinks; when weary he sleeps . . . Then he is . . . the oracle of the district through which he travels — their genealogist, their newsman, their master of the revels, their doctor at a pinch, their divine. (290)

Unlike Oldbuck, whose knowledge derives from written texts, Edie is a store of oral knowledge, "the news-carrier, . . . the historian" of the region (33). When Oldbuck declares a grass-covered elevation to be a remnant of an ancient Roman encampment, Edie debunks the theory, saying he remembers the "bourock" [mound] being built; "I mind [remember] the bigging [building] o' t" (30). As Edie is able to particularize his recollection with convincing detail, his version wins the day, suggesting a valorization of personal oral, local truth over written, theoretical knowledge. Later, because of his intimate knowledge of local terrain (an example of *mētis*), a rocky coastal stretch, Edie is able to save two figures from certain death from the incoming tide (55–7). But when one of the persons he rescued, Isabella Wardour, wants to reward him by providing him with a permanent home, he refuses, saying,

> I downa be bound down to hours o' eating and sleeping . . . I could never bide the staying still in ae place, and just seeing the same joists and couples aboon my head night after night . . . And than what wad a' the country about do for want o' auld Edie Ochiltree, that brings news and country cracks frae ae farm-steading to anither, and gingerbread to the lassies, and helps the lads to mend their fiddles, and the gudewives to clout their pans . . . and has skill o' cows and horse, and kens mair auld sangs and tales than a' the barony besides . . . ? — troth, my leddy, I canna lay down my profession it would be a public loss. (92–3)

A female counterpart to Edie is Elsbeth o' the Craigburnfoot, an old crone who likewise has a store of local lore and knowledge. Edie says of her,

> auld Elspat is like some of the ancient ruined strengths and castles that ane sees among the hills. There are many parts of her mind that appear . . . laid waste and decayed, but there are parts that look the . . . strong, and the grander, because they are rising just like to fragments among the ruins of the rest — She's an awesome woman. (228)

A nearly allegorical figure, sitting like an ancient Sybil in the peasant Meiklebackit home, Elsbeth spends her time spinning, her mind seemingly elsewhere. When asked a question,

> the old woman paused in the act of twirling the spindle, . . . lifted her withered, trembling, and clay-coloured hand, raised up her ashen-coloured and wrinkled face, which the quick motion of two light-blue eyes chiefly distinguished from the visage of a corpse . . . as if catching at any touch of associations with the living world. (213)

Most of the day, "the ancient grandame . . . resumed her eternal spindle, wholly unmoved" by the chatter about her (217). She rarely speaks but before she dies, Elsbeth reveals that she'd had a hand in the absconsion of Lovel as an infant, which she'd done in a spirit of revenge against his mother, an Englishwoman, her employer, because "she gecked [mocked] and scorned at my northern speech and habit . . . Yes, she scorned and jested at me — but let them that scorn the tartan fear the dirk [dagger]!" (261). Elsbeth's actions thus may be seen to reflect vengeful Highland culture in resistance against English colonial contempt. Before she dies Elsbeth takes to chanting old Gaelic ballads. Unlike Macpherson's fake Ossian translations, hers are "a genuine and undoubted fragment of minstrelsy" handed down through the ages (310). When she dies, and when Edie dies, all that oral knowledge will be lost. Scott's novel is in part an attempt to preserve and honor that ancient culture.

As noted in previous chapters, the issue of women's place in society raised by the Enlightenment concepts of personhood, rights, and citizenry — all of which challenged the primacy of the traditional kinship identity of women — was a central question in the early nineteenth century. Many if not most of the local-colorists deal with the issue in one way or another — whether by tacitly questioning women's subordination — which we saw in Irish writers Maria Edgeworth and Lady Morgan — or by depicting powerful women characters. Indeed, compared with other fictional genres, such as the epic or the novel of manners, local-color literature distinguishes itself by the array of memorable, powerful women characters encountered therein.

Sir Walter Scott raised the issue of women's place in society in *The Antiquary*. First, there is Oldbuck's misogyny, a peculiarly regressive and anomalous trait — given his otherwise sophisticated outlook. He treats the women of his household (his sister and niece) with contempt, using them as virtual slaves. He "kept no male servant . . . under the pretext that the masculine sex was too noble . . . [for] personal servitude, which in all early periods of society, were uniformly imposed on the female" (44). "All ancient legislators," he says, "agree in putting [women] in their proper and subordinate rank" (44).

A further discussion about women's place occurs later in the novel in a local fisherman's cottage. One woman, Oldbuck's servant Jenny, argues that fish-wives are nothing but "puir slaving bodies" (213). But Maggie, one of the wives in question, retorts, "Slaves? Gae wa', lass — Ca' the head o' the house slaves? Little ye ken about it, lass . . . Na, na, lass — thae that guide the purse rules the house" (212). Since the fish-wives sell the wares and control the household income, they hold power in the house — a materialist political theory. While the issue isn't settled, it at least suggests Scott's interest in the subject.

Rob Roy (1817), Scott's succeeding novel, seems, as a rehearsal of a young hapless Englishman's embroilment in Highlander rebellion, a reprise of *Waverley*. As in the earlier novel, a contrast is drawn between a shallow, commercial culture seated in England and a rich, passionate — albeit violent — Highlander world. Frank Osbaldistone, in line to follow in his father's business footsteps, renounces his mercantile heritage and journeys north, first to stay with relatives in northern England and thence to Scotland. There he encounters the celebrated outlaw Rob Roy Magregor Campbell, who typifies the warrior code of the Highlands — honorable but ferocious. But, as usual in Scott, it is the side characters who are the most interesting.

In *Rob Roy*, continuing Scott's interest in the "woman question," the two most intriguing characters are women: Diana Vernon and Helen Campbell, Rob Roy's wife. Diana Vernon might well be termed "the wild Scottish Girl" (though she is part English), for she resembles in many ways Lady Morgan's Glorvina — although perhaps more fiercely independent and, as a Catholic Jacobite, more politically engaged than her Irish counterpart. Like Glorvina she's been educated like a man — "science and history are my principal favorites" (92). And she has a reading knowledge of Greek and Latin, "as well as most of the languages of modern Europe" (92). Like Glorvina, Diana has a "powerful mind" such that "the rapidity of [her] progress in knowledge" was "almost incredible" (129). The traditional female skills have been neglected — "I can neither sew a tucker, nor work cross-stitch, nor make a pudding" (92), and the author emphasizes that she was "encouraged . . . [to] despise . . . the forms and ceremonial limits which are drawn round females in modern society" (129). Indeed, Diana ridicules the trivial knowledges women were often limited to: "the mysteries of washing lace-ruffles, or hemming cambric-handkerchiefs" (93). Instead she has been trained in masculine military practices. "I learned out of doors to ride a horse, and saddle him . . . and to clear a five-barred gait, and fire a gun without winking" (93). Her feminist resentment at the traditional limitations to women's education come across when she sarcastically explains, "I wanted . . . to read Greek and Latin . . . and make my complete approach to the tree of knowledge, which you men-scholars would engross to yourselves, in revenge, I suppose, for common mother's share in the great original transgression" (93) — the latter an allusion to Eve and the apple, a common justification for women's subordination.

Diana asks Frank to treat her as an equal, "a friend and companion" (50), and warns him not to take her forthright outspokenness as coquetry. "You think me a strange bold girl, half coquette, half romp; desirous of attracting attention by the freedom of her manners and loudness of her conversation . . . [Y]ou were never more mistaken" (50). Frank comes to admire her austere independence, "the unshaken constancy of her own mind" (123). "[T]here was an expression of dignity in her contempt of ceremony — of upright feeling in her disdain of falsehood — of firm resolution . . . [as] she contemplated . . . dangers" (123).

Though Diana is not marginalized by virtue of class, education, and ethnicity, like many of Scott's other memorable characters, she is by gender a kind of outlaw, expressing authenticity and integrity that the more assimilated characters lack. Predictably, even though he doesn't entirely approve of her "masculine" education, Frank falls for her and in the end marries her, thus allying himself permanently with the noncommercial, nontraditional world he sought in escaping from his father's domain.

Even more of an outlier than Diana and a literal outlaw is Helen Campbell. But as with Fergus and Flora in *Waverley* her ferocity is adjudged too extreme, indeed barbaric. A "female leader of [the] band" (301), she heads a clan sept in the Highlands, which is, we are reminded, "lawless" (239) and "uncivilized" (241). She is a real "Amazon" (293).

> I have seldom seen a finer or more commanding form than this woman. She . . . had a countenance which must once have been of a masculine cast of beauty; though now . . . its features were only strong, harsh, and expressive. She wore her plaid, not drawn around her head and shoulders, as is the fashion of women in Scotland, but disposed around her body as the Highland soldiers wear theirs. She had a man's bonnet . . . an unsheathed sword in her hand, and a pair of pistols at her girdle. (293)

Helen speaks in Scots dialect but her native tongue is Gaelic. "The language rendered by Helen . . . out of her native and poetical Gaelic, into English, which she acquired . . . was graceful, flowing and declamatory" (357). (By contrast, the highly educated Diana declaims in highly sophisticated — indeed artificially Shakespearean — sentences. At times indeed she seems to have walked out of a Shakespearean play.)

Animated by outrage at the deplorable treatment her people have received from the English, Helen has become merciless and vindictive. "You have left me and mine neither house nor hold, blanket nor bedding, cattle to feed us, or flocks to clothe us — Ye have taken from us all — all! . . . and now ye come for our lives" (293). "All may be forgotten," she says, "but the sense of dishonor, and the desire for vengeance" (359). Her ferociousness leads her to order a merciless execution by drowning of a pathetic English prisoner.

The proper role and power of women continues as a subtext in *The Bride of Lammermoor* (1819), while the principal theme concerns a conflict over property between a representative of the old traditional feudal order, Edgar Ravenswood, and of the new commercial world in the person of Sir William Ashton. The plot itself is a Romeo-and-Juliet situation where Ashton's daughter Lucy and Ravenswood fall in love but are thwarted because of the hereditary enmity between the two families.

Sir William resembles Sir Ulick in Maria Edgeworth's *Ormond*; an oily operator, a "silver-tongued lawyer" (156), "bred to casuistry" (65), and a political opportunist — "It had . . . been [his] policy . . . to watch the changes in the political horizon, and . . . to negotiate some interest for himself" (161) — he has managed to obtain ownership of the Castle of Ravenswood through legal machinations. As a "skilful fisher in the troubled waters of a state . . . [he] contrived to amass considerable sums of money," which he knew how to use "as an engine of increasing his power and influence" (27). Ravenswood by contrast, untrained in legalities, is rash, impetuous, and highly resentful of his dispossession. "The lands which you now occupy were granted to my remote ancestor . . . How they have glided from us by a train of proceedings . . . — all this you understand better than I do . . . [B]ut to my ignorant understanding [they] seem very little short of injustice and gross oppression" (171). Thus, though not a Highlander, Ravenswood's situation and character resemble the Highlander's in that he has been dispossessed of his ancient land by modern Anglo machinations because of which he is passionately vengeful. Also, tellingly, he is a Jacobite, while Sir William is a Whig. The author notes the "advantages which the cool lawyer and able politician . . . [possessed] over the hot, fiery, and impudent [Ravenswood] whom he had involved in legal toils and pecuniary snares" (28).

The issue of women's status is raised by the contrasting characters of Lady Ashton and her daughter Lucy — one, the extreme of domineering assertiveness, and the latter, a model of crippling passivity. Lady Ashton is a Lady-Macbeth type: ruthlessly willful — she "no more lost sight of her object than a falcon . . . turns his quick eyes from his destined quarry" (30). With an "ambitious and undaunted disposition" (41), she holds sway over her husband and daughter through intimidation.

Lucy is almost the complete opposite: anemic, will-less, meek. She is, the author tells us, bound "by the ideas of the time [early eighteenth century], which did not permit a young woman to offer her sentiments on any subject of importance" (54), and so keeps silent much of the time. She "did not speak much . . . and what she did say argued a submissive gentleness" (156). As for her preference in marriage, "the suitor expected little more from his bride than a silent acquiescence in the will of her parents" (303). Because of the mother's machinations Lucy is forced against her wishes to marry an arriviste, Bucklaw — with tragic consequences.

The issue of women's place is also raised in an otherwise irrelevant quasi-comical domestic scene in the Girder household in a village near the castle. Ravenswood's servant, desperate to provide some food for his master, steals a roast fowl from the Girders. When Mr. Girder finds out, he blames his wife and "raised his riding whip" about to beat her "but she stood firm . . . and undauntedly brandished the iron ladle" (149). "Am I no to chastise my ain wife?" he exclaims (149), but backs down under pressure from others present. Later the servant asserts that "woman hath dominion over all men" (188) — a peculiar misreading of patriarchal scripture but relevant to the novel's subtext.

The tragic denouement — in which the passive Lucy erupts in violence on her wedding night, stabbing her new, undesired husband to death — seems to result from the imbalances in women's power. On the one hand, the mother is seen as too powerful and too willing to use that power to control and force others against their will; on the other hand, Lucy is too oppressed and controlled, her own unexpressed will so frustrated that it bursts forth in passionate vengeance. Here again one senses a parallel to the political oppression of the Highlanders with an implicit assertion that people's wishes must be respected, heard, and acted upon, not denied and run over, a repression that can only lead to a violent counterreaction.

One other female character is worthy of note; namely, Alice, an old blind woman who lives on Ravenswood's estate. She is thought by some to be a witch (199) and has prophetic powers, warning Ravenswood not to wed the daughter of his house's ancient enemy. Later when Ravenswood is kicked out of the Ashton estate, he sees the ghost of Alice who has just died. He then wakes her body along with three old crones who are likened to the witches in *Macbeth*. While Ravenswood "despised most of the ordinary prejudices about witchcraft, omens, and vatication, to which his country still gave such implicit credit" (252), and deplored the seventeenth-century witch persecutions, he feels nevertheless haunted by the strange vision he had of the dying Alice (252). And on Lucy's wedding day, one of the three remaining witch-crones predicts doom: "'I tell ye,' said the Sibyl, 'her winding sheet is up as high as her throat already . . . Her sand has but a few grains to rin out'" (334). Lucy indeed dies shortly thereafter.

Contemporary with Scott but much less well known is the author of numerous local-color stories, as well as poems, James Hogg (1770–1835), the "Ettrick Shepherd." Although friends with Scott and influenced and supported by him materially and morally (see MacLachlan), Hogg appears to have sought to portray rural Scotland less romantically than Scott. The narrator in "Highland Adventures" (1811), a story collected in Hogg's *Winter Evening Tales* (1820), debunks the picturesque view of the Highlands found in Scott's poem "The Lady of the Lake" (1810). Its "greatest fault," he objects, is that it's not "founded on a fact," is "without the bounds of probability," even of "*possibility*" (108). A "crusty old Highlander" in the same story similarly complains that there's nothing special about the nearby Trossacks mountains except that "a Mr. Scott had put all the people mad by printing a *lying poem* about a man that never existed, — 'Wat the d— was to be seen about the Trossacks more than in an hundred other places? A few rocks and nothing else'" (109). The narrator says it helps to have imbibed "a little Highland whisky" to appreciate the mountain scenery. "[W]ithout a drappie in his noodle; he may as well stay at home" (111). Regarding another landmark, "the Craig of Glen-Whargen," he found it "much more striking" when viewed with "a bottle full of whisky . . . The rock continued to improve . . . and by the time the bottle was empty, we were fixed to the spot in amazement at that stupendous pile" (111).

Unlike most local-color writers, Hogg was not a middle-class observer of rural folk, he was one of them. Largely self-educated, indeed mostly illiterate until his late teens, Hogg spent his youth as a shepherd in the Borderlands region where he heard many of the stories he later wrote down and published. In an early query (1813) to a publisher Hogg explained, "I have for many years been collecting the rural and traditionary tales of Scotland and I have of late been writing them over again and new-modelling them" (Duncan xiii). The idea of "new-modelling" his material suggests an oral methodology where bards revised and added to the material they transmitted (see Duncan xiii). In an early advertisement he drafted for his collection of tales, Hogg said, "these tales have been selected . . . among the shepherds and peasantry of Scotland and are arranged so as to delineate the manners and superstitions of that class" (xvii) — suggesting a work aimed at a metropolitan readership, their interest in alien "manners" and "superstitions" having by this time (1820) been aroused. Hogg was nurtured by the Blackwood's publishing house and journal in Edinburgh, which promoted works about provincial Scottish culture, reflecting the idea that "as we [Scots] became absorbed into Britain, we naturally came to feel that if our culture had an essence, it lay in now bygone idioms and cultures" (D. Craig 161).

Hogg began publishing his stories in periodicals (first in *The Spy* and later in *Blackwood's Magazine*) in 1810 and continued publishing them regularly until 1820 when 18 were published as *Winter Evening Tales: Collected among the Cottagers in the South of Scotland*, later reissued as *Tales and Sketches of the Ettrick Shepherd*. (Hogg had originally proposed as the title *The Rural and Traditionary Tales of Scotland*.)

Although Hogg claims to have reworked the stories, which he had received orally, for print circulation, much of the original material appears to have been transmitted directly without much doctoring. Ian Duncan notes, Hogg gives us the "ethnographic raw material of the national tale, not yet ideologically and aesthetically processed" (xxvi). Indeed, compared with that of Scott and other writers of the national tale, Hogg's perspective is less political and historical; it is rather of a timeless peasant world, one in which one hears "popular voices telling their stories in their own words, as opposed to their absorption into a polite master narrative" (Duncan xxv). Hogg refuses to submit and "assimilat[e] . . . local episodes to a general (national and historical) purpose" (xxv).

In an effort to highlight the authenticity of the narrative sources of his stories, Hogg details their transmission history more than most other local-color writers. While Scott offered oral sources as verification in foot-notes and prepared lengthy prefaces, only in his later Scottish novels does he explain the narrative source of his story. In *The Bride of Lammermoor*, for example, we learn that a Dick Tinto heard the story from an "aged goodwife" (25); he then wrote it down in a few notes which he passed on to Peter Pattieson, who allegedly wrote it up as the novel's narrative. (Pattieson was the fictional narrator of the several Scott novels published under the rubric *Tales of My Landlord* [which included *The Bride of Lammermoor*].)

In Hogg's "Bridal of Polmood" (1820; probably written 1813), the "edi-tor" claims to have heard the story in a carriage headed for Edinburgh from an "old gentleman" full of "traditionary knowledge" (259). Once in Edinburgh the editor "wrote it down," noting, "I have retained all his senti-ments . . . [and] expressions to a degree which the present taste for abstract knowledge will scarcely justify" (261). Here Hogg seems conscious that he is going against the Enlightenment grain of generalized theoretical knowl-edge in providing a narrative that is rooted in particularized Scottish history and orally — that is associatively — organized. (The story itself, however, which concerns hijinks in James IV's court, is not a typical local-color tale but rather more like a Renaissance novella.)

The narrator of "The Wife of Lochnaben" (1810) claims "the story was related to me by a strolling gypsy of the town of Lochnaben, pretty nearly as follows" (426). It concerns a murder, which is revealed when the victim's ghost speaks to a former friend, which then leads to the punishment of the murderer, the victim's husband, who is dunked publicly and run out of town. "Tibby Johnston's Wraith" (1820) opens with the narrator explain-ing how when he "was a tiny boy" "herding cows" an old man — David Proudfoot — used to "tell me old stories . . . and this was one among the rest" (500). This story too involves ghosts: David once met a man whose wife had died of fright after seeing the ghost of Tibby Johnston who herself had just died. David then interviewed Tibby's husband who reminisced affectionately about his wife and sadly about her death. "An Old Soldier's Tale" (1820; probably written in 1817/18) is narrated orally to his wife by Andrew Gemble, a beggar, recalling his youthful military adventures. The recorder/narrator notes he had to anglicize Gemble's Scots dialect: "were I to tell it in his own dialect, it would be unintelligible to the greater part of readers" (99). As it is, part of his story takes place in the Highlands where during the 1745–46 uprising he is captured. His captor speaks in a heavy Gaelic brogue: "Surcheon . . . you heffing peen tahken caring te harms . . . akainst our most blessit sohofrain" (104) [Sergeant, . . . you having been taken carrying arms . . . against our most blessed sovereign]. He is sentenced to death by decapitation but moves his head at the last minute and wrestles the executioner down, which impresses his captors so much they all celebrate together and the sentence is lowered to imprisonment.

Most of the storytellers in Hogg's stories speak in Scots dialect while the frame is in standard English. Hogg reveals a sensitivity to the variety of Scots dialects in "Love Adventures of Mr. George Cochrane" (1810). One old woman "spoke the border dialect in all its primitive broadness and vulgarity, which I thought the sweetest dialect on earth" (209). Another woman is described as "not speak[ing] with such a full Border accent as either her husband or daughter" (216). The narrator concludes with a note to the editor, saying he forwards this tale because "you are so fond of all narratives that tend to illustrate Scottish manners" (227).

"The Renowned Adventures of Basil Lee" (1810), possibly Hogg's first story, which the "editor" says he received as a manuscript "in the summer of 1810, [from] an old man . . . a decayed gentleman . . . Basil Lee" (3), also records diverse dialects, including an Irish brogue, "a broken Highland jargon" (18), and "the broadest border dialect" (18). An example of Highlander Scots occurs in an anecdote about a customer to whom the protagonist accidentally served vitriol instead of whiskey. The imbiber liked it so much he came back for more: "an it pe your vill, let her have te same tat she gat fan she vas here before" (11). (*She* was used as a generic pronoun; *p* substitutes for *b*; *v* for *w*; *t* for *th*; *f* for *wh*.)

The world Hogg depicts resembles that found in William Carleton's works more than that encountered in Scott or the other Scottish writers — an unreconstructed peasant world on the fringes of civilization replete with ancient beliefs and superstitions. Basil Lee, for example, on his return from America where he fought in the Revolutionary War, lands on the west coast of Scotland on the Isle of Lewis in the town of Uig where none of the inhabitants speak English, only Gaelic, and where the people have "second sight" — the ability to see beyond the here and now. They "have no communications with the rest of the world; but with the beings of another state of existence they have frequent intercourse" (49). While there he himself sees apparitions and hears stories about mermaids and a lake monster. He encounters an old Gaelic-speaking woman who claims to be visited every night by her dead son's spirit. Lee sees the son's corpse but the next day "I could not tell whether I saw these things in a dream, or reality" (58). (A place somewhat similar to the town of Uig is described in American local-colorist Sarah Orne Jewett's *Country of the Pointed Firs* [1896].)

In "Love Adventures of Mr. George Cochrane" we encounter another of the powerful Amazon women seen in other local-color works. Jessie (aptly named) Armstrong chooses her lovers through trials-by-ordeal (wrestling matches with her, for example). She is seen winning a throwing match with a suitor. Her father says, "Very little wod hae meade my Jainny a man, for she wants neane o' the spirit o' ane" (213). The preponderance of these premodern "gender benders" lends credence to the Foucaultian theory noted in the Introduction, that it was the instantiation of pseudoscientific sexological norms that imposed a narrow modern grid on premodern sex-gender diversity.

The same might be said of species distinctiveness, which was much less rigid in premodern thinking. As seen in previously mentioned works, in Hogg's stories humans' bond with animals, who are not seen as radically *other*, is taken as a given. "Duncan Campbell" (1811) deals largely with the tribulations of the protagonist and his "colley," Oscar. The two are deeply bonded but Duncan has to leave Oscar behind in the Highlands when he goes to Edinburgh for schooling. When this doesn't work out, Duncan runs away to the countryside where he encounters a "drove of Highland cattle" with whom he identifies. "They were all in the hands of Englishmen; — poor exiles like himself; — going far away to be killed and eaten, and would never see the Highlands again" (81). Suddenly, among them he sees Oscar, "hungry and lame," having been beaten and abused by the Englishmen. Duncan eventually rescues Oscar and they travel together for years as vagabonds. "The sagacity which this animal possesses is almost incredible . . . [having] undaunted spirit and generosity" (87). The dog finally dies of old age at 16. The story ends with Duncan's *Heimkehr* to the Highlands. (The aspersion of the English suggests a political angle unusual in Hogg.) Hogg wrote a personal essay about his own dogs, "Further Anecdotes of the Shepherd's Dog," which appeared in *Blackwood's Edinburgh Magazine* in March 1818. (Scott was also a great dog-lover; see Harriet Beecher Stowe's essay "Sir Walter Scott and His Dogs.")

"The Shepherd's Calendar" (1819), narrated by a shepherd, describes a terrible winter storm that occurred in 1794 in which he managed to save most of his sheep with the help of his "colley" Sparkie (384). In its powerful description of humans and animals struggling against the elements the piece anticipates Tolstoy's "Master and Man" (1895).

In "Highland Adventures" (1811), a Highlander recounts a tale about a local named Duncan who shoots a deer several times but the deer refuses to die, instead turning into a white-bearded old man (to whom Duncan had earlier given some food). The man/deer says, "Go home, and let the remains of my exhausted herd rest in peace" (110). Duncan gives up hunting thenceforth. (This story too anticipates a Tolstoy story, "Esarhaddon, King of Assyria" [1903]. I do not know whether Tolstoy was acquainted with Hogg's works.)

Far different from both Hogg's peasant world and Scott's Highlands is that reflected in the charming works of John Galt (1779–1839) and D. M. Moir (1798–1851), both of whom, however, were, like Hogg, members of and promoted by the Blackwood publishing circle. Galt and Moir detail the petty-bourgeois little people of Lowland villages with humor and affection, concerned like the other local-colorists about the changes being wrought in their lives by the advent of modernity, in particular capitalist industrialism and in Galt's case, the "jacobin spirit" (*Annals* 193) of the French Revolution. Both Galt and Moir were of upper-middle-class background and well educated. Galt's father was a shipmaster and Moir was a doctor.

Galt claimed as his model Oliver Goldsmith's *Vicar of Wakefield* (1766). ("I wished to write a book that would be for Scotland what *The Vicar of Wakefield* is for England" [*Annals* Appendix 208].) True, Galt's *Annals of the Parish: Or the Chronicle of Dalmailing during the Ministry of the Rev. Micah Balwhidder Written by Himself* (1821) — the best of Galt's Scottish works — resembles its English model in that it is a first-person account by a rural minister, but Goldsmith's novel is a sentimentalist saga with stock characters about a family's victimization, whereas Galt's work is a largely plotless chronicle of a parish and its transformations over a 50-year period, 1760–1810. The work it most resembles is Mary Leadbeater's *Annals of Ballitore*, treated in the previous chapter, though Galt's work is fiction or fictionalized, unlike hers, and unified by the comical narrative voice of Micah Balwhidder, the parish minister. As her work came out after Galt's, if there was any influence it was from him to her. Galt's *Annals* was apparently completed in 1813 but a publisher rejected it on the theory that readers had no interest in Scottish material (*Waverley*, which was a huge popular success, had yet to appear), so its publication was delayed until 1821.

As in other local-color works, we encounter in Galt's *Annals* a number of memorably eccentric characters. There is Mizy Spaewell, "one of the best howdies [midwives] in her day," who "had a wonderful faith in freats [omens], and was just an oracle of sagacity at expounding dreams" (18). There is Nance Birrell, "a distiller of herbs, and well skilled in the healing of sores" (39). "It was only with great ado that I could get the people keepit from calling her a witchwife" (39). Miss Sabrina Hookie, the schoolmistress, performs a successful Caesarian on a duck who had eaten too many uncooked beans (66). Jenny Gaffaw is the village madwoman whose "idiot daughter" (70) Meg commits suicide in grief over a hopeless infatuation with an aristocrat who is oblivious to her.

As Galt explains in a note in a later work, deviants like Meg and Davie Gellatley in *Waverley* were by the early nineteenth century no longer readily seen in villages where they used to wander at will. "[P]oorhouses and asylums . . . have hidden away, and . . . blotted out, the race of Naturals — weak-minded persons, 'innocents,' — who were of considerable importance in the social economy of an earlier day" (Galt *Works* 2:295). "Intercourse with towns and villages beyond their own being restricted, their eccentricity was not easily rubbed out, and, indeed it was fostered by the freedom that was allowed them" (*Works* 2:296).

One of the most striking figures in Balwhidder's parish is Betty Pawkie who with her sister establishes a retail tea business. "Betty . . . was of a manly stature and had a long beard, which made her have a coarse look, but she was, nevertheless, a worthy well-doing creature" (92). As with Jewett's transvestite militia captain discussed in Chapter One, here too we find an acceptance of deviancy that would be corrected or in some way normalized in the modern world. Rather than stigmatize or segregate her, the villagers in this premodern era accept the bearded Betty — even admire her. When an exciseman tries to assess her stores of tea, Betty destroys the stock rather than let him to it, "which was thought a brave action of Betty" (94).

Balwhidder duly notes somewhat wistfully the introduction of new industrial and capitalist developments in the parish. At first he is enthusiastic about their effects on the town but soon grows uneasy and skeptical. He calls new coal pits dug nearby "a Godsend to the parish, and the opening of trade and commerce, that has . . . brought gold in gowpins [handfuls] among us" (31). But in looking back he comes to feel the new wealth was a mixed blessing. "For with wealth come wants . . . and it's hard to tell wherein the benefit of improvement in a country parish consists" (50).

A Mr. Cayenne, a Tory refugee from America, arrives in town in 1785 with his black slave, Sambo, who then becomes his servant. Cayenne is "a hot and fiery" entrepreneur (118) and soon builds a cotton mill with a new town "Cayenneville" for the mill workers (127). But the parishioners remain somewhat indifferent to "the craft of merchandize. The only man interested in business . . . was Mr. Cayenne himself" (176). Still, Balwhidder notes a new spirit of enterprise in the air: "The minds of men were excited to new enterprises; a new genius . . . an erect and out-looking spirit that was not to be satisfied with the taciturn regularity of ancient affairs" (128). Even Miss Sabrina Hookie has caught the capitalist spirit, saying, "that, if more money could be made by a woman tambouring than by spinning, it was better for her to tambour than to spin" (128). (*Tambouring* was embroidering on circular frames [235 n.1].) And Balwhidder realizes how through the cotton mill and Cayenneville, "we were become part of a great web of commercial reciprocities, and felt in our corner and extremity, every touch or stir that was made on any part of the texture" (197). But the minister is concerned that "in the midst of all this commencing and manufacturing, [there were] . . . signs of decay in the wonted simplicity of our country ways" (128). "In that spirit of improvement, which was so busy everywhere I could discern something like a shadow . . . Accordingly, I began a series of sermons on the evil of vanity of riches" (137).

Balwhidder is also upset about the radical ideas emanating from the

French Revolution. He preaches against those Enlightenment theories — the "infidel philosophy" — which under the name of "universal benevolence, philanthropy, utility" have appropriated Christian virtues of "charity, brotherly-love, and well-doing" (147). "I told my people . . . [not] to secede from Christianity to become Utilitarians" (147). (Apparently, John Stuart Mill picked up the term *Utilitarian* from Galt [237n].) Meanwhile, the Cayenneville workers have become "afflicted with the itch of jacobinism" (179) — a radical egalitarianism. "The infidel and jacobin spirit of the French Revolution had corrupted the honest simplicity of our good old hameward [sic] fashions" (193). Rather than the drastic changes of revolution, Balwhidder favors gradual evolution. "I considered that the best reformations . . . proceed step by step" (188). Suspicious of the French Enlightenment emphasis on reason as a guide for social improvement and progress, the minister notes that the "birds and beasts" are "governed by a kindly instinct in attendance on their young," which suggests "that love and charity, far more than reason or justice, formed the tie that holds the world, in social dependence and obligation together" (157). Balwhidder is, in short, a Burkean conservative, distrustful of radical and abrupt change and rationalist schemes of capitalist and industrial "improvement."

The Ayrshire Legatees, which was actually published before the *Annals*, serially in *Blackwood's Magazine*, 1820–21, is a comical, epistolary novel about a Scottish family, the Pringles, who remove to London to process a legacy. In letters back to their Scottish community, Garnock, the four Pringles — Zachariah, the father, a minister; Janet, his wife; Rachel, the daughter; Andrew, the son, a lawyer — express their reactions, mostly dismay, at the hubbub and harshness of their urban locale and nostalgia for the "primitive simplicities of my native scenes," as Rachel puts it (*Ayrshire Legatees* 2:152). Zachariah deplores the new industrialism and mechanization; even in Edinburgh, he finds, "the houses [are] grown up as if . . . sown in the seed-time . . . by a drill machine" (2:81). Andrew sees London as a "Babylon," "a multitudinous assemblage of harsh alarms, of selfish contentions, and of furious carriages driven by a fierce and insolent race, [which] shatter the very hearing" (2:88).

Mrs. Pringle, who unlike the others, is barely literate (typical of a woman of her status) and writes with crude spelling, is alarmed by the insolence of servants, infected with libertarian ideas: "we are all seething in the pot of revolution, for the scum is mounting uppermost" (2:195). One morning at breakfast,

who shoud com intil the room but Andrew's grum, follo't by the rest, to give us warning that the were all going to quat our sarivice, becas they were starvit. I thocht that I would have fentit cauld deed . . . It was . . . a rebellion waur than the forty-five [an allusion to the 1745–6 uprising] . . . So you see how dangerous it is to live among this piple, and their noshans of liberty. (2:196)

The servants are pacified when Mr. Pringle gives them a keg of ale.

Once their inheritance is secured, the Pringles happily return home to Scotland. "The leaves had fallen thickly, and the stubble-fields were bare; but Autumn, in a many-coloured tartan plaid, was still walking with matronly composure in the woodlands" (2:266). They are returning to a beloved close-knit community, whose members Galt particularized in the course of the novel through scenes of social gatherings where they read aloud the Pringle letters to one another and comment upon them.

The Provost (1822), Galt's next work, is narrated by a local politician, Mr. Pawkie, in an inadvertently self-satirical mode not unlike that of Micah Balwhidder. In recounting the gradual transition of his village to a more liberal reform-minded regime, he reveals his own opportunistic Machiavellianism along with the petty bribery and cronyism that character-ized the village's political behavior. As village provost, he learns to appear to adapt to new demands for reform without succumbing to "Jacobinism" (*Works* 10:144). In deciding to run for office, he realizes that playing coy will be the most effective tactic. "I looked warily about me before casting my nets, and therefore I laid myself out rather to be entreated than to ask . . . I therefore assumed a coothy [affable] and obliging demeanor" (10:7), maintaining "an outward show of humility and moderation" (10:11).

Once in office Pawkie enacts certain reform moves, mostly those to his own advantage, such as enclosing a fifty-acre common tract as his own property. "There were not wanting persons, naturally of a disloyal opposi-tion temper, who complained of the enclosure as a usurpation of the rights and property of the poorer burghers" (10:44). He also bans the practice of pigs running loose, "ordering them to be confined in proper styes" (10:164). Both of these moves were examples of modern agricultural practices being imposed, as we have seen, on rural areas at the time. He also introduces contract bidding for town projects instead of cronyism — "by which loose manner of administration great abuses were allowed" (10:81) — as well as the sale of bonds to finance repairs and the installation of street lamps. For these innovations "all the inhabitants of the town gave me credit for intro-ducing such a great reformation into the management of public affairs" (10:85).

He acknowledges, however, his own complicity in past embezzlement, arguing that it "seemed to be the use and wont of men in public trusts . . . to indemnify themselves in a left-handed way . . . I must confess that I myself partook . . . [in] doings that are now denominated corruptions" (10:118). But despite continuing "calumnious innuendoes to my disadvantage"

(10:128), he learns how to ingratiate himself with the radicalizing populace, who, inspired by the French and American revolutions, are demanding more voice in their government and more accountability in officials. "I had learnt . . . that the secret of the new way of ruling . . . was to follow, not to control, the evident dictates of the popular voice" (10:143). "This was a new era in public affairs" (10:146), in which

> the peremptory [sic] will of authority was no longer sufficient for the rule of mankind. Therefore, I squared my own conduct more by a deference to public opinion than by any laid-down maxims and principles . . . The consequence of which was that my influence still continued to grow and gather strength in the community and I was able to accomplish many things. (10:148)

Galt produced several more Scottish novels, including *The Entail* (1823) and *The Last of the Lairds* (1826).

The Life of Mansie Wauch, Tailor in Dalkeith, Written by Himself (1828) by D. M. Moir, continues in the antiheroic mode initiated by Hogg and developed by Galt. Indeed, *Mansie Wauch* is dedicated to Galt; the two men were friends and Moir is thought to have had a major hand in writing Galt's *Last of the Lairds* (Aldrich 86–8). As in Galt's work, in Moir's novel we find a detailed description of village life through the eyes and voice of a tailor in a tone of affection and gentle humor. While the novel is loosely organized as an autobiography, the narrator apologizes for his roundabout narrative style. "It behoves me . . . to beg pardon for not being able to carry my history aye regularly straight forward, and for being forced whiles to zig-zag and vandyke" (80) — images appropriate for a tailor.

As the case in other local-color literature, love of the homeland is the dominant theme. During his apprenticeship in Edinburgh, for example, Mansie longs for his home village.

> I used to look out at the window, where I could see thousands and thousands of lamps spreading for miles . . . where I did not know a living soul . . . Then would the memory . . . return to me . . . pleasant Dalkeith! Ay, how different, with its bonny river Esk, its gardens full of gooseberry bushes and pear-trees, its grass parks spotted with sheep. (25)

Unlike in Scott (though Scott's protagonists are themselves not very warlike) Moir's tailor is comically antiheroic; indeed the notion of the Highlander warrior cult is mocked. On hearing of a threat of a French invasion (during the Napoleonic Wars) Mansie bravely announces, "I, for one, kept up my pluck, like a true Highlander. Does any living soul believe that Scotland . . . could be conquered . . . ?" (194). However, when he is dragooned into the local militia, "I was seized with a severe shaking of the knees and a flaffing [sic] of the heart" (77). He imagines "going out to scenes of blood, bayonets, and gunpowder, none of which I had the least stomach for" (78), and when he is knocked off his feet while trying to fire a gun, his fellow soldiers laugh at him (79).

As with Galt's Balwhidder, Mansie deplores the introduction of revolutionary ideas, including communism.

> Everything was to be divided, and every one made alike; houses and lands were to be distributed by lot; and the mighty man and the beggar — the auld man and the hobble-dehoy — the industrious man and the spendthrift . . . made all just brethren, and alike. Save us! But to think of such nonsense!!" (75)

Like many other local-color characters, Mansie is sensitive to animals and recoils at animal abuse, deploring a race in which an exhausted mare is forced to run, which leads to her death. "I turned round my back, not able to stand it" (88). This incident occurs in a distant city, and Mansie implies it would never have happened in his native Dalkeith. "This spectacle gave me . . . insight . . . [into] the selfishness, the sinfulness, and perversity of man, that I grew more and more home-sick" (88).

One of the most touching episodes in the work concerns an apprentice, Mungo Glen, who is himself homesick for his rural home but dies of consumption before he can return there.

> Ye was never brought up in the country — ye never kent what it is to wander about in simmer glens, wi' naething but the warm sun looking down on ye, the blue waters streaming over the braes, the birds singing, and the air like to grow sick wi' the breath of blooming birks. (149)

But leaving home has broken his heart: "I'll never be as I was before . . . The thoughts of my heart have been broken in upon, and nothing can make whole what has been shivered to pieces" (148).When Mansie finally retires and faces the prospect of moving to a new locale, he laments,

> I could not think of leaving my auld house — every room, every nook in it, was familiar to my heart. The garden trees seemed to wave their branches sorrowfully over my head, as bidding me a farewell . . . the mist of gushing tears bedimmed my eyesight. (224)

Mansie's and Mungo's comments might well serve to characterize the underlying general mood of Scottish local-color literature — indeed all local-color literature — nostalgia for a vanishing but beloved home world. "Nothing can make whole what has been shivered to pieces."

CHAPTER 4

Dorfgeschichte

The German Village Tale

Sir Walter Scott was one of the most popular authors in Germany in the first decades of the nineteenth century. A recent study of German circulating libraries (*Leihbibliotheken*) of the time by Albert Martino (1990) reveals that nearly every town in Germany had at least one such library and that they all included multiple volumes of translations of Scott's novels, which were among the most read. A summary of 62 of these libraries' catalogs from 1815–48 lists 4,332 volumes by Scott, making him the second highest in popularity (Martino 276). By 1823 the library in Frankfurt-am-Main, for example, held 56 Scott translations (220); by 1828 Köln had 98 (227).

The impact of Scott on German literature was considerable. In particular, he provided a model for the German local-colorists, the writers of *Dorfgeschichten* [village stories], who emerged in the 1830s and 1840s, notably Jeremias Gotthelf (1779–1854), a Swiss-German writer, and Berthold Auerbach (1812–82), a Swabian, the leading figures in the German regionalist movement, as well as Annette von Droste-Hülshoff (1797–1848), a Westphalian, and Josef Rank (1816–96), an Austro-Bohemian, also important progenitors of the genre. As one literary historian notes, "the representation of [German] folk-life without the example of Walter Scott is hardly imaginable" ["die Darstellung des Volksleben ohne das Vorbild Walter Scott kaum denkbar ist"] (Baur 195). Auerbach, who has been described as the "Walter Scott of his hometown" ["Walter Scott seines Heimatsdorf"] (Baur 195), acknowledged Scott's influence on him, noting, "I know of no narrative writer whom I hold higher and also Walter Scott has influenced me as no other. I learned from him to see in a literary perspective and to create first Jewish and then peasant life" ("Ich weiss auch keinen erzählenden Dichter, den ich höher halte, und auch auf mich hat Walter Scott eingewirkt, wie kein Anderer. Ich habe von ihm gelernt, zuerst das jüdische Leben und dann das Bauerleben in dichterischer Perspektive zu sehen und zu fassen"] (Baur 195).

It was Scott's ethnographic approach — what German critics called his "footnote realism" ["Fussnoten Realismus"] (Baur 195) — in describing Scottish communities in exact historical, cultural, and geographical detail that most impressed the German writers. At the time the dominant conception of the novel in Germany stemmed from Goethe's *Bildungsroman, Wilhelm Meister's Lehrjahr,* which focused solipsistically on the evolution of one individual. Scott offered a drastically different kind of novel, one conceived "as a collective, 'public' form," unlike the "elitist individualism" of Goethe's "'Privatform'" (McInnes, "Realism" 42–3). As we have seen, Scott's characters were not depicted as transcendent egos but as embedded in historical social context. "No novelist before [Scott] had made such sustained efforts to penetrate the inward dependence of his characters on the body of interacting beliefs, assumptions and customs controlling their self-awareness and attitudes" (McInnes, "Realism" 44). German critics of the time recognized Scott's work as part of a democratizing trend and "praised his respect for the humanity of his most insignificant characters and his concern to stress the strength, dignity, and courage which lay in simple lives" (McInnes, "Realism" 45).

Scott was not alone among the Scottish and Irish local-colorists in having an enthusiastic reception among German readers. Many of the writers treated in preceding chapters appeared in German translation soon after their original publication. Maria Edgeworth's *Castle Rackrent* appeared in 1802 as *Schloss Rackrent: Eine Erzählung* [Tale] *aus dem Jahrbüchern* [Annuals] *Irlands vor der Union.* Her *Ennui* was translated as *Denkwürdigkeiten* [Memoirs] *des Grafen von Glenthorn* in 1814, the same year as a German translation of *The Absentee* appeared.

Lady Morgan's works were especially popular. *The Wild Irish Girl* appeared in two separate editions in 1809: *Glorwina, das Naturmädchen* [Nature-girl] *aus Irland* and *Glorwina, das wilde Mädchen* [Wild Girl] *in Irland.* Goethe himself read the novel apparently, making several references to it in his notebooks (Hennig, "Goethe" 367). *Florence Macarthy* appeared in German translation in 1822, and *Die O'Briens und O'Flahertys* in 1829.

Even less well-known works, such as Christian Isobel Johnstone's *Clan-Albin,* appeared (in 1821) with the subtitle *Ein Schottisches National-Gemälde nach dem Englischen des Walter Scott Esqr* [A Scottish National Portrait in the English Manner of Walter Scott]— a misconstrual of Scott's nationality but an attempt to trade on his popularity. James Hogg's tales appeared the following year as *Die Wanderer im Hochland* [the Highlands]; *Winter-abend Erzählungen* [Winter Evening Tales]. In 1828 John Galt's *Ayshire Legatees* came out as *Die Erben: ein Familiengemälde nach dem Englischen bearbeitet* [The Inheritors: a Family Portrait done in the English Fashion]. Michael Whitty's *Tales of Irish Life* appeared in 1826 as *Irlandisches Erzählungen: zur Kenntnis der Sitten, der Gebräuche und des Volksleben in Irland* [Irish Tales: Toward a Knowledge of the Customs, Usages and Folk-Life in Ireland]. Several of William Carleton's stories were included in *Skizzen aus Irland oder Bilder aus Irlands Vergangenheit von einem Wanderer* (1838) [Sketches of Ireland or Pictures of Ireland's Past by a Traveler]. Even S. G. Hall's work was published as *Skizzen aus Irland* in 1850.[1]

It is perhaps not surprising that these Irish and Scottish works would have had such an appeal, for the historical political and cultural processes occurring in German-speaking regions during the early nineteenth century paralleled in certain respects those occurring in the Celtic lands. As there, the German provinces were dominated by a succession of imperial authorities whose direction came from distant metropoleis. The first and perhaps most important of these was the French empire under Napoleon established in the wake of the French Revolution. By 1796 the west bank of the Rhine, which included several German states, was under French military control, an authority that continued to expand through the first decade of the nineteenth century. In 1806 a "Confederation of the Rhine" was established under French control; it included Bavaria, Baden, Westphalia, and Hesse, and eventually much of present-day Germany with the exception of Prussia — the region around and to the east of Berlin. By 1807 Napoleon occupied much of this region as well and the Treaty of Tilsit ratified his control as far east as the Elbe River. By 1809 the French had captured Vienna and thus occupied a significant part of the Austrian Empire — the other major European imperial power of the day. With the defeat of Napoleon in 1814–15 the French military control receded, but the impact of the French occupation and the liberal ideas of the French Revolution promulgated by the French continued to have their effect in the territories that had been occupied. During the period 1815–71 the German Confederation — a loose network of regional states — remained the political unit for much of Germany, but Prussia and the Austrian Empire remained the most powerful political entities until the First World War ended in 1918. During the period 1848–71 Prussia began to exert its influence over the Confederation, a process that culminated in the establishment of the Second Empire in 1871 with Berlin as its capital.

As in Ireland and Scotland, the German regions resisted the political and cultural control imposed on them by the imperial authorities — whether French, Austrian, or Prussian. And, as elsewhere, the cultural hegemony imposed by the empires entailed the introduction of modern ideas and institutions — liberal political theories, Enlightenment methodologies, and capitalist industrialism — which upset, challenged, and often displaced traditional premodern ways of thinking and being. As in the Celtic countries, the German regions had their own unique cultures and their own locally specific dialects. In some parts of the Austrian empire, such as Moravia and Bohemia, or in Jewish *shtetls*, regional peoples spoke not just dialects but entirely different languages from the standard imperial tongue

(*Hochdeutsch*). Scholars have in fact recently begun characterizing the cultural subordination of these regions as an "inner colonization." (See Metz.)

German regional writing took the form of *Dorfgeschichten* (village stories) or *Bauernromane* (peasant novels). In addition to Gotthelf, Auerbach, Droste-Hülshoff, and Rank, noted above, the principal writers in the genre included Alexandre Weill (1811–98), an Alsatian who wrote in both German and French; Adalbert Stifter (1805–68), Austro-Bohemian; Leopold Kompert (1822–86) and Karl Emil Franzos (1848–1904), who focused on Jewish ghettos in the Austro-Hungarian Empire; Marie von Ebner-Eschenbach (1830–1916), Austro-Moravian; and Gottfried Keller (1819–90), Swiss. (Because the latter two wrote after the genre was well established, detailed discussions of their work will not be included here.) The genre was extremely popular; literally hundreds of collections of village tales appeared in Germany in the nineteenth century (Jürgen Hein lists nearly 300; Uwe Baur lists over ninety stories in the decade of the 1840s alone).

The heyday of the German local-color movement was the 1840s, sometimes referred to as the "*Vormärz*" period — *März* being an allusion to the revolutionary uprisings (the March Revolution) in 1848, whose failure to dislodge regressive imperial regimes marked the onset of a reactionary era in continental Europe. After 1848, according to Baur, regional writings became more political and tendentious, devolving, especially in northern Germany, into the social novel that dealt with conditions of the industrialized proletariat (39). Carl Arnold Schloenbach's *Die Weber und die Mucker* (1848), which depicts the "epochal transition from an agricultural to an industrial society" ["der epochal Übergang von der Agrargesellschaft zur industriellen Gesellschaft" (quoted in Baur 162)], marks the endpoint, according to Baur, of the *Dorfgeschichte* of the *Vormärz* period. The peasant's story has become "a rural proletariat story" ["eine dorfliche Proletariergeschichte" (Baur 162)].

While not overtly political, German local-color fiction nevertheless generally shared the anti-imperial, antimodern view of local-color works elsewhere. And, as elsewhere, the *Dorfgeschichte* focused sympathetically on peasants or villagers as ethnic minorities, presenting their point of view, detailing their customs, representing their dialogue in dialect, and locating them in accurate historical time and geographical space. While the writers themselves were for the most part well educated and had traveled beyond their region, they, like their Irish and Scottish predecessors, retained emotional ties to their home region and wrote out of a desire to preserve the uniqueness of its ethnic character as against the homogenizing sweep of modernity.

Most of the writers were themselves liberal, against feudal political and social arrangements, and in favor of democratizing tendencies. They thus wrote in part so as to elevate the status of peasants, to establish them culturally as worthy human beings, not slaves or serfs. Baur proposes anti-feudalism as a necessary precondition for the emergence of the German *Dorfgeschichte* ["eine wesentliche Vorbedingung für das Enstehen der Dorfgeschichte" (173)]. German local-color writers, therefore, like their predecessors, evinced the characteristic dual vision noted in earlier chapters of the colonial/postcolonial writer, seeing the world "not from the point of view of the castle" (though they may have been closer socially to its inhabitants) but having their "perspectival standpoint in the peasant village" ["Der Erzähler sieht die Welt nicht aus dem Blickfeld des Schlosses, sondern hat seinem perspektivischen Standpunkt im bäuerlichen Dorf" (Baur 173)]. Their goal was to "relate the empirical historical reality of the contemporary everyday life of the social underclasses" to an "educated public" ["für ein aufgeklärtes Publikum" "historische-empirische Wirklichkeit zu erzählen, das zeitgenössische gewöhnliche Leben der gesellschaftlichen Unterschichten" (Baur 192)].

But for the local-colorists the concern was not primarily with class oppression but with the suppression and devaluation of ethnicity. Many German local-color writers were, for example, focused centrally on validating ethnic Jewish culture; such that the Jewish *Dorfgeschichte* became an important subdivision of the German local-color tradition (see further discussion below).

The underlying tension in German regional writing, however, remained that of the resistance to state-imposed modernity. In his study of German regional literature, *Erzählte Provinz* (1982), Norbert Mecklenburg remarks that nineteenth-century regional genres such as the *Dorfgeschichte* or *Bauernroman* reflected the "regions' battle against the central power of the state" ("Kampf der Regionen gegen staatliche Zentralgewalt" [9]). "Literary regionalism is determined . . . by its oppositional relation to modernity" ("Literarische Regionalismus bestimmt sich . . . durch seine Widerspruchsvolle Beziehung auf die Moderne" [11]) and may be seen "as an 'answer' to specific challenges of our modern civilization" ("als eine 'Antwort' auf spezifische Herausforderung unserer modernen Zivilisation" [9]). In particular, Mecklenburg notes, regional literature reflects an early response to and "compensation for the gradual shrinkage of the preindustrial agrarian small-town way of life with its relative cohesion, autonomy, and 'rootedness'" ("Kompensation des allmählichen Schwundes vorindustrieller, agrarisch-kleinstädtischer Lebensweise mit ihrer relativen Geschlossenheit, Autonomie, und 'Bodenstandigkeit'" [72]). The emphasis on regional difference — in particular, regional dialect, Jürgen Hein notes, may be seen as a reaction against the "'homelessness' of the industrial world" ("'Unbehausbarkeit' der industriellen Welt" [Hein 42]). Jürgen Hein also emphasizes that the regional genres expressed an opposition to "a dark superior power with which the bearers of technical civilization threatened to destroy the old values and ways" ["eine dunkle Übermacht des Technisch-Zivilisatorischen, das die alten Werte und Ordnungen zu zerstören drohte" (Hein 37)].

In Germany the history of the local-color movement has been distorted by twentieth-century developments in German regional writing, notably the so-called "blood and soil" [*"Blut und Boden"*] literature of the Nazi era. Indeed, because of its unjust association with *Blut-und-Boden* fiction, the nineteenth-century *Dorfgeschichte* tradition was largely "repressed and forgotten" ["in Vergessenheit geraten, bzw. 'verdrangt'" (Hein vii)] by post-war German critics (Mecklenburg 17, 87). "The regional was equated with the homeland novel and it with the 'Blood-and-Soil' novel, and thereby rendered taboo" ["Der regionale wurde mit dem Heimatroman und dieser mit dem 'Blut-und-Boden'-Roman gleichgestellt und damit tabuiert" (Mecklenburg 19)]. (The *Heimatroman* was a regionally chauvinistic form that emerged out of the *Dorfgeschichte* tradition around the turn of the nineteenth century.) Studies of *Dorfgeschichten* are few therefore because "the fascist Blood-and-Soil cult so thoroughly discredited peasant litera-ture" [Der faschistische Blut-und-Boden-Kult habe die Bauernliteratur so gründlich diskrediert" (Hein 133)] that it has since 1945 been "excluded from the canon" ["entkononisiert" (Hein 133)].

However, Hein argues, the rural world depicted in the *Dorfgeschichten* was actually falsified ["verfälscht"] in *Blut-und-Boden* ideology, indeed "defamed" by it ["schliesslich verfielen . . . literarische Provincialismus der Diffamierung" (37)]. Instead, regional particularities and differences — so stressed in *Dorfgeschichten* — were erased, according to Mecklenburg, in the *Blut-und-Boden* literature. In the Third Reich regional particularity was forced to conform ["'gleichgeschaltet'" (Mecklenburg 100)] to an ideologi-cally driven ideal of peasant life. One might say indeed that Nazi ideology constituted another colonization and repression of the regional differences so celebrated by the writers of *Dorfgeschichten*.

The *Dorfgeschichte* tradition also posed a problem for Nazi theorists because many of its central writers were Jewish, including perhaps the most celebrated, Berthold Auerbach, as well as Alexandre Weill, as noted, another progenitor of the genre. (Both Auerbach and Weill were trained as rabbis.) In addition, there was a subgenre of village stories that focused on Jewish communities in Eastern Europe, seen in works by Karl Franzos and Leopold Kompert — both of whom were, like Auerbach, widely read and popular, and Droste-Hülshoff's *Die Judenbuche* deals centrally with

Jewish characters. Rudolf Zellweger in his definitive study of the origins of the genre emphasizes how strong the Jewish component was in the earliest German examples (261). But because of the anti-Semitism inherent in *Blut-und-Boden* theory (and to a lesser extent in the *Heimatdichtung*), Jewish predecessors like Auerbach were erased and by the turn of the century relegated to obscurity and forgotten (Hein 78, 112).

Thus, while *Heimat* literature (and later *Blut-und-Boden* literature) focused on rural life, that is where its similarity to the *Dorfgeschichten* ends. As one writer put it, the Nazi emphasis was more on "blood than soil" (Dominick 85; see also 99, 101), idealizing peasant life for its rootedness and alleged racial (Aryan) purity and setting up the Jew as a scapegoat for the problems of modernity (Mecklenburg 100). The orientation in the early *Dorfgeschichten* was, however, quite different. While they did focus, in most cases positively, on local customs and manners, they did so as a subversive gesture against or in negotiation with externally mandated regulation handed down from centralized political or economic authority. To a great extent the central issue was resistance to *Gleichschaltung*. And many works included positive representation of Jewish customs and traditions as an integral part of the provincial scene. (The exception here is the Jewish usurer who appears in Gotthelf's work; see below.)

While the main flowering of the German local-color tradition occurred around 1840, it was preceded by several earlier works of fiction that initiated the serious treatment of peasants and rural life. Until the late eighteenth and early nineteenth century, writers in the Western literary tradition generally followed the Aristotelian classification of literary subjects, according to which the lower classes are considered to be suitable subjects only for comedy or idealized pastoral romance. But as the classical *Stiltrennung* broke down, realistic treatments began to appear.

One of the first of these was *Lienhard und Gertrud* (1781) by the Swiss Johann Heinrich Pestalozzi (1746–1827), a pedagogical temperance novel that purports to instruct peasants somewhat à la Elizabeth Hamilton's Scottish *Cottagers of Glenburnie* (1808) and Mary Leadbeater's *Cottage Dialogues* (1811), which, as noted, it likely influenced. However, while set in a village and dealing with peasant characters, Pestalozzi's setting is too abstract — lacking, as Rudolf Zellweger notes, "la couleur locale" (24) — to be considered a harbinger of the genre.

A more immediate predecessor was the *Schatzkästlein des rheinischen Hausfreundes* (1803–11) [The Treasure Chest of the Rhinelander Family Friend] by Johann Peter Hebel (1760–1826), a selection of short fables and anecdotes originally published in an almanac. In an enthusiastic essay the Marxist critic Ernst Bloch linked Hebel with Jeremias Gotthelf as examplars of an era "still untouched by capitalism." Both writers sought to "preserv[e]

. . . indigenous folklore on the eve of capitalist incursion" (*Literary Essays* 323, 325). For

> in the aftermath of 1789, the peasants were not only liberated from feudal overlords, but also from their old customs, their folklore, their spinning rooms . . . And along with the spinning room, the art of storytelling also passed from the scene. (323)

The *Schatzkästlein* is rooted, Bloch notes, in just such spinning-room conversation and oral culture. "[E]ven words printed in High German [*Hochdeutsch*] seem imbued with a style of speaking . . . Hebel's voice is one of the least affected by the print medium" (147). While thus dedicated to preserving a world that was being superceded by modern ways, Hebel was nevertheless an enthusiastic supporter of the liberal ideas of the French Revolution, because they promoted peasant liberation, as well as women's and Jewish rights. (Although a Protestant minister, Hebel "openly acknowledged his Jewish background," according to Bloch [153].) In this, Hebel anticipated the succeeding Jewish writers in the *Dorfgeschichte* tradition, notably Auerbach, Weill, Kompert, and Franzos — all of whom evinced a desire to preserve local ethnic particularity while embracing the emancipatory ideals of modernity.

The *Schatzkästlein* consists of short pieces, some only a paragraph long, others one to three pages. Most are pinpointed historically to an exact date (in the early 1800s), many deal with "little people" and how they were affected by the Napoleonic Wars. "Der schlaue Husar" ("The Clever Hussar"), for example, opens, "A hussar in the last war . . ." ["Ein Husar im letzten Kriege . . ." (*Erzählungen* 68)]. The entire story "Misverstand" ("Misunderstanding") is set during the war.

> In the 1790 war, as the Rhine on one side was occupied by French sentries and on the other by Swabian district soldiers, a Frenchman to pass the time called to the German sentry, "Filu! Filu!" which means in good German: "rascal!" The honest Swabian . . . thought the Frenchman asked, "What time is it?" and goodhumoredly answered "three thirty". [Im 90er Krieg, als der Rhein auf jener Seite von franzosischen Schildwachen, auf dieser Seite von schwäbischen Kreissoldaten besetzt war, rief ein Franzos zum Zeitvertreib zu der deutschen Schildwache herüber "Filu! Filu!" Das heisst auf gut deutsche: Spitzbube. Allein der ehrliche Schwabe . . . meinte, der Franzose frage, Wieviel Uhr? Und gab gutmütig zur Antwort, "Halber Vieri".]
>
> (*Erzählungen* 75)

Most of the pieces have a moral point, usually endorsing a character's tolerant, sensible behavior. For example, "Einer Edelfrau schlaflose Nacht"

("A Noblewoman's Sleepless Night") (*Erzählungen* 276–9) concerns the protagonist's change of heart regarding her servant's illegitimate pregnancy. "Seltsame Ehescheidung" ("A Unique Divorce") defends a woman against an abusive, oppressive husband, promoting in effect women's rights. The moral of the story is: "A husband should never beat his wife, lest he dishonor himself" ["Ein Mann soll seine Frau nie schlagen, sonst verunehrt er sich selber" (*Erzählungen* 153)].

Several of the stories have Jewish characters, some register criticisms of anti-Semitism. "Einträglicher Rätselhandel" ("Profitable Riddle Business"), which concerns a Jew who wins some bets against his fellow travelers by solving several riddles, notes his estrangement from and abuse by the others. "The Jew had to endure the way they sometimes treated these people [Jews] and thus wronged him" ["der Jude . . . musste viel leiden, wie man's manchmal diesen Leuten machte und versündigt sich daran" (*Erzählungen* 114)].

Hebel's concern about the status of Jews in Western culture is most fully expressed in his *Schatzkästlein* essay "Der grosse Sanhedrin zu Paris" ("The Great Sanhedrin in Paris"), which reports on a Jewish proclamation issued March 2, 1807, under Napoleon's aegis, that lays out the principles by which Jews may live in gentile lands, noting "that since the destruction of Jerusalem . . . the Jews have lived in diaspora without fatherland and without citizen rights" ["Dass die Juden seit der Zerstörung Jerusalems . . . ohne Vaterland und ohne Bürgerrecht . . . in der Zerstreuung leben" ("Der grosse Sanhedrin")]. The gist of the document is that "Christians and Jews are brothers . . . and . . . the Jew shall live with the French and Italian and the oppressed in whichever land they live as with brothers and fellow citizens" and "should consider such land as their fatherland" ["Die Christen und die Juden seien Brüder . . . und . . . der Israelite soll mit dem Franzosen und Italiener und mit den Untertanen jedes Landes, in welchem sie wohnen, so leben als mit Brüdern und Mitbürgern" und "solches Land als ihr Vaterland anzusehen" ("Der grosse Sanhedrin")]. These principles were, the document implies, to be carried forth by Napoleon into the German provinces as well. (Jews in fact were granted equal rights in the French-occupied territories.)

Although Hebel paved the way for the *Dorfgeschichte* in his serious treatment of "little people," in his oral narrative style, in his historical specificity, and liberal perspective, his works are not geographically specific. Though they are usually set in a particular named place, they lack local color and a detailed, contextually specific representation of that place; nor is Habel concerned beyond abstract general principles with representing ethnically specific details. Indeed, as the Sanhedrin piece indicates, Hebel was more concerned with generic Enlightenment concepts that apply to all people than with particularizing and preserving the differences among peoples.

Another early predecessor of the *Dorfgeschichte* was Caroline Pichler (1769–1843), an Austrian, whose *Das Husarenoffizier* (The Hussar Officer) appeared in 1816. While the work depicts an alpine valley realistically it remains more of a travelogue, seen through the eyes of an outsider-visitor, than an authentic expression of an indigenous perspective. The urban visitor, according to Uwe Baur, "remains a tourist collecting curiosities" ["er bleibt Tourist, der Kuriosa sammelt" (Baur 205)], who sees the rural scene as "through a telescope" ["durch ein Fernrohr" (Baur 206)].

The "Oberhof" section of *Münchhausen: Eine Geschichte in Arabesken* (1838) by Karl Immermann (1796–1840) in its realistic description of upper-end peasant life is often cited as another work that anticipates the *Dorfgeschichte*. That section opens with a vignette depicting a horse sale in which the seller, a peasant, is saying good-bye to his horse: "It always saddens one when one sells a creature one has raised, but what can one do?" ["Es tut einem immer leid, wenn man eine Kreatur, die man aufzog, losschlägt, aber wer kann wider?" (*Münchhausen* 3:141)]. The horse looks back wistfully ["als wollte sie klagen" (3:141)] and when a boy observes that a cow too is mournful at the departure ["Das Vieh grümt sich" (3:141)], the farmer answers, "why shouldn't she? . . . we're all mourning" ["Warum sollte es nicht . . . grämen wir uns doch auch" (3:141)]. The local perspective, reflecting the characteristic attachment to animals, is thus presented. The author reveals his own affection for the rural world in noting that there one still finds a sense of "Mother Earth as the All-Nourisher, from whom one wants and asks nothing more than the gift of the field, the meadow, the pond, the forest" ["Diese halten vielmehr die Stimmung zur Mutter Erde als zu Allernährerin fest, wollen und verlangen nichts von ihr, als die Gabe des Feldes, der Viehweide, des Fischteiches, das Wildforstes" (3:157)]. Because it lays out a "counter-picture" ["Gegenbild"] for the urban reader, the Oberhof piece has been seen as the first German example of peasant-focused literature (Hein 73).

The most significant forerunner of the *Dorfgeschichte*, however, remains Heinrich Zschokke (1771–1848)'s *Das Goldmacher-Dorf* (1817). Although too didactic to be considered the first of the genre, it nevertheless lays out many of the thematic issues that dominated the *Dorfgeschichte*, notably the clash between modern and premodern ways. The novel's plot indeed concerns the introduction of the former into a small village, Goldenthal, by a resident, Oswald, who returns to his hometown (the *Heimkehr*) after 17 years abroad as a soldier in the Napoleonic Wars, full of new ideas spawned by the French Revolution and capitalist industrialism. The town is depleted economically because of the wars; "it was occupied by foreign troops who used up town provisions and townspeople were forced to pay taxes and duties to the ruling authorities" ["Unser Dorf hat vom Kriege viel gelitten . . . Es lagerten sich fremde Truppen bei uns und verzehrten unsere Vorräte; . . . wir mussten der Obrigkeit Zins und Steuer zahlen" (Zschokke, *Das Goldmacher-Dorf* 246)].

As a follower of Enlightenment theory, Oswald believes the way to prosperity is through instituting new household and civic management techniques, such as accurate accounting, and new agricultural and forest management methods, using accurate land measurement. He also proposes more radical ideas, such as equalizing wealth, progressive taxation, leasing the commons, and communal household labor. But his ideas are resisted by both the lower and upper classes. When he tries "to give good advice or criticize [people's] lack of household management and order, he received surly looks for thanks" ["guten Rat geben wollte, oder wenn er die Unhäuslichkeit und Unordnung tadelte, so bekam er nurrische Gesichter zum Dank" (243)]. They tell him to mind his own business: "Steck du die Nase in deinem eigenen Dreck!" (243).

When he proposes leasing out the common grazing area so the poor can use it, the upper classes accuse Oswald of being "French, a New Ager, a Jacobin, a Bonapartist' ["ein Franzose, ein Neuerer, ein Jakobiner, ein Bonapartler" (316)]. But Oswald persists: the commons is now only used by the wealthy who squander the income which should be used for infrastructure, such as a ditch to drain a boggy area, which would benefit all (250). The bottom line is "some . . . have too much land; others, none whatsoever" ["die einen . . . haben zu viel Land, die andern gar keines" (250)].

Gradually, the townspeople come over to Oswald's side; acknowledging the wisdom of some of his ideas, they ask him if he knows how to make gold. This he seizes as an opportunity to introduce capitalist financial methods, teaching the people how to figure out their debts and pay them off, how to save and accrue interest, and how to reinvest it — thus in a sense "making gold." "When . . . interest accrued, one put it out again as small capital; thus it was that the interest brought in more interest" ["Wenn . . . die Zinsen einkamen, that er sie wieder als ein kleines Kapital aus, also, dass die Zinsen wieder Zinsen eintragen müssten" (286)]. The town thus transitions to capitalism, becoming a "gold-making village" [*Goldmacher-Dorf*].

Berthold Auerbach's *Samtliche Schwarzwälder Dorfgeschichten* [Black Forest Village Stories] is considered the premiere example of the genre, both in the sense of initiating the tradition and in remaining its exemplification. It was also the most popular, establishing a model followed by literally hundreds of successors — and not just in Germany. Auerbach received considerable international attention — from Russia to France and the United States. Ivan Turgenev is said to have been influenced by him; Leo Tolstoy visited him in his home village in Baden, as did George Sand, herself a major author of French peasant novels (see Chapter Five).

The work first appeared in 1843 in two volumes — the first containing seven stories or novellas and the second, four. (Some of the stories had been published separately in 1842.) The stories are set during the early 1800s in Nordstetten, a village in Swabia, the Black Forest region of southwestern Germany. The stories are thus linked by the continuing temporal and geographical setting and also by the recurrence of certain characters in different stories. Many of the stories refer to the historical background of the era, in particular the aftermaths of the Napoleonic Wars and occupation and the succeeding Austrian imperial control. In "Die Kriegspfeife" ["The War Pipe"] (1842), for example, the narrator laments how during the war years (the story is set in 1796), it was

> first the Austrians . . . who marched through the Black Forest, then the French . . . then again the Russians . . . and in between the Bavarians, Wurtemburgers, Hessians . . . The Black Forest was an always open door for the French and only now are we finally putting an end to it. [Ueber den Schwarzwald zogen bald die Oesterreicher . . . bald die Franzosen . . . dann wieder die Russen . . . und zwischendrein steckten die Bayern, Würtemburger, Hessen . . . Der Schwarzwald war das allzeit offene Thor für die Franzosen, und jetzt eben is man endlich daran, einen Riegel vorzuschieben.]

> (Auerbach 1:27)

The take-over of the area by the Austrian Empire in the wake of Napoleon's defeat, however, only replaced one alien authority with another. "Befehlerles" ["Silly Regulations" (loosely translated)] deals centrally with the clash between local customs and practices, on the one hand, and edicts issued by a translocal authority, in this case Austrian, on the other. The plot concerns the arrest and trial of a young local, Matthes, for setting up a maypole in front of his fiancée Aivle's house, which is strictly forbidden ["streng verboten"] as it requires poaching in a ducal forest ["Waldfrevel"] (1:88). The arresting magistrate, having only recently been appointed, is "so eager to please his Austrian superiors ["der österreichischen Herrschaft"] that he feels he should affect an Austrian dialect" ["in seiner Dienstbeflissenheit glaubte er auch den österreichischen Dialekt sprechen zu müssen" (1:89)], saying "I sog es" instead of colloquial dialect for "I say it."

The legal hearings reflect the culture clash in the conflict of dialects. The presiding official addresses Matthes familiarly with "Du" and "scolded him in high German, just as the mayor had the day before in peasant German" ["schimpfte ihn auf Hochdeutsch ebenso, wie gestern der Schultheiss auf Bauerndeutsch" (1:91)]. The proceedings are seen as unfair and the narrator notes that "so long as judicial proceedings are not public — as they generally were in the old times in Germany — so long will an official always be able to do with an accused what he will" ["Solange die Gerichtsverhandlungen nicht öffentlich sind, wie sie es zu alten Zeiten in Deutschland überall waren, solange wird ein Beamter immer mit einem Angeklagten machen können, was er will" (1:91)].

Matthes is briefly imprisoned, denying his guilt, but his girl, Aivle (Eva), is brought before the judge and tricked into implicating him. She speaks in local dialect while the court proceedings are in *Hochdeutsch*. Her testimony "is translated into high German and rescripted in connected periods" ["in hochdeutsche Sprache übersetzt und in zusammenhängende Rede gebracht waren" (1:95)] for the written record, with all her "tears and suffering" ["dem Weinen und den Qualen" (1:95)] expunged. When her testimony is read back to her she is "astonished over all that she had said" ["erstaunte über alles das, was es da gesagt hatte" (1:95)]. The bewilderment of the provincial before an alien-speaking court anticipates Kafka's *Der Prozess*.

The maypole tree adds a symbolic dimension to the story in that it takes root and continues to grow, suggesting an alignment between the villagers and the natural world, drawn in contrast to urban bureaucracy. When in prison Matthes comes to prize a fir twig, a token of the natural world that he identifies with against the oppressive imperial authorities who have imprisoned him. Meditating on this "relic of the green world" ["ein Ueberrest aus der grünenden Welt" (1:91)], he saw now for the first time how beautiful a sprig is: underneath the nuts were hard and darkgreen but still so soft and light-colored near the point" ["er sah jetzt zum erstenmale, wie schön so ein Reis ist; unten waren die Nadeln dunkelgrün und hart, nach der Spitze zu aber waren sie noch so sanft und hellfarbig" (1:91)]. In Auerbach, as in certain Celtic predecessors, notably William Carleton, the natural world is a place of spiritual presence. Auerbach was himself, according to Uwe Baur, a Spinozaist pantheist (Baur 128–9). Matthes is eventually freed and marries Aivle.

Part Two of the story further explores the clash between local custom and imperial edict when a judge bans the Black Forest practice of carrying axes in the left hand. The peasants protest with rallies and, led by the village mayor, Buchmaier, confront the judge, complaining against the constant regulation enforced from on high, oblivious to local conditions. "The community now counts for almost nothing, everything is disposed of in bureaucratic offices" ["Die Gemeind' soll jetzt gar nichts mehr gelten, alles soll in den Beamtenstuben abgetan werden" (1:100)]. Pretty soon, Buchmaier claims, petty bureaucrats will be "prescribing . . . how the hen must cackle when she lays an egg" ["schreiben . . . vor, wie die Henn' gackern muss, wenn sie ein Ei legt" (1:100)]. Indeed, he says to the judge, "you'll end up putting a policeman under every tree to keep it from quarreling with the wind and from drinking too much when it rains" ["Zuletzt stellet ihr noch an jedem Baum einen Polizeidiener, damit er keine Händel kriegt mit dem Wind und nicht zu viel trinkt wenn's regnet" (1:100)]. He suggests finally it would be better if the villagers had a hand in running their own affairs which they could do capably even though their ordinances won't be written "in officialese" ["im Amtstil" (1:100)]. The villagers continue to carry axes in the left hand and eventually the matter is dropped.

On another occasion (in another story) Buchmaier notes the resistance of local farmers to new sowing machines. When the local teacher, taking the side of modernity, deplores this as opposition to progress, Buchmaier retorts, "believe me, if the peasants were not so stiff-necked and adopted the experiments that the learned men concoct, we'd soon go hungry many a year" ["Glaubet mir, wenn die Bauersleut' nicht so halsstarrig wären und jedes Jahr das Versucherles machen thäten, das die studierten Herren aushecken, wir hätten schon manches Jahr hungern müssen" (2:96)].

"Der Lauterbacher" (1843), another novella in the *Schwarzwälder Dorfgeschichten*, represents the clash between urban metropolitan and rural cultures through the intermediary of the schoolteacher — an educated outsider — who has come to the village bent on reforming the peasantry by educating them in modern ideas. In the process, however, he himself is won over to village ways, cemented by marrying a local girl. Thus, Auerbach reworks Zschokke's plot ironically. Indeed, in one of his attempts to educate the locals, the teacher, referred throughout as the Lauterbacher, starts a reading group in which participants read the *Goldmacher-Dorf* (as noted, one of the earliest proto-*Dorfgeschichten*, in which a pedagogue convinces villagers to modernize). In Auerbach's story the villagers in the reading group are critical of Zschokke's reformer, Oswald, saying an outsider has no business telling villagers how to live (2:123–4).

The mayor, Buchmaier, and the teacher have several arguments over the question of introducing modern methods. Buchmaier protests, for example, to the Lauterbacher against animal welfare regulations issued by urban bureaucrats who don't, he claims, understand farm animals and farmers' relationships with them. "I have seen that people cry more when an ox passes on than when one of their children dies" ["ich hab' schon gesehen, dass die Leut' mehr heulen, wenn ihnen ein Rind draufgeht, als wenn ihnen ein Kind stirbt" (2:68)]. He remarks sarcastically that "official folks now want to regulate cattle. Before long you'll see a man . . . ordered as to what he can sow on his land" ["Die Amtleut' wollen jetz gern auch über das Vieh regieren. Ihr werdet sehen, wenn's so fort geht, wird man . . . einem befehlen, was er auf seinem Acker säen darf" (2:68)]. The teacher argues back that "the state is obliged to establish the good through penalties" ["ist der Staat verpflichtet, das Gute durch Strafen einzuführen" (2:69)].

Buchmaier strenuously objects. This debate neatly encapsulates the central problem posed by modernity to the provinces — whether its ideas (in this case efficient market-oriented management of agriculture) should override time-honored local practices in raising produce. We have seen the issue articulated forcefully in the Scottish resistance to the Highland Clearances.

Until his conversion to provincial ways near the end of the story, the Lauterbacher holds the locals in contempt. He is amazed at their lack of a sense of historical perspective. When he asks who built the church, the villagers are dumbfounded; for "they could hardly imagine that there could have been a time when the church was not yet there" ["sie konnten sich gar nicht denken, dass es . . . eine Zeit gegeben haben könne, da die Kirche noch nicht da war" (2:66)]. When early on it is suggested that he should marry a local girl, he thinks, "rather an ape for a wife than one of these stocky peasant women" ["lieber eine Aeffin, als so eine vierschrötige Bäuerin zur Frau" (2:64)]. And he resolves never to sink to the peasants' level ["Ich will alle meine Kraft zusammenhalten, um mich gegen das Verbauern zu wahren" (2:65)]. "I want to remain free from the influence of my surroundings" ["Ich will frei bleiben von dem Einfluss meiner Umgebung" (2:65)]. In the discussion about agriculture regulations he dismisses the villagers' opinions as evidence of their "coarseness" ["die Roheit dieser Menschen" (2:68)].

The narrator, on the other hand, sees the community in utopian terms as one governed by common tolerance. A central aspect of its utopian character is that it embraces Jews and Christians as equals, and part of the teacher's own education and transformation involves his overcoming his anti-Semitism. Here Auerbach obverts the later stereotyped association of Jews with urban modernity. In his stories Jews are country people and it is the urban-educated avatar of modernity who is anti-Semitic, not the local villagers.

Another participant in the tavern discussion about agricultural regulations is the Jew Mendel, who, we are informed, though he speaks high German (*Hochdeutsch*), speaks it in "the singing tones of the Jewish dialect" ["in dem singenden Tone des jüdischen Dialekts" (2:69)]. Significantly, the gentile teacher ignores the Jew during the discussion, and the narrator sarcastically observes, "it is not to be supposed that he, like other learned men, cared to treat the reply of a Jew as if it had not been proposed" ["Es ist nicht wahrscheinlich, dass er, wie die gelehrten Herren pflegen, auf die Gegenrede eines Juden that, als ob sie nicht vorgebracht worden wäre" (2:69)].

Shortly thereafter, the Lauterbacher meets a Jewish teacher through whom he begins to overcome his anti-Semitism. Upon being introduced, however, the Jewish teacher hesitates whether to shake hands, fearing to appear too pushy ["zuverdringlich"] but at the same time feeling offended at not having the ritual observed. "These two feelings," the narrator observes, "fear of obtrusiveness and disrespect on the one hand and of a sensitivity carried too far on the other — those are the two thieves between which the Jew in social life is crucified" ["Diese beiden Gefühle — Furcht vor Zudringlichkeit und Missachtung auf der einen, und vor zu weit getriebener Empfindlichkeit auf der andern Seite — das sind die beiden Schächer, zwischen denen der Jude im gesellschaftlichen Leben gekreuzigt ist" (2:71)]. The gentile teacher is impressed, however, by the Jew and soon comes to reflect on the anti-Semitism he learned as a boy, noting in his diary: "Heretofore I've never thought about Jews, although they also lived in my birthplace. I remember only as a small child I mocked the Jewish kids . . . and . . . hit them." ["Ich habe früher nie über Juden nachgedacht, obgleich in meinem Geburtsorte auch Juden wohnten; ich errinere mich nur, dass ich als kleines Kind auch die Judenknaben . . . verhöhnte und . . . schlug" (2:79)].

The Lauterbacher's reflections here recall those of the narrator in Edgeworth's novel *Harrington* (though to my knowledge that novel was never translated into German).

In the tavern discussion Mandel laments the lack of legal rights afforded Jews in Germany, highlighting the question of discrimination. In discussing the status of Alsace, a German-speaking province then under French control, the schoolteacher argues it should be returned to Germany but Mandel objects: "Most Jews in Alsace would rather be massacred than become Germans; over there they're completely the same as Christian citizens; whereas we pay the same taxes, serve as soldiers like Christians but have only half the rights" ["die vielen Juden im Elsass liessen sich eher massakrieren, ehe sie deutsch werden thäten; drüben sind sie vollkommen gleich mit den christlichen Bürgern; wir, wir bezahlen alle Steuern gleich, werden Soldaten wie die Christen und haben doch nur die halben Rechte" (2:68)].

One of the distinguishing features that differentiates the educated teacher (and the narrator) from the locals is that the latter speak in dialect, whose "coarse sounds" ("groben Lauten" [2:61]) initially grate on the teacher's ears. In introducing Hedwig, a local girl the teacher courts, the narrator in a footnote explains that although she speaks in dialect her speech will be translated henceforth into *Hochdeutsch* (88 n.1) — this undoubtedly because his primary audience were educated speakers of standard German who would have had difficulty understanding the local dialect. In his Preface to the first edition of the *Dorfgeschichten*, Auerbach noted that in order to reach an urban audience he had attempted only to give "the essential impression" ["das wesentliche Gepräge"] of "the particularity of the dialect and speech" ["die Eigentumlichkeit des Dialekts und der Rede" (Hein 78)].

As the Lauterbacher becomes serious about Hedwig, he attempts to correct her dialect, saying "it's a pity that you speak in that rough peasant German" ["es jammerschade ist, dass Ihr das holperige Bauerndeutsch sprecht" (2:102)]. It would be far more becoming ["das würde Euch viel besser anstehen" (2:102)], he tells her, if she adopted standard *Hochdeutsch*. She rejects the idea, saying it would "shame her" ["in die Seel' . . . schämen" (2:102)] to talk otherwise. Eventually, he comes to see Hedwig's speech as charming and even resolves to study writings in the region's Upper Swabian dialect ["oberschwäbischen Dialekte" (2:113)].

In the end the teacher comes to have doubts about his civilizing mission, realizing that "the modern culture has taken a great deal from the people, but what real joy has it given in return? Can it be a substitute? And how?" ["Die neue Bildung hat dem Volke viel . . . genommen, was hat sie ihm von wirklichen Freuden dafür gegeben? — Kann ihm ein Ersatz werden? und wie?" (2:114)]. In this story, then, the educated representative of modernity succumbs to the attractions of the region, becoming in a sense one of the natives.

"Ivo der Hajrle," another important novella included in Auerbach's *Schwarzwälder Dorfgeschichten*, further explores the tension depicted in the genre between regional customs and ways and an externally imposed elite culture issued by an alien officialdom located elsewhere. The plot concerns Ivo, a young man torn between following his father's wishes that he become an educated gentleman (*Hajrle*) and his own desire of remaining tied to the regional peasant folk he has grown up with. As a child he had bonded with a farm larborer named Natzi, "who cannot write and can barely read" ["der nicht schreiben und kaum lesen konnte" (1:123)]. Like Carleton's Phil Purcel and James Hogg's shepherds, Natzi's closest companions are the farm animals he tends. He laments, for example, that pigs are only on earth to be slaughtered. "That is why the sow cries and screams the most when she is slaughtered," he says ["dessenthalben auch so eine Sau am ärgsten schreit und heult, wenn man's metzget" (1:126)]. And he tells Ivo about a shepherd dog he once had who "was smarter than ten doctors" ["gescheiter war als zehn Doktoren" (1:125)] and who could read his "innermost thoughts" ["verborgesten Gedanken" (1:125)]. Through his friend Ivo comes to love animals too, saving a calf on one occasion from slaughter (1:133). "Natzi . . . encouraged him in this care for the defenseless enslaved creatures" ["Zu dieser Sorgfalt für die wehrlos Angejochten hielt ihn Natzi . . . an" (137)].

Natzi represents the premodern in conflict with authorities who would impose modern knowledges on the local populace. As a practitioner of herbal medicine, for example, he is chastised by the local doctor and receives official notice that he will be fined a heavy penalty if he continues his practice, which is labeled "quackery" and verboten ("Damals hat der Doktor erfahren und hat mich bei Amt angezeigt. Es ist nur bei hoher Straf' das Quacksalbern verboten worden" [1:202]).

Ivo's father, bent on his son becoming a gentleman, forbids him to see Natzi, chasing him out of the stables and sending him back to his studies. "Get out of here, . . . go back to your books . . . you are to become a gentle-man" ("Fort, . . . gang du zu deinem Büchern . . . du musst Hajrle werden" [1:149]). Ivo begins to feel a "stranger in his own house" ("entfremdete . . . vom elterlichen Hause" [1:149]), an estrangement that intensifies when he is sent to boarding school. When he writes home in *Hochdeutsch*, his mother finds it so alien she can hardly believe the letter is from her own son and has to remind herself that he's becoming a university man ("ihr Kind war ihr hierin so fremd, dann aber besann sie sich wieder, dass der Brief eben von einem 'G'studirten' sei" [1:169]).

While in school Ivo develops a romantic friendship with a schoolmate, Klemens. On one occasion on a group outing the two leave the trail and "behind a blooming blackthorn bush, where no one could see them, they fell upon one another . . . and kissed and embraced ardently" ["hinter einen blühenden Schlehdornhecke, wo es niemand sah, fielen sie . . . sich um den Hals und küssten und herzen sich inniglich" (1:189)]. A similar rela-tionship develops between two women in Alexandre Weill's story "Udilie und Gertrude" (see below). Both serve as further examples of the fluidity of sexual orientation in the premodern era.

On his return to Nordstetten, the *Heimkehr*, a central feature in many *Dorfgeschichten*, Ivo delights in recognizing old familiar faces. "Oh, home! You holy, trusted place . . . there are the roots of one's being . . . every hedge, every stack of wood seemed friendly" ["O heimat! du heiliger, trauter Ort! . . . da sind die Wurzeln des Daseins . . . [J]eder Zaun, jede Holzbeuge schaute ihn traulich an" (1:174)]. Significantly, he praises his native village as a place "where everyone was so good, Christian and Jew all alike" ["lobte Ivo innerlich sein liebes Nordstetten, in dem alle Menschen so gut waren, Christ und Jud, alles gleich" (1:172)]. On his return he had hitched a ride with Jewish villagers and observed them praying. The narrator notes that "he respected every creed, especially venerable was the Jewish as it was the old-est" ["er achtete jedes Glaubensbekenntnis, und besonders das jüdische als das uralt ehrwürdige" (1:172)], and he is pleased that he can read Hebrew.

Eventually, Ivo gives up his studies, joins up in business with his child-hood friend Natzi, and marries a local girl. Like the Lauterbacher he finds happiness in embracing the premodern ways of the province. While himself educated and knowledgeable about urban modernity, Auerbach thus, like other local-colorists, retained a strong emotional tie to the premodern world of the province. He once stated that he wrote the *Dorfgeschichten* "out of the deepest homesickness" ["aus tiefstem Heimweh" (Hein 75)].

Alexandre Weill and Auerbach apparently exercised mutual influence upon each other. They met in Frankfurt-am-Main, where both were living, in 1837. Weill wrote his first village story, "Stasi," in 1836 in Frankfurt in German (though after 1840 Weill, an Alsatian, wrote mostly in French and published in Paris). According to Rudolf Zellweger, it was Weill who actually coined the term *Dorfgeschichten*, proposing for the title of his collection *Elsässische Dorfgeschichten* [Alsatian Village Stories], but his editor deleted the term from the title, changing it to *Sittengemälde aus dem elsässischen Volksleben* [Pictures of Manners from Alsatian Folk-Life]. Auerbach then apparently took over the term *Dorfgeschichten* (suggested to him by the same editor) and used it for the title of his first collection. Weill came to resent Auerbach's success and felt in later life that not only had the term been stolen from him, but his pioneering role in creating the *Dorfgeschichte* genre had been neglected (Zellweger 38, 83–4). Indeed, unlike Auerbach, Weill is virtually unknown today, despite his contribution to the genre.

Like Auerbach, Weill (who, as noted, was Jewish and likewise trained as a rabbi) includes Jewish characters and issues prominently in his work, depicting Alsace as a tolerant, peaceful province. In "Stasi: Ein Sittengemälde aus Elsass" [Stasi: A Picture of Customs from Alsace] (Weill 1:7–104), a central character is the Jew Gumper, who serves as a kind of confidant and advisor to Stasi, the heroine, and her mother. Gumper had served along with Stasi's father in Napoleon's army (the father was fatally wounded in the Battle of Marengo). The plot concerns the seduction of Stasi, a peasant girl, by an upper-class roué, against whom Gumper vainly warns her (see further discussion below).

In "Frohni" (1840), another story in the *Sittengemälde*, we learn that Jews who settled in the Alsatian town before 1789 had to pay "*Schutzgeld*," a special "protection" tax, but that under the new enlightened regime that practice has been abolished. Now indeed a Jew owns a local *Schloss* (Weill 1:283). The main character Frohni's best friend, Elly, is Jewish and Ambrosi, Frohni's sweetheart, tells her, "To me the Jew is like Christ . . . when the need is greatest, the help is at hand" ["mir ist Jude wie Christ . . . wenn die Noth am höchsten, ist die Hülfe am nächsten" (Weill 1:350)]. The narrator offers the comment that all people are brothers underneath; all share the same fate, the same pain, the same joy ["Da ist alles Bruderherz, Juden, Katholiken, Protestanten theilen ein Loos, haben einem Schmerz, eine Freude" (Weill 1:348)].

The main character in "Der Bettler und sein Kind: Elsässische Dorfnovelle" [The Begger and His Child: an Alsatian Village Story], a gentile, Dollinger, whose best friend, Lase, is Jewish, speaks out directly against anti-Semitism: "basically there is no difference between Jews and Christians. A Christian is nothing other than a baptized Jew. To be sure the idiots in Jerusalem did crucify the Lord, but Lase was not there" ["im Grunde ist nicht viel Unterschied zwischen Juden und Christen. Ein Christ is weiter nichts als ein getaufter Jude. Die Dummköpfe in Jerusalem haben zwar unsern Herrgott gekreuzigt, aber der Lase war nicht dabei" (Weill 2:93)]. He expresses a liberal view, contending that "no one is bad by nature but only [so because of] relationships and external social influences" ["von Natur is kein Mensch böse, nur Verhaltnisse und äussere soziale Einflüsse . . ." (Weill 2:98)]. It is acknowledged, however, that Jews are hated by some in Alsace but the hope is that with their new freedoms they will be able to fight back and assert their rights (2:142).

At the time of Weill's writing, Alsace was a province of France but had long been under German cultural domination. Weill's stories present the point of view of the German-speaking Alsatian peasant in conflict with dominant French authority. (The province was retaken by Germany in 1871, and returned to France in 1919 where it remains.) Interestingly, Weill wrote the first three of the stories included in the collection ("Stasi," "Frohni," and "Udilie und Gertrude") in German (and in Germany) but the rest in French. The collection as a whole was translated into French as *Histoires de village* in 1853. (Weill also wrote some plays in Yiddish.) In his Preface to the French edition, Weill emphasized his deep connection to and understanding of peasant life: "I have seen my peasant men and women in flesh and bones" ["Mes paysans et mes paysannes, je les ai vus en chair et en os" (Zellweger 311)].

In Weill's Alsace the primary issue is defense of German customs and language against French imposition. "The Alsatian is and remains a German; no matter how frenchified, he still curses and loves in German" ["Der Elsässer ist und bleibt ein Deutscher, und wenn er noch so sehr französiert ist, flucht und liebt er auf deutsch" (1:132)]. The first story, "Stasi," while a traditional seduced-and-abandoned tale, is cast in terms of German-speaking peasants versus the French-speaking educated elite. Stasi is a simple peasant woman who doesn't "understand French at all" ["verstand nicht einmal die französische Sprache" (1:11)] and writes only in "bad German" ["in schlechten Deutsch" (1:11)]. Her seducer, Marzolf, is associated with France; he affects the French name Marceau and returns to the Alsatian village from France proper where he entraps Stasi. She is avenged by her brother who kills Marzolf and himself.

Most of Weill's stories deal with love thwarted by parents who insist on the old custom of arranged marriage, which is seen as destructive. In this respect, Weill strikes a modern note. "Udilie und Gertrude," for example, one of the most interesting of Weill's stories, has a decidedly feminist cast

— as do certain later *Dorfgeschichten,* such as those by Karl Franzos and Marie Ebner-Eschenbach. As women's status in the new social relations established under modernity involved drastic change, it was an aspect of the transition to modernity that invited treatment.

"Udilie und Gertrude" concerns two couples who are forced into arranged marriages foregoing their true loves. The two women involved, Gertrude and Udilie, form a romantic friendship that is so intense one wonders if their real "true love" is for each other.

> The two virginal girls had already undressed, and the one silently marveled at the attractiveness of the other . . . As they lay in bed, Gertrude said to Udilie, "Udilie, do me a favor and give me a kiss." A lover couldn't have made the request more tenderly. Without hesitation Udilie threw her beautifully formed arms around Gertrude's neck, and kissed her over and over, as if she were in love with her. [Sie hatten sich bereits entkleidet, die keuschen Jungfrauen, und eine bewunderte im Stillen die Reize der andern . . . Als sie im Bette lagen, sagte Gertrude zu Udilien: "Udilie thu' mir einen Gefallen, gieb mir einen Kuss." Ein Verliebter hätte nicht in einem weichern Ton diese Gunst verlangen können. Unwillkurlich schlang Udilie ihren schön geformten Arm um Gertrudens Hals, und küsste sie Schlag auf Schlag, als wäre sie verliebt in sie.] (1:159)

That Weill does not comment on this relationship, which is seen as secondary to their heterosexual loves, suggests that as in Auerbach's "Ivo der Hajrle" such relationships were part of the provincial norm and that stigmatization of them as deviant came in with the modern pseudoscience of sexology, as proposed by Michel Foucault (see especially *Histoire de la sexualité* 35, 59–60). Gertrude is moreover seen as physically powerful; she rides a horse "like a man" ["ein Bein rechts, das andere links, wie ein Herr" (1:114)] and can best all the men of the village in wrestling matches (1:146–7), recalling James Hogg's Jessie Armstrong, Galt's Betty Pawkie, as well as some of Sir Walter Scott's strong women characters. In addition, she has feminist inclinations: "Udilie! If I were a boy, I would already be long gone into the wide world. But if a girl ventures out into the world, right away they say she's worthless" ["O Udilie, wäre ich ein Bursch, ich wäre schon längst in der weiten Welt. Wenn aber ein Mädchen in die Welt läuft, sagt man gleich, es wäre nichts werth" (1:161)].

"Frohni" (1840) sets up a plot somewhat similar to Ebner-Eschenbach's "Die Unverstandene auf dem Dorfe" discussed below, except in reverse: it is the male character who courts two different women (on different occasions): the one represents the premodern; the other, the modern. The first woman, Frohni, is not literate and passively follows her husband's direction ["die Frohni widersetzt sich nie dem Willen ihres Mann" (1:386)]. The more modern woman, Kettel, reads German fluently ["Kettel las auch geläufig

Deutsch" (1:434)] and has an independent mind, shown in her skeptical attitude toward a gypsy's fortune-telling (1:423). That the premodern woman dies and that Ambrosi, the protagonist, marries Kettel — seen as a happy ending — suggests that Weill endorses the supersession by the modern.

The question of land ownership is a central issue in the transition from feudalism to capitalism. Several *Dorfgeschichten* focus on the issue of forestland ownership and wood- and animal-poaching as a central aspect of this transition. Under feudal law, forestland was controlled by the aristocracy (the crown in England) but with commoners allowed certain foraging rights. By the early to mid-1800s, however, the extent of that foraging had become a political issue. Defenders of the poor claimed the gathering of wood for subsistence ("use-value production" in Marxist terms) was necessary. Marx himself in early writings, "Debatten über das Holzdiebstahlsgesetz"["Debates over the Wood Theft Law"] published in the *Rheinische Zeitung* in 1842, defended the rights of the poor against a 1841 law passed by the Rhine parliament which made the gathering of dead wood — along with the poaching of animals — a crime. Such a law, Marx argued, usurped "folk customary law" ["volkstümliche Gewohnheitsrecht"], which dated back to the *leges barbarorum* (Weber 206; see also Gray 518–19).

Among the *Dorfgeschichten* that treat this issue is Weill's "Der Bettler und sein Kind" (1847), in which the villagers support wood-poaching, arguing "why shouldn't the poor devil who has four children to feed fetch a bundle of wood to warm himself and his family?" ["warum soll der arme Teufel der vier Kinder zu ernähren hat, nicht eine Welle Holz holen dürfen um sich und seine Familie zu wärmen?" (Weill 2:103)]. In Auerbach's "Befehlerles," which was published two years after the Rhenish vote, we have seen the main character, Matthes, called before a magistrate for violating a law against poaching in a ducal forest. Another Auerbach story in the *Schwarzwälder Dorfgeschichten*, "Tonele mit der gebissener Wange" ["Toney, With the Bitten Cheek"] also concerns poaching. In this case a gamekeeper kills a rare bird, a red kite ["die Gabelweihe" (1:71)]. An onlooker says "he should have let the creature live on Sunday" ["Er hatt' doch das Tier am Sonntag leben lassen können"] and another complains that gamekeepers "do nothing but throw poor peasants in prison for poaching and [themselves] take the lives of innocent animals" ["sie können nichts als die armen Bauern wegen Holzfrevel in den Turm und die unschuldigen Tiere ums Leben bringen" (1:71)]. In Jeremias Gotthelf's "Der Besenbinder von Rychiswyl" [The Broommaker from Richiswyl] (1852) the protagonist has a personal attachment to the trees: "he knew his birches, indeed he had given specific names to all the individual trees [and] treats them with tenderness" ["Seine Birken kannte er . . . alle, ja, für sich hatte er . . . einzelnen Bäumen bestimmte

Namen geben . . . behandelte die Baume mit Zärtlichkeit"]. It makes him furious when poachers ["Frevler"] harm them (2:104).

Those critical of the traditional poaching rights considered that they no longer subtended subsistence but rather were being used to permit large-scale proto-capitalist exploitation of the woodlands. A later story, "Das verlorene Lachen" (1874), in *Die Leute von Seldwyla* [The People of Seldwyla], by the Swiss Gottfried Keller, for example, makes the point that the rural world is falling prey to capitalist modernity by dramatizing the destruction of an ancient oak. In none of these stories, however, is wood-poaching or its expansion into capitalist exploitation blamed on Jews. And while valuing profit over personal commitments is deplored in numerous *Dorfgeschichten* — indeed it is a central theme (see, for example, Auerbach's "Die feindlichen Brüder"; Weill's "Stasi" and "Selmel, die Wahnsinnige"; Keller's "Romeo und Julia auf dem Dorfe") — in none of these are the profit-mongers Jewish; thus the stories implicitly counter another central popular stereotype of the Jew.

Annette von Droste-Hülshoff's novella *Die Judenbuche: Ein Sittengemälde aus dem gebirgigten Westphalen* (1842) [The Jew Beech-Tree: A Picture of Manners from Mountainous Westphalia], published the year after the Rhenish laws were passed, was the first of the *Dorfgeschichten* to deal centrally with the wood-poaching issue. It must therefore be seen in the context of the shifting status of land and forest occurring at the time. As Betty Nance Weber points out in a perceptive article, the conflicting views on the issue are central to the novella: "While the aristocrats contend that poaching and stealing wood constitutes criminal activity, the populace views such appropriation as a legitimate practice" (207). By Droste-Hülshoff's time, therefore, it is clear that the feudal system of land ownership is beginning to transmute into a capitalist system, and hereditary aristocrats are becoming capitalist entrepreneurs — something Marx clearly understood. That the locals resent and resist this aspect of modernity is implicit in her novella, which opens on a satirical note, describing the town "Dorfe B," as "one of those closed-off corners of the earth without factories and manufacturing" ["einer jener abgeschlossenen Erdwinkel ohne Fabriken und Handel" (Droste-Hülshoff, *Judenbuche* 11)] where "a strange face" ["ein fremdes Gesicht" (11)] still disturbed people and where a trip of 30 miles was considered an odyssey. It is ruled by lax laws and by public opinion ["ein Recht der öffentlichen Meinung" (12)], because of which "the inhabitant's conception of the difference between right and wrong became somewhat confused" ["der Begriffe der Einwohner von Recht und Unrecht einigermassen in Verwirrung gerathen" (12)]. In other words, village "B" was a backwater rural area where state and feudal authority had broken down, and toward which the narrator takes an ironic perspective.

Droste-Hülshoff shows how the local populace comes to blame Jews, while making it clear that those most responsible for mercenary exploitation of the forest are the indigenous non-Jewish locals themselves (as Richard T. Gray demonstrates in a recent article). (Up until 1841 peasants in Droste-Hülshoff's Westphalian locale had held wood-gathering rights, according to an 1828 ruling in Paderborn, but that right had been rescinded shortly before she published *Die Judenbuche*.)

Gray notes:

> *Die Judenbuche* concerns itself centrally with the question of economic transformation, the shift among the populace of Droste's native Westphalia from an agrarian economy based primarily on the use-value of the surrounding natural world, to a proto-capitalist, industrially managed economy in which the natural world is assessed solely in terms of its exchange-value on the worldwide colonial market. (523)

The plot concerns the corruption of Friedrich Mergel by his maternal uncles who are connected to a band of wood- and deer-poachers known as the *Blaukittel* (Blue Shirts). When told by the boy Friedrich that one of the poachers, Hülsmeyer, is a thief who steals wood and deer, his mother Margareth defends the practice, taking a position similar to Marx's, that "God lets the wood grow free and the game animals move from one gentleman's land to another's; they can't belong to anyone" ["das Holz lässt unser Herrgott frei wachsen und das Wild wechselt aus eines Herren Lande in das andere; die können Niemand angehören" (18)]. She also, when told by the boy that Hülsmeyer had beaten a Jew, Aaron, and stolen his money, defends him, saying Hülsmeyer is a "regular" ["ordentlich"], "settled man" ["angesessener Mann" (17)] "and the Jews are all scoundrels" ["und die Juden sind alle Schelme" (18)], thus sounding the note of anti-Semitism that has concerned numerous critics (see especially Doerr).

To be sure, certain Jewish characters, notably Aaron, are treated viciously by townspeople. At a wedding in 1760 at which Aaron shows up demanding that Friedrich pay him a debt, the other revelers mock him and throw him out, associating him with swine — a stock anti-Semitic slur ["Packt den Juden! Wiegt ihm gegen ein Schwein!" (*Judenbuche* 43)]. On the other hand, as the Jewish characters are otherwise treated similarly to the gentile in the narrative and as there is an attempt to faithfully replicate Yiddish dialect, the anti-Semitism is not embedded in the narrative perspective but rather in that of certain characters, all of whom are otherwise reprehensible (being associated with theft, murder, etc.).

Gray argues that while it is the native Paderbornians — in particular the wood-poaching gang the *Blaukittel* — who are destroying the forest, the natives project their guilt onto Jews like Aaron.

Anti-Semitism thereby serves as a convenient way for the Paderborn populace — who, after all, covertly support the activities of the *Blaukittel* and themselves participate freely in profit-mongering acts of wood poaching — to ignore their own complicity with the destructive dialectic of exchange-value economics and transfer guilt to a convenient Other . . . [They] exculpate themselves from complicity with the ecological destruction caused by the capitalist commercial economy by shifting guilt and responsibility to the Jews . . . *Die Judenbuche* is not so much a manifestation of anti-Semitism as it is a *critical representation* [of it]. (529–30)

Like the *Dorfgeschichten* by Auerbach and Weill, therefore, *Die Judenbuche* may be read as a rejection of the traditional anti-Semitic view of the Jews as bearers of the nefarious aspects of capitalist modernity. The novella, which includes five murders (three of the deaths on the solitary beech-tree of the title — solitary because the surrounding area has been denuded by exploitation, as with Keller's oak) ends on September 1788, the eve of the French Revolution, the beginning of a more liberal era for Jews, which suggests that the author may have viewed the events of the story as belonging to a benighted past. In Westphalia, for example, in the wake of the French occupation, Jews received equal rights in 1808 (though these were rescinded at the Congress of Vienna in 1815. It was not until 1871 that Jews in Germany were granted full civic rights (Helfer 230). *Die Judenbuche* thus deserves its reputation as one of the earliest *Dorfgeschichten* depicting as it does the clash between locals governed by traditional custom (which in the end Droste-Hülshoff seems to consider retrogressive) and regulations enacted under the new regime.

A nonfictional essay Droste-Hülshoff wrote at about the same time as *Die Judenbuche* would seem to further indicate that her own attitude was more or less pro the Enlightenment ideals of modernity associated with the French Revolution. In "Bilder aus Westphalen" (1842), a sketch of peasant customs from the point of view of an educated writer schooled in Enlightenment perspectives, the narrator refers to the French occupation ["französischen Regierung" (4:219)] and laments the ensuing loss of regional customs ["dass alle diese Zustande am Verloschen sind und nach vierzig Jahren vielleicht wenig mehr davon anzutreffen sein müssen?" (4:220)], but these provincial beliefs are nevertheless stigmatized as "harmless superstitions" ("Der Münsterländer ist überhaupt sehr abergläubisch, sein Aberglaube aber so harmlos wie er selber" (4:215)].

At about the same time as Auerbach, Weill, and Droste-Hülshoff in Germany, Albert Bitzius (1779–1854), a Protestant minister, began writing peasant stories in the Emmental region of Switzerland, a German-speaking part of the country. Bitzius wrote under the pseudonym Jeremias Gotthelf, the protagonist of his first novel *Der Bauernspiegel: oder Lebensgeschichte des Jeremias Gotthelf, von ihm selbst beschreiben* [The Peasant's Mirror: or the Life Story of Jeremias Gotthelf Described by Himself] (1836), a *Bildungsroman*.

Heavily influenced by Pestalozzi and Zschokke, Gotthelf's writings are inclined toward didacticism, imbued with strong moral and political messages. But because of his detailed and realistic presentation of well-developed characters, their relationships, and their historical, geographical, social, and political milieux, the works remain as rich representations of the nineteenth-century rural world, beyond whatever pedagogical purposes the writer may have had in mind.

Today Gotthelf is considered perhaps the most authentic of the German local-colorists, the least assimilated into urban modernity, and the closest to the folk he wrote about (Hein 48). In part, this is because he envisaged as his audience peasant readers, unlike the others who wrote largely for a metropolitan educated readership (Zellweger 290–1). Gotthelf stated in fact that he wrote "for the uncultured" ["fürs grobe Volk" (Hein 75)] and saw himself as a "folk-writer" ["Volksschriftsteller"] who (like Pestalozzi and Zschokke) wrote for the betterment and instruction of the lower classes (Waidson, *Jeremias Gotthelf* 51). He wrote therefore in a clear, simple style with a heavy use of Bernese (Swiss German) dialect (*Schwitzerdütsch*), especially in later works. The dialect is so far removed from *Hochdeutsch* as to require a special dictionary today (one was published in 1858 [von Rütte], another in 1972 [Juker]). Following is an example of Gotthelf's dialect taken from *Die Käserei* [The Cheese Dairy] (1850). It occurs in a letter written by a peasant woman inviting a friend to buy some cheese.

> Geliebter Fründ!
>
> Hurti, hurti, chumm u chauf dr Käs. Es ist scho en angere da gsi u het ne welle, u dr Att hätt ne fast gäh . . .
>
> [Dear Friend,
>
> Hurry, Hurry, come and buy the cheese. Another has already come and wanted it and Father almost gave it to him . . . .]

> (Zellweger 74 n.2)

Of the German local-colorists Gotthelf was also the most ambiguous about modernity (Zellweger 298) and, though opposed to contemporary radical political movements, such as French liberalism and Marxism, he himself expressed a certain radicalism, Uwe Baur notes, in "his permanent opposition to the political praxis of the Bern liberals" ["seine permanent

Auseinandersetzung mit der politischen Praxis der Berner Liberalen" (87)].
Gotthelf was particularly animated against the ruthless mercenary aspects
of capitalism with his works reflecting, Hein notes, "an anticapitalistic
standpoint" ["Standpunkt gegenüber der kapitalistischen Entwicklung"
(Hein 110)]. The Marxist Ernst Bloch, an enthusiastic reader of Gotthelf,
considers that he portrayed a world "still untouched by capitalism" (323),
"a still (partly) precapitalist stage: a land of laborers not yet alienated from
themselves" (338).

Following *Der Bauernspiegel*, Gotthelf published *Leiden und Freuden
eines Schulmeisters* (1838–39) [Sorrows and Joys of a Schoolteacher], which
follows the pattern established by Zschokke (and seen in Auerbach's "Der
Lauterbacher") of an educated outsider attempting to teach and modernize recalcitrant locals. Gotthelf's first *Dorfgeschichte* followed: "Wie fünf
Mädchen im Branntwein jämmerlich umkommen: Eine merkwürdige
Geschichte" ["How Five Girls Came to a Miserable End on Account of
Spirits: A Noteworthy Story"] (1838), thus published (in Bern) at about the
same time as Weill and Auerbach were publishing their first stories further
north. A didactic temperance tale, the story nevertheless has many of the
hallmarks of the classic local-color story, in particular the conflict between
official authorities and resisting, critical locals. An educated traveler stop-
ping at an inn notices the five girls drinking and misbehaving. He blames
(in part) state officials for not properly educating people in the dangers of
drink, stipulating that they should not only promulgate laws and decrees
but should also give out (to the populace) copies of *Lienhard und Gertrude*
(Pestalozzi's temperance novel) (Gotthelf, "Wie fünf Mädchen" 2:611).

The narrative structure also follows a common local-color format of an
indigenous figure narrating the story to the outsider (recall this pattern
especially in Hogg's works). In this case the local is a "philosophizing peasant" ["philosophierenden Bauer" (2:631)]. The traveler takes the occasion
to note how, like this old man, uneducated rural folk often have more
worthwhile things to say than the educated: in the canton of Bern he found
many people "who, in terms of deep sense and sound thoughts, were worth
more than ten . . . professors, together with their . . . crazy theories and
incredible arrogance" ["deren an einer tiefem Sinn und gesunden Denken
mehr wog als zehn . . . Professoren samt ihren . . . verrückten Theorien
und fabelhaften Arroganz" (2:631)]. The philosopher-peasant proceeds to
tell the traveler the sad fates of the drunken girls (all of whom died young).

Beginning in 1839 Gotthelf began publishing stories in Bernese calen-
dars, a popular annual collection of stories. Among the first, appearing in
1840, was "Marei, die Kuderspinnerin, und ihr Tröster" ["Marei, the Flax
Spinner, and Her Consoler"]. This story, in which Gotthelf atypically presents a positive case for capitalism, also has a pedagogical format. A spinster

woman is despairing because a spinning factory ["eine Spinnerei" (Gotthelf *Sämtliche Werke* 1921, 22–4:183)] is being built nearby and she fears it will cut into her business, which is home-based, hand-loomed production. An educated traveler explains to her the mechanics of global capitalism: that the new factory won't hurt her if she retools and adjusts her work; that locating the factory nearby will benefit the local economy by eliminating the middlemen who import materials from England, making the whole system more efficient and cheaper.

> Through the machine a hundred pounds of raw flax yields 180,000 more than it currently does. Think Marei, what that may bring. If one figures only six kreuzer to the thousand, one makes from 100 pounds more than eleven kroner. [. . . gibt der Zentner roher Flachs durch die Maschine hundertachtzig Tausende mehr, als er jetzt gibt. Denk doch, Marei, was das bringen mag. Wenn man das Tausend nur zu sechs Kreuzer rechnet so macht das vom Zentner ja mehr als elf Kronen.]

(*Sämtliche Werke* 1921, 22–4:189)

(A *Zentner* equaled 100 pounds; one *Kroner* equaled 100 *Kreuzers*.) Marei is somewhat mollified by the traveler's disquisition but remains uncertain about her future.

Gotthelf's first peasant novel, indeed the first German novel to feature a peasant as the protagonist (*Bauernroman*) (though several Irish and Scottish works — *Castle Rackrent* and works by the Banim brothers, William Carleton, and James Hogg — may be considered predecessors in this) appeared in 1841. *Wie Uli der Knecht glücklich wird* [How Uli, the Farmhand, Becomes Successful; usually translated as *Uli, the Farmhand*] was another pedagogical work on the order of Pestalozzi et al. It concerns the education of illiterate Uli, who drinks too much, by his master Johannes, who preaches the usual virtues of hard work, frugality, and orderliness, which in the end pay off. Uli is promoted and marries well, the happy ending. In the process, Gotthelf conveys many details about farm life, such as birthing a cow, which give the novel an interest beyond the heavy moralizing.

Far more rich and complex was Gotthelf's next novel *Wie Anne Bäbi Jowäger haushaltet und wie es ihm mit dem Doktern geht* [How Anne Bäbi Jowäger Kept House and How She Got Along with Doctors], which was published in two parts in 1843–44. The central issue in this work is the clash between traditional customs, such as herbal medicine, and modern science. As in Mary Leadbeater's *Annals of Ballitore* and *Cottage Dialogues* and Elizabeth Hamilton's *Cottagers of Glenburnie*, the issue is drawn over the question of smallpox inoculations. Anne Bäbi, the family matriarch, has refused to have her son Jakobli vaccinated and when he comes down with smallpox ["die rechten Blattern" (Gotthelf, *Anne Bäbi* 32)], neighbors criticize her. "Did you not have him given the cowpox when he was still young?" ["Habt ihr ihm die Kuhblattern . . . nicht geben lassen, wo er noch jung gewesen ist?" (32)], a neighbor asks, suggesting further that if "he is inoculated, he will get well" ["wenn er geimpft ist, so wird es wohl sein" (32)]. Hansli, the father, replies that that is not their way; their ancestors didn't do it ["es ist nicht der Bruch gewesen in unsere Haus; der Ätti hat es nicht getan und der Grosätti nicht" (32)]. Moreover, he claims fatalistically, "there is not much we can do to change things; we can do it this way or that, but it still comes out the same" ["öppe viel an der Sache machen wir nicht; wir können es dä Weg oder diese Weg machen, es kömmt öppe aufs Gleiche heraus" (44)].

They finally call in a doctor who "couldn't understand how parents could allow their children such misery when they could have spared it them" ["er begreife nicht, wie Eltern ihren Kinder solches Leiden antun mögen, wenn sie es ihnen doch ersparren könnten" (*Anne Bäbi* 34)]. Despite their failing to follow the doctor's orders, the boy recovers but is weakened and retains pockmarks. Neighbors taunt him about his looks and he shrinks from people (43), finding companionship with the farm animals who seem to commiserate with him. The hens and doves "flocked near him and pecked out of his hand" ["flogen neben ihn und pickten ihm aus der Hand" (42)]. The sheep "also had not forgotten his voice and they sprang at him, and the rams rubbed their heads against his weak little legs" ["hatten auch diese seine Stimme nicht vergessen, und sie springen an ihn hin, und die Widder rieben ihre Köpfe an seinem schweichen Beinchen" (42; see also 86–7)].

Anne Bäbi is seen as a domineering matriarch, referred to throughout as "die Meisterfrau," a little Napoleon. "She ruled the roost like the emperor Napoleon during his time in Germany" ["das fuhr ganz herrisch im Hause herum wie der Kaiser Napoleon zu seiner Zeit in Deutschland" (139)]. She "came . . . out of the field full of pride like a general after a successful battle" ["kam . . . das Feld auf ganz stolz wie ein Feldherr nach gewonnener Schlacht" (146)]. What Anne Bäbi "thought good, so should the others think good" ["gut dünkt, soll andere auch gut dünken" (212)]. Ernst Bloch comments on the "matriarchal character" of Gotthelf's work, noting numerous examples of "feminine dominance," which he says is characteristic of "archaic agricultural society" with its "Demeter-like" figures (327–8). In *Geld und Geist*, indeed, a later novel (see below), Gotthelf states: "In the peasant home it is the woman who leads and makes the rules" ["in Bauernhaus ist es die Bäuerin, welche der führt und die Regel macht" (169)].

However, in this novel Anne Bäbi's truculence more often has baneful results. Her continuing use of traditional medicine and quacks

["Wundermänner" (232)] only succeeds in making her son sicker and eventually leads to the death of a grandchild. Although the peasants' faith in traditional remedies is seen as harmful and retrogressive, the doctors' contemptuous attitude toward them compounds the problem. The one who treats Jakobli declares that "the peasants are hopeless" ["Es ist mit dem Bauern nichts zu machen"]. And he despairs of how peasants have more faith in old wives than in himself ["die glauben jedem altem Weibe mehr als mir" (67)]. On the other hand, the peasants themselves sense the doctors' condescension and distrust them, feeling that they are helped more by traditional "Elixieres" (63–4)].

The narrator, meanwhile, worries that the loss of traditional religion is making people more vulnerable to quack remedies.

> The farther they are from Christ, the more thoroughly and modernly they are brought up, the greater credence astrologers and fortune-tellers have. Faith is innate in people; if God's son doesn't appear within, the devil haunts therein [Je weiter sie von Christus sind, um so fester, und je neumodischer sie erzogen sind, desto grössern Verdienst haben Zeichendeuter und Wahrsager wieder. Der Glaube ist dem Menschen angeboren; scheint aber Gotts Sohn nicht hinein, so spuckt der Teufel darein.] (231)

Indeed, the more secular the state, he suggests, the more prominent is quackery. "Where do fortune-tellers have more status than in enlightened Paris?" ["Wo haben die Wahrsagerinnen mehr Verdienst als im aufgeklärten Paris?" (230)]. Gotthelf thus proposes a reliance on traditional religion, is distrustful of Enlightenment secularism, but at the same time is open to modern medical advances, deploring hidebound traditionalism in matters of health and welfare.

Published at about the same time as *Anne Bäbi Jowäger* (1842–44) was *Geld und Geist oder die Versöhnung* [Money and Spirit; or Reconciliation; usually translated as *Wealth and Welfare*]. Here again Gotthelf proposes Christian values as an antidote to rising capitalist materialism. The novel centers upon a farm family that falls into financial difficulty, which creates animosity between wife and husband until her Christian faith is reanimated, which leads to forgiveness, reconciliation, and household peace. The main plot concerns the courtship of the son Resli of a girl, Anne Mareili, whose father is a cruel mercenary who wants to marry her off for money. Her family indeed forms a negative counterpart to Resli's. "Money is all they care for, and they treat me," Anne Mareili says, "as one sticks the poor worm on the hook, when one wants to catch fish" ["Darum fragen sie allen nichts nach als dem Gelde alleine, und mich geben sie dar, wie man arme Würmer an die Angel steckt, wenn man Fische fangen will" (180)]. Unlike Resli's mother, who has equal access to family funds and equal, if not dominant say in household management, Anne Mareili's mother is a virtual slave: "For forty years she has never had her way" ["Vierzig Jahre sei es nie gegangen, wie sie gewollt" (206)]. "I didn't have it good with him, and if ever I needed a Kreuzer myself . . . he would remonstrate for two hours" ["habe ich es bei him nicht gut gehabt, und wenn ich einen Kreuzer habe brauchen müssen, . . . so hat er für zwei mit mir aufbegehrt" (203)]. Thus, like several other local-colorists, Gotthelf affirms women's social (if not, in his case, political) equality, while deploring the instrumental mentality of capitalism, valuing "Geld" over "Geist."

His strongest condemnation of modernity appears in the novel *Zeitgeist und Berner Geist* (1852) [The Spirit of the Times and the Spirit of Bern], which like *Geld und Geist* draws a contrast between two sets of characters, one of which exemplifies a correct (resistant) attitude toward modernity, the other of which succumbs to its blandishments, only to perish as a result. In his Foreword, Gotthelf makes clear his opposition to secular modernity, which he casts as a "snake" ["diese Schlange"] and "the scourge of Europe" ["diese Landplage Europas" (Gotthelf, *Zeitgeist* 9)]. It has "destroyed the sanctuary of the family, undermined all Christian elements" ["das Heiligtum der Familien verwüstet, alle christlichen Elemente zersetzt" (*Zeitgeist* 9)].

"Anyone who ardently supports the people . . . must above all encounter radical politics with hostility, for it is really not a political movement but a separate life- and world-view" ["Wer mit Liebe am Volke hängt . . . der muss überall mit der radikalen Politik feindlich zusammentreffen, denn dieselbe ist eigentlich keine Politik, sondern eine eigene Lebens- und Weltanschauung" (*Zeitgeist* 9)]. It is to this end that he has written the novel. "Against all these sects which destroy the people's happiness the author has written his book" ["Gegen diese alle Volksglück zerstörende Sekte hat der Verfasser sein Buch geschreiben" (*Zeitgeist* 9)]. In the course of the novel the narrator amplifies these ideas, seeing radical politics as a disease, a cholera (38) that must be countered before it infects the rural village.

The radicalism Gotthelf deplores is clearly that spawned by the French Revolution and the Enlightenment. An antimodern preacher (perhaps representing the author's ideas) laments how

> in the previous century the Enlightenment emerged out of France and with it the delusion that whoever claims to be educated may no longer be Christian . . . Most government officials . . . [see religion as useful only as] a rein on the people . . . [But] the state cannot be God . . . State religion and state teaching cannot bring contentment. [Im vorigen Jahrhundert kam von Frankreich her die Aufklärerei und mit ihr der Wahn, wer Ansprüche auf Bildung mache, dürfe kein Christ mehr sein . . . Der grösste Teil der

Staatsbeamteten . . . es sei ein Kappzaum für das Volk . . . Der Staat kann nicht Gott sein . . . Staatsglaube und Staatspädogik geben kein Befriedigung.] (125)

The pro-Englightenment position is given by a government administrator ("der Regierer"), who believes in natural law, progress, political and religious freedom — all hallmarks of Western liberalism. "There is no other ground for just laws than Nature; only laws which are grounded in Nature are rational, that is the true natural law" ["Es gibt für rechte Gesetze keinen anderen Boden als die Natur, und nur die Gesetze sind rationell, welche auf die Natur gegründet sind, das ist das wahr Naturrecht" (191)]. Progress will not occur until preachers leave off teaching about theological matters and adopt Enlightenment views, so that the people are no longer made "to concern themselves with dogma and religious teaching but with becoming enlightened and educated through a beautiful morality, which is grounded in Nature and natural law" ["zu plagen mit Dogmatik und Glaubenslehren, sondern sie aufzuklären und zu bilden durch eine schöne Moral, gegründet auf Natur und Naturrecht" (193)]. The administrator even goes so far as to exclaim, "Man is God!" ["Der Mensch ist Gott!" (193)].

Another character articulates a libertarian vision of radical democracy where the nobility will be overthrown and "Europe will be a grand republic . . . where everyone can live like princes" ["würde Europa eine grosse Republik, wo es alle . . . leben könnten wie die Prinzen" (332)]. The peasant will be free and "can do what he wants and not what he is ordered to do from on high . . . the lords [will] kneel before him and not he before the lords" ["mit seinem Sachen machen kann, was er will, und nicht, was ihm von oben herunter befohlen wird . . . die Herren vor ihm knien und nicht er vor den Herren" (332)]. Through public humanist education ["die freie Bildung und echt menschliche Erzeihung" (414)] — the primary means by which the ideals of modernity have been inculcated in populations by modern states — there will be "liberation from preachers and aristocrats, . . . personal freedom in all things, liberation from superstitions" ["die Erlösung von Pfaffen und Aristokraten . . . die persönliche Freiheit in allen Dingen, die Erlösung aus dem Aberglauben" (414)].

The plot concerns how two contrasting peasants, Benz and Hans, react to these new ideas and developments. Benz favors the old ways and customs ["mir ists wohl bei der alten Gewohnheit und dem alten Glauben" (194)]. In resisting public school education, Benz worries that "school makes children haughty instead of humble, alienates them from home, teaches them to look down on their parents" ["die Schule . . . mache die Kinder hochmütig statt demütig, entfremde sie dem Hause, lehre sie die Eltern verachten" (28)]. Significantly, Benz like all the other peasant characters speaks in *Bärndütsch*, a Bernese dialect, whereas his interlocutor, the local schoolteacher, speaks in *Hochdeutsch* (and the narrative itself is in standard German). Thus Benz, the rooted rural peasant, resists French-derived notions about Enlightenment and modernity that authorities are attempting to impose on the local populace.

Hans, on the other hand, is taken in by the new radical ideas, believing that "this is a new day . . . one is no longer servant and underling but free and oneself lord" ["Es sei jetzt eine andere Zeit . . . man sei nicht mehr Knecht und Untertan, sondern frei und selbts Herr" (34)]. In the end Benz is successful and Hans comes to grief, taken in by a Jewish usurer (who is described in anti-Semitic terms as "a parasitic insect" ["dieses Ungeziefer" (372) — the term used by Kafka in his novella *Die Verwandlung* [*Metamorphosis*]). Hans's wife also dies as a result of his neglect of her in his pursuance of radical ideas (see *Zietgeist*, Chapter 15), by which the author suggests that ordinary human obligations are often forgotten in the utopian abstractions of Enlightenment schemes.

A charming and poignant story that appeared at about the same time as *Zeitgeist und Berner Geist* is much less polemical while illustrating Gotthelf's continuing empathetic concern about rural "little people." "Das Erdbeeri-Mareili" [Strawberry Mareili] (1851) features a rustic woman who makes a living picking and selling wild strawberries. The narrative format is similar to "Marei, die Kuderspinnerin": a judicial official from Bern comes to a rural town to certify Mareili's death and is told her story by a local pastor. Mareili is a natural; she spends much of her time in the woods, communicating with the animals, as well as with the spiritual world through angels she claims to see. After a period spent in devoted service to a noble girl who becomes an angel figure to Mareili and "whose presence filled her heart with joy" ["das Fraulein bleib sein Engel, dessen Erscheinung sein Herz mit Freuden füllte" (Gotthelf, *Kleinere Erzählungen* 2:38)] — a relationship that prefigures that seen in Sarah Orne Jewett's story "Martha's Lady" (1897) — Mareili, drawn by homesickness, returns to her native area ["eine Art von Heimweh es wieder dahin zog" (47)]. Hoping to resume her berry-gathering, she is distressed to find that developments have subdivided the fields; the strawberries have been displaced by agricultural improvement.

> What a sad sight she now saw! The fields where the first strawberries ripened were no more . . . Nothing but potatoes for people and grass for cows. She cried for the old wilderness which civilization had swallowed up. [Es den Schaden nun sah! Es fand die Weiden nicht mehr, wo früher die ersten Erdberren reiften . . . [N]ichts als Erdäpfel für die Menschen und Gras fürs Vieh. Es weinte über die alte Wildnis, welche die Kulture ihm verschlungen.] (48)

She dies soon after this.

Writing contemporaneously with the German and Swiss local-colorists were regional writers in the Austrian Empire, Adalbert Stifter and Josef Rank, both of whom wrote about Bohemia, now part of the Czech Republic. Stifter's first novel, *Das Haidedorf* [The Heath Village] (1840), which first appeared in a Viennese newspaper (the *Wiener Zeitschrift*), follows a *Heimkehr* plot, the return of the educated son to the homeland, seen in many local-color works (William Carleton's "Going to Maynooth," for example). A country boy, Felix, who tends goats and sheep on the heath, leaves home for education and travel, returning only to find himself a stranger ["ein fremdes Ding" (Stifter, *Gesammelte Werke* 1:189)] among his people, and that the heathland has been taken over by capitalist development. "Many men had suddenly come and measured out a piece of the heathland, which from time immemorial had never been the property of any man" ["Es kamen einmal viele Herren und vermassen ein Stück Haideland, das seit Menschengedenken keines Herrn Eigentum gewesen war" (1:185)]. Characteristically, Stifter provides much lush description of the heathland and includes an interesting portrait of Felix's grandmother, who is half-gone mentally — like Scott's Elsbeth o' the Craigburnfoot, "a powerful ruin" ["eine machtige Ruine" (1:197)] — who communicates with the spirits and expresses herself in poetic ways that only Felix can understand (1:197).

Jürgen Hein considered *Das Haidedorf*, along with Stifter's next novel, *Die Mappe meines Urgrossvaters* [My Great-Grandfather's Papers] (1841), the best Austrian *Dorfgeschichten* of the *Vormärz* period (Hein 86). The latter novel is a narrative purportedly written by the great-grandfather in 1739 and discovered in an attic by his descendant, who adds an occasional comment of his own. The great-grandfather was a doctor, who had received his medical education in Prague but returned to practice in his beloved rural Bohemia where "people had never seen a doctor before" ["Die Menschen standen alle herum und schauten mich an, weil sie noch nie einen Artz gesehen hatte" (Stifter, *Gesammelte Werke* 1:509)]. "Many who succumbed to serious illness, died deep in the forest wilderness where an educated man could have saved them" ["Mancher, der in eine tiefe und heftige Krankheit verfiel, starb auch in der Einöde der Wälder dahin, wo ihn ein Mann, der Erfahrung hatte, hätte retten können" (1:507)]. Although thus a believer in scientific medicine, the doctor comes to feel that generic book-learning is not sufficient; that healing requires something beyond materialistic science, a sympathetic energy that God gives to all living things: "one must learn the prescripts of natural things" ["Man muss die Gebote der Naturdinge lernen" (1:630)]. A doctor, he feels, must develop a holistic knowledge of the region, its animals and how they heal, and its medicinal plants (1:630).

And is it not clearly observable that God has planted our health within the great composition of matter . . . How then would the deer heal and the dog and the snake in the woods . . . ? It is something in the cool flowing water . . . in the blowing air . . . [which] through the correspondence of all things is received and vibrates in our being every hour, every minute. [Und ist es nicht klar abzumerken, dass Gott in die grossen Zusammensetzung der Stoffe unser Heil gelegt hat . . . ? Womit würde sich denn der Hirsch heilen, und der Hund, und die Schlange des Waldes . . . ? Es wird ein Ding in dem kühlenden fliessenden Wasser sein, es wird eins in der wehenden Luft sein, und es werden . . . aus der Eintracht aller Dinge jede Stude, jede Minute in unser Wesen zittern und es erhalten.] (1:631)

The doctor thus comes to think that medicine must be rooted in a sympathetic knowledge of local ecology (or what is today called bioregional knowledge).

He develops an intense connection with nonhuman creatures. "The voice of the cricket . . . throbs in my heart — likewise . . . the neglected animal beats in my heart, as if he were speaking to me in clear human words" [die Stimme der Grille . . . klopfte . . . an mein Herz — gleichsam . . . klopfte das misachtete Tier an mein Herz, als sagte er mir deutliche menschliche Worte" (1:469)]. He especially loves his horses: "O, these good, these true, these willing animals — in the end they are the only ones on earth who love me so truly from the ground up" ["Ach diese guten, diese treuen, diese willigen Tiere — sie sind am Ende doch das einzige auf dieser Erde, was mich so recht vom Grunde aus liebt" (1:646)].

There is, moreover, he notes, a general sense of community among humans in the country. "With us everyone knows and takes a sympathetic interest in one another" ["Bei uns alle Leute sich kennen und Anteil an einander nehmen" (1:510)]. The narrator contrasts the homelessness of the urban dweller to that rural sense of community. "The big city resident has . . . no home, and the peasant son, when he himself has become an urbanite, harbors a secret gently painful nostalgia for a poor old house" where his forebears lived ["Darum hat der Grossstädter . . . kein Heimat, und der Bauersohn, selbst wenn er Grossstädter geworden ist, hegt die heimliche, sanft schmerzende Rückliebe an ein altes, schlechtes Haus . . ." (1:449)].

Treating roughly the same region as Stifter but from a more ethnographic point of view was Josef Rank, also a German-speaking native of Bohemia. The first portions of *Aus dem Böhmerwalde* [From the Bohemian Woods] began appearing in a Viennese journal, the *Österreichische Morgenblatt*, in 1840. Its editor, L. U. Frankl, encouraged Rank to write more stories about "the folk-life of his Bohemian woods home" ["das Volksleben der Böhmerwald Heimat"]. The resulting work was published in 1843 in Leipzig, where at about the same time Rank met and became friends with Berthold Auerbach.

Aus dem Böhmerwalde is a patchwork quilt of essays, stories, fairy tales ["Märchen"], fables ["Sage"], superstitions ["Aberglauben"] and collections of folk songs ["Nationalliedern"] with the note scales printed. The stories are labeled "Volksnovellen." The only link among these disparate patches is that they concern German settlers in Bohemia, who spoke in a Bohemian-German dialect, which, like Gotthelf's *Schwitzerdütsch*, would have been virtually incomprehensible to the middle-class German reader but which is faithfully reproduced in the text with translations (either in footnotes or parenthetically) into standard *Schriftsdeutsch*. As an example, in the story "Die Auswanderung in das Banat" [The Emigration to Banat], which concerns a migration some Germans made to another region, a husband explains why he has decided not to leave, as follows:

m'a hômâ râ Hôâmat, a Hôs und kôi Schuld'n –wôs?–Sôllmâ dafôgei und d' hôâmat fôlauss'n?

[In German: wir haben eine Heimat, Kinder, ein Haus und keine Schuldern — was?– Sollen wir davon-gehn und die Heimat verlassen?]

[In English: We have a home, children, a house and no debt. So? Should we go away and abandon the home?]

(Josef Rank, Aus dem Böhmerwalde 148)

Aus dem Böhmerwalde opens with several nonfictional essays describing the region's people, their customs and practices ["Sitten und Gebrauche" (29–112)]. A section entitled "Ein Winterabend" ["A Winter Evening"] (possibly influenced by the Scot James Hogg's title) follows (113–30). Its setting is of several women spinning in a peasant house, where in the evening tales, fables, and songs are told or sung (four are included).

In describing the German-Bohemians, Rank notes the tension that existed between them as colonial settlers and the Czech natives ["Tschechen"], who are the underclass ["Untertan" (24)], very poor and oppressed (23), and who behave much like Edgeworth's Irish peasants: they're suspicious ["argwöhnisch"], stiff ["starr"], or "when they do loosen up" ["oder wenn sie auftauen"] are "tediously fawning" ["lästig schmeichelnd" (19)]. He notes that the German settlers prefer to avoid the Czech neighbors and to deal rather with the nearby Bavarians. But Rank urges his German-Bohemian readers to be more mindful of the Bohemian Czechs and their oppressed conditions (although he himself dwells mainly on the German-speaking ethnic community, which differentiates him from most other local-colorists who deal with the oppressed natives rather than the colonizers, although, of course, Edgeworth and Scott mediated that focus through Anglo figures).

The German Bohemians nevertheless feel Bohemia to be their home and are homesick whenever they leave the area, Rank says. Indeed, "their love of home grows all the stronger . . . And this condition makes them all the happier to return home again the farther they travel" ["lebt die Liebe zur Heimat um so tiefer . . . Und dieser Umstand lässt sie ebenso freudig wieder heimkehren, als sie fortwandert sind" (24)].

In "Die Auswanderung in das Banat," which is based on a historical event that occurred in 1829, Rank criticizes those who decided to leave their home region. Lured by promises of riches, they thought they would "return home laden with money" ["mit Geld beladen in die Heimat zurückzukehren" (150)] but instead return impoverished. But Rank asks, how could they "throw away their attachment to all the familiar mountains, woods, hills, and brooks like old clothing?" ["die Anhänglichkeit an all die bekannten Berge, Wälder, Hügel und Bäche abwerfen wie ein altes Kleid?" (146)]. Speaking directly to the emigrants, he continues, "Where is your sensitivity to the sweet deep-rooted habits and manners of the homeland, which every native . . . traveling abroad brings back again with homesickness" ["Wo ist eure Empfänglichkeit für die süssen, tiefwurzelnden Gewohnheiten und Sitten der Heimat, welche alle Eingeborene, wenn sie . . . durch die Fremde gewandert, wieder mit Heimweh zurückbringt?" (146)].

The first Jewish *Dorfgeschichten* were also set in the Eastern European regions of the Austrian Empire. In these works "home" is an ethnic Jewish community, a *shtetl*, but the genre otherwise shares the features of other *Dorfgeschichten*: the focus on local manners, customs, and dialect (in this case, Yiddish); geographical and historical specificity; and thematic engagement with the clash between old ways and modernity, and between ethnic identity and conformity to, or assimilation into, the dominant imperial culture. The inaugural work in this tradition was *Geschichten aus dem Ghetto* [From the Ghetto] (1848) (an evident echo of *Aus dem Böhmerwalde*) by Leopold Kompert, like Rank an Austro-Bohemian (Rank and Kompert met near Vienna in 1844). Kompert and later Karl Emil Franzos carried on the *Dorfgeschichte* tradition established by Auerbach and Weill (both Kompert and Franzos were familiar with Auerbach's work). As one critic notes, Auerbach's "*Dorfgeschichten* . . . for Jewish writers . . . provided a model for the ghetto tale" (Kahn 44). As W. G. Sebald points out in his study of the *Ghettogeschichte* genre, the audience for their stories was the non-Jewish bourgeoisie ["das nichtjüdische Bürgertum" (162)] and the aim was to correct anti-Semitic misapprehensions about Jewish life; thus, continuing the thematic seen in the earlier *Dorfgeschichten*.

The tension between loyalty to traditional Jewish roots and the liberative attractions of urban modernity are seen in both Kompert and Franzos, though Kompert's attitude toward the *shtetl* is more sentimental than

Franzos's. "Der Dorfgeher" (1851) ("The Peddler"), for example, which appeared in *Böhmische Juden: Geschichten* [Bohemian Jews: Stories], concerns the *Heimkehr* of an educated, assimilated Jewish son who returns to his home in disguise, planning to study his family almost as an anthropologist. In letters to his urban girlfriend, Clara, Emmanuel (he had changed his name from Elije in order to better assimilate into modern urban culture) is at first scornful of his family's ways and traditions (his father is a rabbi who has to work during the week as a peddler to support his family).

In the course of accompanying his father on his rounds, Emmanuel feels himself split between someone allied with his father and someone distantly observing his behavior.

> So confused [was Emmanuel] through the division in his soul that he often forgot the natural relationship to his father and saw before him a completely strange person whose mysterious being he must research and investigate in order to prepare interesting remarks for his Clara. [So verwirrt (war Emmanuel) durch den Zwiespalt (sic) seiner Seele geworden, dass er oft das natürliche Verhältniss zu seinem Vater vergass und eine bloss fremde Person vor sich sah, deren geheimnissvolles Wesen er erforschen und durchwühlen musste, um interessante Bemerkungen für seine Clara zu bereiten!] (71)

In the end Emmanuel/Elije comes to feel he has betrayed his people and determines "to overcome the betrayal" ["dass es den Verrath überstrahlen sollte" (77)] henceforth.

Karl Emil Franzos's *Die Juden von Barnow* [The Jews of Barnow] (1876) is set in the Jewish *shtetls* of Galicia, a region now part of Poland. In addition to his knowledge of Auerbach's work, Franzos was also familiar with Droste-Hülshoff's *Die Judenbuch* and wrote a positive review of it, praising its realism, where "Jews and peasants [were] made to seem as they were at the time" ["Juden und Bauern so erscheinen zu lassen, wie sie damals waren" (Doerr 463)].

Like his predecessors, Franzos embraced the liberative ideals of modernity while remaining sympathetic to concerns about preserving ethnic identity. He nevertheless was more vociferous than earlier writers in the genre about rejecting what he saw as regressive provincial customs and was implicitly critical of Jews who continued to adhere to them. Franzos in short rejected the religious customs of the premodern *Ostjude* or Eastern European Jew from the point of view of an assimilated *Westjude*. (On this issue see Robertson 405–13, Kahn 50–4, and Sebald.) On the other hand, Franzos was sympathetic to the idea of remaining faithful to one's authentic ethnic roots, as can be seen in such stories as "Das Christus Bild" [The Picture of Christ] (Franzos 227–57), which involves a *Heimkehr* of an educated assimilated Jew to his Galician ghetto where he reconnects with his Jewish identity.

However, in several of his stories regressive superstitions and customs — especially those restricting women's place — are condemned. In "Der Shylock von Barnow" (1873), a traditional Jewish father refuses to allow his daughter a modern Western education but her uncle, a "Meschumed" [Apostate] (Franzos 18), who speaks in *Hochdeutsch*, influences her toward secular enlightenment. But, because of the father's intransigence, the girl dies alone and abandoned. In "Nach dem höheren Gesetz" [According to a Higher Law] husband and wife come to the realization that their marriage has foundered because it was arranged. The woman says, "you ask why I then became your wife. Ach! Did you ever then consult my wishes?" ["Warum ich dann Dein Weib geworden bin, fragst Du? Ach! Habt ihr mich denn je nach meinem Willen gefragt?" (Franzos 82)]. He reflects,

is then a wife a thing that one possesses like a jewel or a house? Doesn't she have free will? And did we consult her will at that time? That was a crime . . . and what is happening now is just recompense. [Ist denn ein Weib eine Sache, die man besitzt wie einem Schmuck oder ein Haus? Hat sie nicht einen freien Willen? Und haben wir sie denn damals nach ihrem Willen gefragt? Damals ist ein Verbrechen begangen worden. Was jetzt geschieht, ist nur die gerechte Vergeltung.] (84)

In "Ohne Inschrift" [Without Inscription] (258–89) Franzos deplores not only that sinners' gravestones are left blank but how petty the sins were, one woman's sin having been that she kept her hair long when she married, thus violating the custom that married women wear it short and cover it with a *scheitel* (284). In another story, "Das Kind der Sühne" [The Child of Atonement] (142–68), a woman defies rabbinical superstition and consults with a professional doctor in order to save her child's life.

One of the most interesting stories and one that recalls "Der Lauterbacher" is "Esterka Regina" (1872; *Juden* 169–213). In this story a Vienna-educated *Meschumed* courts a provincial girl who only speaks Yiddish, not *Hochdeutsch*. He had changed his name from Aaron to Adolf when he moved to Vienna to study medicine, thus denying his Jewish roots, though as a boy he had attended schools "as a Jew with caftan and curls" ["als Jude mit Kaftan und Schmachtlöcklein" (Franzos 175)]. Even though Adolf and Rachel love each other, she finally turns him down fearing that his career would be impeded by her backwardness. Although once modernized Adolf developed "a burning hatred" for Judaism ["hasste seinem Glauben glühend" (Franzos 184)], he has his mother's "prayer book," which is "written in Yiddish for women" ["ein Gebetbuch für Frauen, im Jüdisch-Deutsch geschreiben" (Franzos 194)], buried with Rachel (213) in a final gesture of reconciliation with his maternal ethnic roots.

Though not herself Jewish, Marie von Ebner-Eschenbach, an Austro-Moravian, features a Jewish physician as the protagonist of the lead story "Der Kreisphysikus" [The Provincial Doctor] of her collection *Dorf- und Schlossgeschichten* [Village and Castle Stories] (1883). Like Franzos, whom she knew, Ebner-Eschenbach is more sympathetic toward modernity than the earlier local-colorists. Her story "Die Unverstandene auf dem Dorfe" [The Misunderstood One in the Village], for example, may be contrasted with both Auerbach's "Der Lauterbacher" and with Franzos's "Esterka Regina." The plot is similar — an educated teacher courts a dialect-speaking peasant woman; however, the narrative point of view is more on the side of modernity than in the others. As "Die Unverstandene" is set like most of Ebner-Eschenbach's work in Moravia (where she was born), a province of the Austro-Hungarian Empire, the dominant metropole is Vienna and the dominant language German.

The novella concerns the courtship drama of an upper-end peasant Marie who works as a laundress in the local manor ["Schloss"]. As in "Der Lauterbacher," a Vienna-educated teacher, Anton, comes to town and resolves to elevate her class-wise by teaching her standard German, repressing her Moravian dialect. Marie's mother resents the girl's abandoning her maternal dialect. "Since [Marie] said 'nicht' instead of 'nit,' 'ist' instead of 'is,' sometimes observed umlauts, and even read books which were not prayerbooks, [her mother] harbored a bitter grudge against her" ["Seitdem (Marie) 'nicht' statt 'nit,' 'ist' statt 'is' sagte, von dem Umlauten manchmal Notiz nahm und sogar in Büchern las, die keine Gebetsbücher waren, nährte die Alten einen bittern Groll gegen sie" (268)].

"Speak as it's appropriate for us to speak!" ["Sprich, wie sich's für unsereins schickt'!" (268)], she admonishes her daughter, resenting "that the teacher presumes to instruct Marie in a language she already learned as a child from her mother" ["dass er sich vermass, Marien in dieser Sprache zu unterweisen, die sie doch schon als Kind von ihrer Mutter gelernt" (267)]. Does she think he wants to marry her? the mother taunts Marie, saying, "I wouldn't be surprised if he wrote you a 'Dear-John' letter even today" ["Wenn er dir heut noch den Abschiedsbrief schreibt — mich wundert's nit" (296)]. (Note how the mother speaks in dialect.)

Unlike Hedwig in "Der Lauterbacher," Marie, who is forceful and self-directed, anticipating the emancipated "new woman," eagerly learns standard German, thus proving herself a woman in transition to modern ways. Moreover, she ultimately rejects the idea of arranged marriage for money (which her mother, upholding time-honored tradition, wants), marrying the teacher instead for love. Thus, like many of the local-colorists, Ebner-Eschenbach endorses modern ideas about women's status.

Adalbert Stifter also concerned himself with country–urban romantic liaisons in both *Das Haidedorf* (where the protagonist is rejected as a suitor of an urban girl by her father because of his country ways) and in *Die Mappe meines Urgrossvaters* (where the physician protagonist eventually marries a local girl). One of Stifter's stories, "Der Condor" ["The Condor"] (1840), however, presents a negative view toward women's emancipation. Cornelia, a young woman with feminist aspirations, takes a balloon ride "to show that a woman can declare herself free from the arbitrary boundaries that harsh man had drawn around her for millennia" ["und die . . . ein Beispiel aufstellen wollte, dass auch ein Weib sich frei erklären könne von den willkürlichen Grenzen, die der harte Mann seit Jahrtausenden um sich gezogen hatte" (Stiften *Gesammelte Werke* 1:17)]. Once aloft, however, she becomes ill, forcing the abortion of the voyage, much to the annoyance of the men involved who say, "woman cannot tolerate heaven" ["das Weib erträgt den Himmel nicht" (1:23)].

Cornelia's ascent in the balloon, however, may be seen as emblematic of not just women's rising modernist aspirations but also of the underlying theme of many local-color works — the problematic cultural departure from home territory, away from the familiar traditional past, toward an uncertain alien future. As the balloon rises, she looks over the rim of the basket, trying to make out familiar places on the "beloved, abandoned, no longer radiant earth" below ["die liebe verlassene, nunmehr schimmernde Erde"], "but their intimate domesticity was already no longer apparent, and therefore also the threads that tie us to a dear little spot, which we call home" ["die vertraute Wohnlichkeit derselben war schon nicht mehr sichtbar, und auch mithin die Fäden die uns an ein teures, kleines Fleckchen binden, das wir Heimat nennen" (1:20)].

NOTE

1 Documentation on translations found in WorldCat (online); O'Neill, "Image and Reception"; Sagarra and Tanzer, "Die Rezeption irischer Autorinnen"; Hennig, "Studien zur deutschsprachigen Irlandkunde"; *The National Union Catalog, Pre-1956 Imprints*; McInnis, "Realism, History, and the Nation"; <http://www.british-fiction.cf.ac.uk> (last accessed 4 September 2007); "Bibliography of Scottish Literature in Translation" at <www.nls.uk/catalogues/resources/boslit/index> (last accessed 4 September 2007).

CHAPTER 5

Romans Champêtres

French Provincial Literature

Lucile-Aurore Dupin, baronne Dudevant (1804–76), who used the pen name George Sand, has been called the "Walter Scott of Berry," her native region of France (Zellweger 136). Indeed, perhaps even more than Scott dominated the field in Scotland, Sand towered over the regional genre in France. She may be said, in fact, to have invented the French *roman champêtre*.

There were, however, other important tributaries of the regional tradition in France, including the realists of the Courbet circle — namely Max Buchon (1819–69), Jules Husson Champfleury (1820–89), and Francis Wey (1812–82) — more or less contemporaneous with Sand but who wrote slightly after most of her peasant novels had been published — and the Occitane school, which included Ferdinand Fabre (1827–98) and Léon Cladel (1835–92), who wrote some years after Sand. The Courbet school, which was centered in Paris around the great painter Gustav Courbet (1819–77), located their fiction in their home region of Franche-Comté, the Jura mountain area, while the Occitane writings were set in the southern region of Languedoc. Sand's own peasant novels take place in the central section of France — Berry and Marche. In addition, Émile Souvestre (1806–54) set his works in Brittany; followers of Alexandre Weill — Émile Erckmann (1822–99), Alexandre Chatrian (1826–90), and Daniel Stauben (1825–75) situated their work in their home province of Alsace; and, much later, Eugène Le Roy (1837–1907) in Dordogne in southwestern France. (As Le Roy falls beyond the parameters of this study, his work will not be treated further here.) With the exception of Sand's Berry, all of these provinces are, significantly, remote from Paris, the metropolitan magnet.

France differs from the countries and regions treated in previous chapters in that it was not dominated by a foreign power (except for a brief period of foreign occupation in 1815–18, following Napoleon's defeat). The provinces of France nevertheless experienced a kind of inner colonization that paralleled in certain respects the imperial domination by metropolitan centers seen in Ireland, Scotland, and various German-speaking lands. In France, the dominant metropole was, of course, Paris, well established for centuries as the political center of the country.

While a succession of monarchs had long since centralized control in Paris, the French Revolution, ideologically driven by the Cartesian perspective of Enlightenment modernity — much of which was formulated in France — strengthened the capital's control over the provinces in that it ushered in a new zeal for national standardization. In the early years of the Revolution, the 1790s, for example, a project was established to standardize the language. The results of the so-called Grégoire Inquiry ["l'Enquête de Grégoire" (Certeau et al. 1975)] were published in 1794 as "Report on the Necessity and Means of Annihilating Dialects and Universalizing Usage of the French Language" ["Rapport sur la nécessité et les moyens d'anéantir les patois et d'universaliser l'usage de la langue française"]. A sort of linguistic "Highland Clearances," the project envisaged eliminating regional dialects in favor of a standardized Parisian French. At the same time, as noted in Chapter One, various standardized measurements were enforced to supercede diverse local customary practices. A character in Sand's novel *La Petite Fadette* (1848–49), for example, mentions having to use meters for the first time (79). As Michel de Certeau et al. note in their study of the Grégoire project, its clear purpose was to effect a "colonization of domestic regions" ["colonisation de terres intérieures" (162)].

French local-color literature arose, as elsewhere, at least in part then in resistance to this dictated homogenization. The French tradition was also inspired, like the German, by the influx of translations of Irish and Scottish works, especially those of the sensationally popular Sir Walter Scott, whose *Waverley* was available in French translation soon after its first publication.[1] Several subsequent editions of the novel appeared through the 1820s. Indeed, it was through the vogue of the *Waverley* novels that the term "local color" (*couleur locale*) came into common use in France (Hovencamp 2). All of Scott's local-color novels appeared in French translation shortly after they were published in English: *Guy Mannering, astrologue, nouvelle écossaise* (1816, with several subsequent printings); *l'Antiquaire* (1816, with several reprints through the 1820s); *Robert le Rouge MacGregor: ou les montagnards écossais* (1818); *La Fiancée de Lammermoor* (1819, also with many editions following). Maria Edgeworth was also very popular in France. *Le Château de Rackrent* appeared in 1813–14; *l'Ennui, ou mémoires du comte de Glenthorn* in 1812; *l'Absent*, 1813; *Harrington* and *Ormond* in 1817. One critic goes so far as to suggest that "without Castle Rackrent and [Edgeworth's] novels of peasant life, who knows if [George Sand's] La petite Fadette would have seen light of day?" (Rafroidi 1:253).

Lady Morgan's *The Wild Irish Girl* was translated as *Glorvina, ou la jeune Irlandaise* in 1813. Two versions of *Florence Macarthy* appeared in 1819, and *Les O'Brien et les O'Flaherty, ou l'Irlande en 1793, histoire nationale* came out in 1829. Other Irish and Scottish works available in French included

John Galt's *Les chroniques écossaises: contenant les annales de la paroisse et le prévôt* (which included *Annals of the Parish* and *The Provost*) (1824); the Banims' *The Nowlans* as *l'Apostat, ou la Famille Nowlan* (1829); and some of William Carleton's stories in *Romans irlandais: Scènes de la vie champêtre* (1861).

The German provincial works, themselves originally written in the 1840s, also appeared in French translation within a few years of their German publication. Auerbach's and Gotthelf's works were translated mainly by Max Buchon of the Courbet circle, who himself wrote several local-color novels (see below) under the influence of Gotthelf (as he acknowledged). Buchon also was an admirer of Hebel, whose works he translated and who had a considerable influence on the French writers, especially those of the Courbet circle but also on George Sand (see Minder 112). *Poésies complètes de J.-P. Hébel*, translated by Buchon, along with his own poetic "Scènes champêtres" [Country Scenes], appeared in 1853.

The earliest Auerbach story to appear in French was "Das Kriegspfeife," translated from *Schwarzwälder Dorfgeschichten* as "La Pipe de Guerre" by Buchon, in a Suisse Romande journal, *La Revue Suisse*, in 1847. *Hebel et Auerbach: Scènes villageoises de la Forêt-Noire* [Village Scenes from the Black Forest] (1853), translated by Buchon, included several Auerbach stories, and a more expansive *Contes d'Auerbach* [Stories by Auerbach] appeared the same year. Gotthelf's *Wie Uli der Knecht glücklich wird* was translated as *Ulric le valet de ferme ou comment Ulric arrive à la fortune* [Ulric the Farmhand or How Ulric Was Successful] and published in Suisse Romande in 1850. A succession of Gotthelf's novels translated by Buchon as *Nouvelles bernoises* began appearing in 1854. A later selection, *Au Village* (1875), included a Preface written by George Sand.

On the question of influence, however, since most of the major French local-color works were published before or at the same time as the German translations, it seems unlikely that they had a direct influence (except, as noted, Hebel and Gotthelf on Buchon and his circle). This notwithstanding, Sand was sufficiently enthusiastic about the German writers to visit Auerbach at his home in Swabia and to laud Gotthelf in the above-noted Preface. She also, according to Robert Minder, "from 1853 on knew of and admired Hebel's work" ["Hebel's werk hat sie erst seit 1853 gekannt und bewundert" (112)].

However, there is little doubt of the influence that Scott and the other Celtic writers had on the French *champêtre* novelists. Émile Souvestre, one of the earliest French local-colorists, for example, in his Preface to *Le Foyer breton: Contes et récits populaires* [Popular Stories and Tales] (1844) acknowledged the influence of James Hogg's *Le Calendrier du berger* [The Shepherd's Calendar] and Scott's "contes populaires" (12 n.1). And in one of Sand's earliest peasant novels, *Jeanne* (1844), a character exclaims that the rural world is so full of curious myths and superstitions that "it would take a Walter Scott to describe them" ["que si nous avions un Walter Scott pour les écrire" (1:105)]. Later in the novel another character remarks of another's mood: "Walter Scott himself could not conjure [it up]" ["Walter Scott lui-même ne pouvait conjurer" (2:52)] — a tribute to her predecessor's narrative powers.

The French local-color tradition was also shaped in part by historical political developments in the France of the time. Of course, the earthquake of the French Revolution continued to reverberate through the nineteenth century, and the liberal ideas it unleashed continued as the ideological context of French literature of the day. Consequently, the French local-color works tend to be more overtly political, express greater indignation about class oppression, and be more inclined toward a socialist solution than any of the preceding local-color literature. While to be sure political implications may be drawn from Edgeworth's, Morgan's, Scott's, and others' works, the resistance and resentment of the peasant "subaltern" is there cast more in terms of ethnic nationality than in terms of class. Similarly, in the German works oppression is largely seen as the result of foreign impositions rather than of class subordination. With the French, however, class warfare is accepted as a fact, and the reality that the revolutionary ideals of "liberté, égalité, and fraternité" have not been realized for the peasantry is seen as a political injustice, the rectification of which is the underlying issue in many of the French regional works.

Through much of the nineteenth century, despite the hopes raised by the Revolution, France was subjected to one dictatorial regime after another — some worse than others. The monarchy was restored after the defeat of Napoleon in 1814 and while the so-called July Monarchy, established under Louis Philippe after the 1830 July Revolution, was relatively benign — a sort of constitutional monarchy — it was overthrown during the 1848 Revolution, which raised hopes again for a socialist democracy but which ended like the 1789 Revolution in a repressive dictatorship under Napoleon III, the so-called Second Empire, which lasted from 1852 to 1870. The local-color writers, most of whom were of liberal, indeed socialist, inclination were deeply disappointed with the failure of the 1848 uprising; some — like Buchon — went into exile abroad; others — like George Sand — went into a kind of inner exile, returning from Paris to her home, Nohant in Berry where she in a kind of escapist vein wrote her remaining local-color novels.

In her December 1851 retrospective Preface to *La Petite Fadette*, which first appeared in 1848, Sand said that she wrote the novel as an escape from the "ill-starred days of June 1848," when "troubled and depressed to the bottom of my heart by external storms, I sought to recover in solitude, if not tranquillity, at least faith" ["C'est à la suite des néfastes journées de juin 1848, que troublé et navré jusqu'au fond de mon âme, par les orages extéri-eures, je m'efforçai de retrouver dans la solitude, sinon le calme, au moins la foi" (1973, 15)]. As Pierre de Boisdeffre notes in his Introduction to the novel, in returning to Berry from Paris, Sand hoped to engage herself "in a new rural novel which would permit her to forget 'this sad political scene'" (as she put it in her *Histoire de ma vie*) ["un nouveau roman champêtre qui lui permettrait d'oublier 'cette triste politique'" (1973, xiii)]. "To the politi-cal deceptions which she had just experienced, to the sterile and murderous ambitions of the city, to the revolution itself, George Sand now opposed the poetry of the country" ["Aux déceptions qu'elle venait d'éprouver dans la politique, aux ambitions stériles et meurtrières de la ville, à la révolution elle-même, George Sand opposait maintenant la poésie de la campagne" (xix)]. There she depicted "a rural humanism" not yet destroyed by urban industrial modernity (Vernois 434).

Sand was also motivated to write her peasant novels in reaction against the unsympathetic and unrealistic characterization of the rural world she saw in the regional novels of Honoré de Balzac, which included his *Les Chouans* (1829), *Le Médecin de campagne* (1833), *Le Curé de village* (1839), and *Les Paysans* (1844). As Rudolf Zellweger explains, with Balzac "the image of the peasant is . . . completely subordinate to the preconceived idea" he brings to the table ["l'image du paysan est . . . soumise entièrement à l'idée preconçue qu'il se propose d'exprimer" (110)]. In *Le Médecin de campagne*, for example, "in no way are the customs of the peasants, their way of life, manner of speaking or thinking in the foreground" ["Nulle part . . . les habitudes des paysans, leur façon de vivre, de parler, ou de penser ne sont au premier plan" (111)]. In other words, Balzac's works lacked the characteristics of local color. Moreover, and perhaps more importantly, Balzac lacked sympathy for his peasant characters, seeing them as unruly representatives of a "retarded stage of civilization" ["un état arrière de la civilisation" (Vernois 28)]. Paul Vernois notes,

> the curse [Balzac] lays upon [his] characters . . . impeded the rise of a rustic social novel because the primary . . . characteristic of this literary genre is sympathy of the author for the disinherited class whose behavior he proposes to depict. [(Le) malédiction dont [Balzac] les accable a . . . entravé la naissance d'un roman rustique sociale . . . [parce que] le premier . . . caractère de ce genre littéraire est la sympathie de l'auteur pour la class déshéritée dont il se propose de dépeindre le comportement.] (28)

By these criteria the works of several other nineteenth-century French writers — writers like Flaubert, Maupassant, and Zola — despite being set in rural areas and including peasant characters, do not properly speaking belong to the local-color or *roman rustique* genre. Zola's *La Terre* (1887), for example, deploys a broad canvas of peasant life but, because "it greatly lacked sympathy for the peasant class," cannot be included in the genre. ["Elle manquait par trop de sympathie pour la classe paysanne" (Vernois 137)]. Indeed, Anatole France said of Zola's rustics: "In their turpitude and bestial promiscuities his peasants are as completely imaginary as d'Urfé's shepherds" — an allusion to a seventeenth-century pastoral romance, *l'Astrée* ["Ses paysans dans leur turpitude et leurs promiscuités de bêtes sont aussi parfaitement imaginaires que les bergers d'Urfé" (quoted in Vernois 137)]. Similarly, a writer like Prosper Mérimée who is often identified with local color may be excluded because his works are not realistic depictions of peasant culture but focus rather on exotic, "picturesque," remote locales and cultures (see Hovencamp).

It was thus to correct Balzac's misconceived view of peasant life that George Sand seems to have been motivated to "sketch a picture of rural society that was more accurate and . . . more sympathetic" ["tracer un tableau plus vrai et . . . plus sympathique de la société campagnarde" (Zellweger 119)]. Unlike Balzac, Zellweger notes, Sand's "point of departure is not an economic or social doctrine but the intimate knowledge of her native region and a feeling of sincere affection for its beauties and the lives of its inhabitants" ["le point de départ n'est pas une doctrine économique ou sociale mais la connaissance intime de sa région natale et un sentiment d'affection sincère pour ses beautés et l'existence de ses habitants" (Zellweger 119)].

Sand may thus be said to have founded the genre of the *roman champêtre* in France (Vernois 11). ["L'honneur d'avoir créé le roman rustique . . . revient tout entier à George Sand" (Zellweger 117)]. She did so not just through her novels, which we analyze below, but also through a series of theoretical prefaces, which helped to explain her intentions and to define the genre.

Perhaps the most revealing of her prefaces is the 1852 "Avant-Propos" to *François le champi* (originally published serially in 1847–48), which is cast as a dialogue between the author ("moi") and "R," "un ami" (xi) on the issue of how as sophisticated urbanites they can enter into, understand, and transcribe rural society — which is seen as primitive, marginally civilized, and more innocent than urban modernity. R notes the difficulties a modern intellectual has in penetrating the peasant mindset. The author, the Sand persona, agrees, observing the contrast between "the *primitive life*" of the peasant "relative to our developed and complicated life, which I will call *artificial life*" ["*la vie primitive*, relativement à notre vie développée et compliquée, que j'appellerai *la vie factice*" (xii)]. How does one bridge the gap between "these two opposite states"? ["ces deux états opposés" (xii)]. The answer, she says, is through feeling, "le sentiment" (xiii). The challenge, R says, is to "translate this candor, this grace, this charm of primitive life to those who only live in an artificial life and who are . . . absolute cretins before nature and its divine secrets" ["traduire cette candeur, cette grâce, ce charme de la vie primitive, à ceux qui ne vivent que de la vie factice, et qui sont . . . en face de la nature et ses secrets divins, les plus grand crétins du monde" (xiii)].

Sand determines that the best way to transcribe the peasant world authentically is to write down as exactly as possible what native narrators have told her orally; in other words, to put into print their oral history, legends, and stories. The story of François le champi, for example, she has just heard from a hemp-worker, "un chanvreur" (xxv), who we learn in the Appendix to another work, *La Mare au diable*, is a local bard/raconteur who transmits ancient songs, legends, and tales (224–6) — similar to the storyteller figures we've seen in Scott (recall the Preface to *The Bride of Lammermoor*), Moome in *Clan-Albin*, and various Hogg figures, among others. In the Preface to the *Mare au diable*, Sand says she envisaged writing a series of novels under the title "Veillées du chanvreur" [Evening Gatherings at the Hemp-Worker's]. In another work, *Les Maîtres sonneurs*, Sand explains further that such *veillées* or evening gatherings (analogous to the Irish *ceili*) are when "one processes the hemp and where each one then tells his/her story" ["Les heures . . . où l'on broie le chanvre, et où chacun alors apportait sa chronique" (*Maîtres sonneurs* i). The author takes from such oral communal storytelling, writing down indigenous material. In the case of *Les Maîtres sonneurs* the author says she heard the story of Étienne Depardieu (the subject of the novel) in her youth, when it was told to her directly by Étienne himself (i).

In her discussion with "R" Sand notes the dialect problem: while she has just heard the champi story told by the *chanvreur*, she can't tell it in his language because her literate (Parisian) readers wouldn't understand the dialect. R suggests that she must narrate it "as if you had on your right a Parisian speaking modern French and on your left a peasant for whom you would not want to say a phrase, a word that he could not understand" ["comme si tu avais à la droite un Parisien parlant la langue moderne, et à ta gauche un paysan devant lequel tu ne voudrais pas dire une phrase, un mot où il ne pourrait pas pénétrer" (xxvii)]. In her *champêtre* novels Sand followed the format used by other local-colorists, writing the text in standard French but having characters use a modernized *patois* in dialogue, with dialect terms explained in footnotes. In her Preface to *Les Maîtres sonneurs* Sand acknowledges the difficulty in transcribing peasant dialect but says she hopes to capture the indigenous narrator's style as exactly as possible ["en imitant sa manière autant qu'il me sera possible" (ii)] "because it is impossible for me to make him talk like us without distorting his mental processes" ["C'est parce qu'il m'est impossible de le faire parler comme nous, sans dénaturer les opérations auxquelles se livrait son esprit" (ii).

Sand's awareness of the complexities of French linguistic history comes across in her discussion of dialect use in La Marche (in the novel *Jeanne*). One elderly woman, the narrator explains, speaks in a "marchois patois" that is "unintelligible to unaccustomed ears" ("inintelligible aux oreilles non exercées" (1:40)]. For the inhabitants of the region use indiscriminately either the regional dialect or an old French dialect, such as they use in Berry, which derives from an ancient version of "langue d'oïl" (1:39 n.1). "But being that 'langue d'oc' was more familiar to the old woman that the 'langue d'oil,'" she uses the former ["Mais soit que la langue d'oc fût plus familière à la vieille femme que la langue d'oil" (1:40)]. (*Langue d'oc* was a language used in southern and western France before it was suppressed in the late Middle Ages by *langue d'oïl*, the northern language, which became the basis for modern French.)

Sand has been and can be accused of idealizing peasant life. There is no question that she conceives the rural in counterposition to the evils of modern industrial capitalism. In that sense she projects there a kind of utopian socialism. Very much under the influence of Jean-Jacques Rousseau and to a lesser extent utopian socialist theorists like Pierre-Joseph Proudhon, Sand envisaged the *champêtre* world as precapitalist, communal, and relatively uncontaminated by the evils of competitive individualism and ruthless exploitation associated with capitalist industrialism.

Indeed, in her Preface to the French translation of Gotthelf's stories, *Au Village*, Sand deplores the arrival of capitalism in Switzerland, saying the value of Gotthelf lies in having captured a precapitalist world where spiritual rather than material values prevailed.

> He described a Switzerland that has already [by 1875] much changed. Railroads and affluence . . . have transformed . . . a significant part of the population. Already today's writers are showing us mountain-dwellers [who are], dare I say, more civilized? Unfortunately, yes, if civilization consists in extending material well-being at the expense of inner serenity . . . The Swiss wants to enrich himself . . . Commerce prompts him to do so. But it's not only in Switzerland where cheap goods have killed *good deeds*. [Il a donc décrit une Suisse qui a déjà beaucoup changé. Les chemins de fer et l'affluence . . . ont transformé . . . une notable partie de la population. Déjà les conteurs . . . d'aujourd'hui nous montrent des montagnards, dirais-je plus civilisés? Malheureusement oui, si la civilisation consiste à étendre le bien-être matériel au détriment de la sérénité intérieure . . . Le Suisse veut s'enrichir . . . Le commerce l'y excite. Ce n'est pas seulement en Suisse que le bon marché a tué le *bien-faire*.] (281–2)

Thus, while perhaps too rose-colored, Sand's view of the rural life is by no means that of the romantic pastoral, but rather a vision of a precapitalist world governed by an ethic of communal care. Because of her scrupulous attention to local realities — details of dialect, as well as of dress, manners, environment — in other words, because of her realistic use of local color, her works have an authenticity that saves them from being reductive utopian idylls.

The first of Sand's *champêtre* novels was *Mauprat*, written between 1835 and 1837 and published that year serially in the *Revue des deux mondes*. It thus antedates the German *Dorfgeschichten* but reflects very much the influence of Celtic predecessors. Indeed, the novel might be subtitled "The Wild French Man" in acknowledgment of the palpable influence of Lady Morgan's *The Wild Irish Girl* (by then, as noted, readily available in French translation) — a work itself imbued, as we have noted, with Rousseauistic romanticism modified to feminist purpose — aspects that would likely have attracted Sand, who herself had feminist inclinations and was well versed in Rousseau.

The plot concerns the education and civilization of the protagonist, Bernard Mauprat, his transformation "from a state of an orang-utan to that of an intelligent man" ["de l'état d'homme des bois à celui d'homme intelligent" (207)]. Even though born into an aristocratic feudal clan, Mauprat starts out as essentially "a savage, a rustic . . . a brute who can scarcely sign his name" ["un sauvage, un rustre . . . une brute qui sait à peine signer son nom" (463)]. But through a Rousseauistic educational philosophy mainly taught by Edmée, his beloved, he is transformed into a worthy, well-behaved citizen. Edmée bears a strong resemblance to Glorvina in *The Wild Irish Girl*. Like her, "she was imbued with [Rousseau's] *Émile* and put into practice the systematic ideas of her dear philosopher" ["elle était imbue de l'*Émile* et mettait en pratique les idées systématiques de son cher philosophe" (236–7)]. She also reads *La Nouvelle Héloïse* but, like Glorvina, from a feminist, critical perspective: "because . . . I have an inflexible pride, I will never endure man's tyranny, no more a lover's violence than the slap of a husband" ["par la raison que . . . j'ai un inflexible orgueil, je ne souffrirai jamais la tyrannie de l'homme, pas plus la violence d'un amant que le soufflet d'un mari" (189)]. Like Glorvina she has a "vast intelligence" (147), and "brought up in the country, she was strong, active, courageous, lively" ["Élevée aux champs, elle était forte, active, courageuse, enjouée" (149)]. As a Rousseauistic natural but highly educated, she gives her name in Latin as *Edmea Sylvestris*, "Edmée of the woods."

Parallel to Edmée is another character lifted from Lady Morgan, the hermit Patience, also a Rousseau follower, "a rustic philosopher" (35), who resembles Terence Oge O'Leary in Morgan's *Florence Macarthy*. Like him, Patience has a pet bird, an owl (whom the yet-to-be-civilized Bernard kills). Patience puts into practice his love of animals by becoming an ethical vegetarian, a follower of the "Pythagorean doctrine": "he felt . . . a secret joy . . . in no longer having occasion to see death delivered . . . to innocent animals" ["il éprouvait . . . une secrète joie . . . de n'avoir plus occasion de voir donner la mort . . . à des animaux innocents" (42)]. Patience is also a pacifist. "Inclined toward Pythagorean ideas, he was horrified by bloodshed. The death of a doe brought him to tears . . . he couldn't bear to contemplate human murders" ["Enclin aux idées pythagoriciennes, il avait horreur du sang répandu. La morte d'une biche lui arrachait des larmes . . . les meurtres humains lui étaient impossible à contempler" (146)].

The values of Edmée and Patience — nonviolence, compassion, living in harmony with nature — are those Sand ascribed in general to the premodern rural world. While *Mauprat* is perhaps too much of a philosophical novel to be considered a local-color work, strictly speaking, lacking the concrete realism of Sand's later *romans champêtres*, it nevertheless remains an important link in the local-color tradition. In Patience, Sand created perhaps her first peasant character and she scruples to replicate his idiom and his thought processes accurately.

> Thus Patience reasoned. Believe me, in translating his speech into our methodical language I eliminate all his grace, verve, and energy. But who could capture the textual expression of Patience? His language was unique to him; it was composed of the limited but vigorous vocabulary of the peasants and the strongest metaphors of the poets . . . To this mixed idiom, his synthetic mind gave order and logic. [Ainsi raissonait Patience; et croyez-bien qu'en traduisant sa parole dans notre langue méthodique je lui ôte toute sa grâce, toute sa verve, et toute son énergie. Mais qui pourrait redire l'expression textuelle de Patience? Son langage n'appartient qu'à lui seul; c'était un composé du vocabulaire borné, mais vigoureux des paysans, et des métaphors les plus hardies des poëtes . . . A cet idiome mélangé, son esprit synthéthique donnait l'order et la logique.] (154)

Elsewhere Sand wrote of "the peasant being an artist who doesn't know it" ["Le paysan étant un artiste qui s'ignore" (Vernois 34)]. She seemed to believe that peasants — the "precivilized" — live in a world governed more by poetry, by the imagination, than by the prose and rationalism of urban modernity. As a character in *Jeanne* (1844), Sand's next (or, as some claim, first) *roman champêtre*, explains, peasants' "minds are more turned toward poetry than ours" ["ils ont l'esprit plus tourné à la poésie que nous" (2:13)].

Jeanne is in fact a rich and complex novel that has received surprisingly little critical attention. Set in La Marche in the period 1816–20, the novel concerns a confrontation between an ancient Celtic-Druidic peasant world, represented by the peasant shepherdess Jeanne, and modern civilization represented by three educated men who court her.

Jeanne, who has "a poetic soul" ["une âme poétique" (1:252)], is illiterate (1:86), uneducated — indeed feels she has no need for education, explaining, "I was brought up with the animals. That is my work" ["J'étais élevée aux bêtes. C'est ça mon ouvrage" (1:92)] — and believes in a Druidic cult of *fades* or fairies similar to those seen in Irish works. They are, she explains, "women whom one doesn't see but who do good or evil" ["femmes qu'on ne voit pas, mais qui font du bien ou du mal" (1:95)], who are presided over by "the Great Fade, the queen of fairies" ["la Grande Fade, la reine des fées" (1:114)], who merges in Jeanne's mind with the Virgin Mary ["la vierge Marie" (1:255)].

She herself, along with her mother and aunt, has a special nonrational, magical knowledge and power called "la Connaissance." "*Women who have 'la Connaissance,'* as we call them here, [are those] who cure the sick, who pray against floods, hail . . . fire," etc. ["*les femmes qui ont la connaissance*, comme on les appelle ici, qui guérissent les malades, qui font des prières contre les fléaux . . . la grêle . . . l'incendie" (1:104)]. Having "la Connaissance" enables communication with the *fades*, who, Jeanne explains, as "daughters of God or of the devil . . . love us or hate us . . . according to how we know them . . . When a person has la Connaissance, she keeps strong by remaining wise" ["filles de Dieu ou filles du diable . . . nous aiment ou nous haïssent . . . selon que nous les connaissons . . . Quand une personne a *la connaissance*, elle fait son salut en restant sage" (2:217)]. And, to be sure, such wise women reject modern medicine; "we don't believe in that" ["nous ne croyons pas à ça" (1:84)]. Nor do they accept modern science. We are told that "the peasant . . . evokes fantastical powers . . . He makes prayers and pilgrimages that are more pagan than Catholic . . . and disdains having recourse to the remedies of science or the precautions of hygiene" ["Le paysan . . . évoque les puissances fantastiques . . . Il fait des vœux et des pèlerinages plus païens que catholiques . . . et dédaigne d'avoir recours aux soins de la science ou aux précautions de l'hygiène" (1:78)].

Jeanne also has no use for money and sees it as a kind of pollution, in an implicit rejection of capitalism. "We believe," she says of money, "that it brings bad luck" ["on croit chez nous que ça porte malheur" (1:98)]. "The day I found some gold [coins] in my hand I immediately threw them far away from me" ["Le jour où je trouvai de l'or dans ma main je commençai par le jeter bien loin de moi" (2:23)].

The novel opens with three young male hunters and tourists who are visiting Jeanne's native locale to see the ancient Druidic altar stones that remain in the area — "les menhirs, les dolmens, les cromlechs des anciens Gaulois" (1:4). The men are all upper class and educated: one is a lawyer, another a British aristocrat, and the third a French baron.

The men exhibit a kind of imperialist superciliousness toward the area and its inhabitants. Marsillat, the lawyer, says at one point to Sir Arthur, the Brit, "You have traveled in distant and savage countries but I bet you

wouldn't have believed that in the middle of France there were such backward superstitions" (referring to the belief in *fades*) ["Vous avez voyagé dans
les pays lointains et sauvages; vous ne vous doutiez pas, je parie, qu'il y eut
au centre de la France des superstitions si arriérées" (1:11)]. Marsillat, an
avatar of modernity, is, typically, "skeptical and even a bit of an atheist"
["skeptique et même un peu athée" (1:66)]. He rejects local pagan beliefs,
saying "I hate superstition and deplore [such] gross error no matter what
form it takes. I never let an opportunity pass to mock it and believe it's one's
duty to reeducate these simple folk" ["Je hais la superstition et déplore
l'erreur grossière, sous quelque form qu'elles se présentent. Je ne laisse
jamais échapper l'occasion de m'en moquer et je crois que c'est un devoir
à remplir envers ces gens simples" (2:12)].

Yet all three men are passionately attracted to Jeanne and compete in
courting her. She, however, has no interest in them, resists all their atten-
tions, and insists that her destiny is to remain solitary. The confrontation
between her and her suitors has allegorical implications. Guillaume, the
French baron, has a special connection to Jeanne in that she is his "sœur
de lait," meaning that her mother nursed them both as infants. (It was
a custom for upper-class French mothers to have their babies nursed by
country women.) That the bond between Guillaume and Jeanne is thus
pre-oedipal is further suggested by the fact that his first language, the *patois*
he learned from his wetnurse (which he has since forgotten), seems to him
"like his maternal language" ["comme sa langue maternelle" (1:40)]. It has
since been repressed by standard French.

Jeanne and her world seem thus to represent a repressed maternal or
matriarchal realm, what modern French theorists refer to as the "Imaginary"
(Jacques Lacan) or the "semiotic" (Julia Kristeva) — a presymbolic, pre-
oedipal, precivilized, and, feminists would argue, prepatriarchal sphere.
That Sand associates this world with the pre-urban, precapitalist countryside adds a new dimension to the local-color genre.

The strong attachment of the men to Jeanne and their desire to capture,
tame, conquer, and thus civilize her also have allegorical implications,
suggesting, on a psychological level, the dominance of masculine, egoistic
rationalism over a feminine, poetic, nonrational, imaginative sensibility;
and, on the historical level, the dominance and suppression by patriarchal
capitalist modernity of ancient rural dialects, traditions, and practices, many
of which we have noted throughout this book.

The novel ends sadly. Jeanne is effectively harassed to death by the continuing unwanted persecution of the three men, including a rape attempt
by Marsillat. When we first see Jeanne early in the novel it is as a solitary
shepherdess; "passionately devoted to the protection of her flock, she went
almost always alone, her staff at her side" ["passionnée pour la garde de ses

troupeaux, elle allait presque toujours seule, la quenouille au coté" (1:76)].
And in the end her one desire is to return to her flock, to be left alone. In
asking Marsillat (and by extension the modern world) to leave her alone,
she explains,

> We are simple . . . but we see out in the fields . . . things that you do not see and that
> you would never understand. Leave us as we are. When you change us, that brings us
> misfortune. [Nous sommes simples . . . mais nous voyons aux champs . . . des choses que
> vous ne voyez pas et que vous ne connaîtrez jamais. Laissez-nous comme nous sommes.
> Quand vous nous changez, ça nous porte malheur.] (2:10)

The year following *Jeanne*'s publication Sand produced her next *roman
champêtre*, *Le Meunier d'Angibault* [The Miller of Angibault] (1845), perhaps the best known of them. Quite different in focus from its immediate
predecessor, the novel nevertheless returns to a familiar local-color thematic,
the *Heimkehr* of educated aristocrats to their country "home," which is seen
as more authentic and ethically progressive than the decadent, upper-class,
urban milieu they seek to escape. Marcelle de Blanchemont and Henri
Lémor, the protagonists of Sand's novel, thus resemble Glenthorn in Maria
Edgeworth's *Ennui* or Henry Mortimer in *The Wild Irish Girl*, in their
relocation from Paris to the Berry region, which — like the western coast of
Ireland — is seen as an unspoiled precivilized realm. Sand's characters in
addition espouse socialist ideas more explicitly than do her Irish predecessors, though they are latent even there (recall especially King Corny's realm
in Edgeworth's *Ormond*).

Marcelle, for example, hopes to "find refuge [in the country] from all
the languors and miseries of aristocratic life" ["à s'y réfugier contre toutes
les langueurs et toutes les tristesses de la vie aristocratique" (16)], noting
the "useless luxury" ["luxe inutile" (20)] of her urban environment. She
takes a vow of poverty (139), saying, "I want to reduce myself to bare necessity, buy a peasant house, live as soberly as I can" ["Je veux me réduire au
nécessaire, acheter une maîson de paysan, vivre aussi sobrement qu'il me
sera possible" (142)].

Her *amant*, Henri, similarly envisages a life of voluntary poverty à la campagne, proposing to distribute his wealth to the poor "like the Communist
Christians of the early days" of the church ["Je crois que je le distribuerais
aux pauvres, comme les communistes chrétiens des premiers temps" (181)].
And in the end, when the two marry, they determine to live in an egalitarian
communal manner where "yours and mine" ["le tien et le mien" (377)],
the ownership of property, is foresworn.

Money and property are indeed the main sources of misery in the novel;
in particular, the insistence of Bricolin, an upper-end peasant, that his

daughters marry for money — a determination that drives one of them, Bricoline, mad and prevents the other, Rose, from marrying Grand-Louis, the miller of the title, who exemplifies the simple virtues of honesty, intuitive wisdom, and natural compassion that Sand ascribes to the peasantry.

Bricoline's situation recalls Scott's Lucie of Lammermoor: forbidden to marry the man she loves (because he is too poor), she becomes "*deranged*, a regional term, which means mad" ["*derangée* (c'est-à-dire folle, en terms du pays)" (115)]. For twelve years she has remained silent, only occasionally issuing senseless utterances (115). Finally, like Lucie, her madness erupts in violence and she torches her father's farm, "her vengeance long premeditated" ["sa vengeance, longtemps méditée" (370)]. In the process she cries out like a Fury, "exhaling the hate that had been accumulating for twelve years in her broken heart . . . this mute victim of her parents' cupidity" ["la Bricoline exhalait la haine amassée depuis douze ans dans son âme brisée . . . cette victime muette de la cupidité de ses parents" (265)].

The father espouses a kind of heartlessly individualistic capitalism where "everyone," he says, "is free to make his fortune" ["tout le monde est libre de faire fortune" (109)]. But what, Grand-Louis asks, of "the poor, the lazy, the weak, the *simple-minded*, what do you do about them?" "I do nothing," Bricolin replies, "because they are worth nothing. Too bad for them" ["Et les pauvres, les paresseux, les faibles, les *bêtes*, qu'est-ce que vous en faites?" "Je n'en fais rien, puisqu'ils ne sont bons à rien. Tant pis pour eux" (109)].

In addition to being a natural socialist, Grand-Louis has a sort of innate emotional wisdom, which Henri remarks by observing, "You feel that the heart is more powerful than science" ["Tu sens que le cœur est plus puissant que la science" (185)]. Grand-Louis acknowledges that he is "like the first apostles" who "had nothing and knew nothing . . . But God breathed into them and they had greater wisdom than all the schoolmasters and priests of their day" ["les premiers apôtres" "étaient gens de rien, ne sachant rien . . . Le bon Dieu souffla sur eux et ils en surent plus long que tous les maîtres d'école et tous les curés de leur temps" (185)]. Henri says it is because he wishes to accede to Grand-Louis's kind of wisdom that "I have burned my books, why I wanted to return to the people" ["j'ai brûlé mes livres, voilà pouquoi j'ai voulu retourner au peuple" (185)].

Like peasants we have met in earlier literature, Grand-Louis is deeply connected with animals, particularly with his horse Sophie. He is distraught when she is missing and explains to Henri the deep attachment peasants have to their animals, something urbanites fail to appreciate.

We relate to animals as to people and we miss an old horse as an old friend. You wouldn't understand that, you city people, but we peasants live with animals from whom we differ little. [On s'attache aux animaux comme aux gens, et on regrette un vieux cheval common un vieux ami. Vous ne comprendriez pas ça, vous autres gens de la ville; mais nous, gens de paysans nous vivons avec les bêtes, dont nous ne différons guère.] (253)

And it's not a matter of Sophie's monetary value, Grand-Louis continues:

> I scorn the paltry amount the old beast would bring at a fair! Do you think I would care so much for 100 francs? Oh no! What I miss is her, and not her price . . . She was so courageous, so intelligent, she knew me so well, [Je me moque bien du peu d'argent que la vieille bête pouvait valoir en foire! Croyez-vous que pour une centaine de francs j'aurais tant de souci? Oh! non pas: ce que je regrette, c'est elle, et non son prix . . . Elle était si courageuse, si intelligente, elle me connaissait si bien.] (255)

Happily, Sophie eventually turns up again unharmed.

Less politically driven but still governed by the thematic ideas seen in her preceding works is Sand's next novel, which she considered the first of her *romans champêtres*, *La Mare au diable* [The Devil's Lake] (1846). The main character, Germain, is a simple, honorable peasant who, like Grand-Louis, represents a premodern, precapitalist ethic. Regarding money and property, he says, "I would rather give it all up than dispute over what's yours and what's mine" ["Quant à l'argent . . . j'aimerais mieux céder que de disputer le tien et le mien" (52)]. Again like Grand-Louis, he is close to his animals, especially his mule, "La Grise," who is treated as a character with equal status to the humans in the novel. Germain sings to his oxen when plowing the fields. And the feelings of the animals are also described: an ox grieving over a lost companion (27–8), the tight bond between La Grise and her mother (69).

Germain also has the unmediated, unreflective emotional knowledge of Grand-Louis, which makes him in his simplicity, the author says, "more beautiful than someone whose feelings have been smothered by science" ["plus beau que celui chez qui la science a étouffé le sentiment" (36)]. The author much prefers "his spiritual simplicity to the false lights" of modern scientific enlightenment ["cette simplicité de son âme que les fausse lumières" (36)].

The critique of modernity is further seen in a harvesting ritual that the peasants engage in which includes a satire of the educated busybody, the Enlightenment professional, who tries to tell them how to do their job. One peasant "performs the office of an *engineer*: [he] comes close, he distances himself, he outlines a plan, he ogles the workers, he draws lines, he acts the pedant, he cries that they are going to ruin everything . . . and . . . directs the project as ridiculously as possible" ["il fait l'office d'*ingénieur*: s'approche, s'éloigne, lève un plan, lorgne les travailleurs, tire des lignes, fait le pédant, s'écrie qu'on va tout gâter . . . et . . . le plus ridiculement possible dirige la besogne" (278)]. This satirical mummery, the author tells us, is "an addition to the ancient formulary of the [harvesting] ceremony, done in mockery of theoreticians in general whom the custom-bound peasant royally detests" ["une addition au formulaire antique de la cérémonie, en moquerie des théoriciens en général que le paysan coutumier méprise souverainement" (275)]. Such rustic theater presents an interesting variation of the resistance to externally imposed Enlightenment schemes seen in peasant culture from Ireland to Germany, as noted in earlier chapters.

François le champi, which may be translated loosely as François the Abandoned Country Child (the author defines "champi," which is a dialect term, as "enfant abandonné dans les champs" [xxx]), first appeared serially between December 1847 and February 1848, the last section thus appearing at the time of the fall of the July Monarchy. Book publication followed in 1850. The story was allegedly narrated orally to several parishioners by the *chanvreur* and another peasant, Monique, and written down by the author (xxv, 102). François is a kind of male counterpart to the shepherdess Jeanne: a simple, saintly, almost preternaturally good figure. He says, "I prefer to endure evil than to inflict it" ["J'aime mieux souffrir le mal que le rendre" (53)]. As in *La Mare au diable*, the central plot is a romance — here between François and a young peasant woman, Madeleine Blanchet, who unofficially adopts him. As she is unhappily married and about 10 years older than he, their love remains unconsummated until the oppressive and unfaithful husband dies and François comes of age. After various impediments, they do eventually marry.

Sand's next novel, *Le Petite Fadette* (1848–49; book publication 1850), was the first written after (and in reaction to) the failed 1848 Revolution. The term *Fadette* is a diminutive of *fade* or fairy (as explained in *Jeanne*). The *chanvreur* who narrates the tale to the author explains that the name is partially based on the girl's family name, Fadet, and partially "on the fact that people held that she was a bit of a witch as well. You know that the fairy or goblin, what elsewhere is also called the sprite, is a very gentle but a bit malicious spirit" ["pour ce qu'on voulait qu'elle fût un peu sorcière aussi. Vous savez que le fadet ou le farfadet, qu'en d'autres divers endroits on appelle aussi le folet, est un lutin fort gentil, mais un peu malicieux" (68)].

La Fadette thus resembles Jeanne in that she belongs to a world of pagan beliefs and powers, but she is more of an uncivilized, wild child than Jeanne and her story is one of her transformation from tomboy into civilized (and marriageable) lady, a story of taming.

Like Jeanne, Fadette lives in a matriarchal household; her grandmother, like Jeanne's mother and other country wise women, has an extensive knowledge of medicinal herbs and is an unofficial local doctor believed to have magical powers (66–7). "In the country in order to be wise one has to be something of a witch" ["dans la campagne, on n'est jamais savant sans être quelque peu sorcier" 967)]. Fadette learns herbal medicine from her grandmother, knowing "to what good ends the meagerest herbs" may be put ["à quoi sont bonnes les moindres herbes" (124)]. Indeed, she is said to surpass her grandmother in herbal knowledge (131). She thus has "la Connaissance," the special knowledge of rural witch-women: "the knowledge of the secrets my grandmother teaches me for healing the human body, flowers, herbs, stones, flies, all the secrets of nature" ["la connaissance des secrets que m'enseigne ma grand'mère pour la guérison des corps humain. Les fleurs, les herbes, les pierres, les mouches, tous les secrets de la nature" (126)].

She is also able to communicate with fairies or sprites (97) and has a special compassion for other creatures. Regarding a caterpillar, she says,

> Me, I am not like those who say: Look, there's a caterpillar, an ugly creature; oh, how ugly! We must kill it! Me, I don't crush God's poor creature and if the caterpillar falls in the water I extend her a leaf so she can save herself. [Moi, je ne suis pas comme ceux qui disent: Voilà une chenille une vilaine bête; ah! qu'elle est laide! il faut la tuer! Moi, je n'écrase pas la pauvre créature du bon Dieu, et si la chenille tombe dans l'eau, je lui tends une feuille pour qu'elle se sauve.] (127)

Because of her wildness, Fadette is demonized and blacklisted by the community, which she resents. "If people were fair and reasonable, they would pay more attention to my good heart than to my ugly appearance and shabby clothes" ["Si le monde était juste et raisonnable, il ferait plus d'attention à mon bon cœur qu'à ma vilaine figure et mes mauvais habillements" (125)].

Her suitor, Landry, tells her the main reason she's scorned by the community is because she's too masculine. Fadette "lived like a boy without caring about her looks and enjoying only fun and laughter" ["vivait comme un garçon, sans souci de sa figure, et n'aimant que le jeu et la risée" (108)]. "You climb the trees like a real squirrel and when you jump on a mare without bridle or saddle you make her gallop as if the devil were on board" ["Tu montes sur les arbres comme un vrai chat-écurieux (écureuil) et quand tu sautes sur une jument, sans bride ni selle tu la fais galoper comme si le diable était dessus" (123)]. "It's because you are nothing like a girl and everything like a boy in your air and manners," Landry explains. "It's that you don't take care of yourself . . . by your clothes and language you let yourself appear ugly . . . The children call you a name even worse than cricket [her nickname]. They often call you le *mâlot*" ["C'est que tu n'a rien d'une fille et tout d'un garçon, dans ton air et dans tes manières; c'est que tu ne prends pas soin de ta personne . . . tu te fais paraître laide par ton habillement et ton langage . . . Les enfants t'appellent d'un nom encore

plus déplaisant que celui du grelet. Ils t'appellent souvent le *mâlot*" (122)].
A footnote defines *mâlot* as "girl who has the demeanor and inclinations
of a boy" ["jeune fille qui a des allures, des goûts de garçon" (122 n.1)], in
other words, a gender deviant.

Fadette's physical strength and masculine demeanor recall other examples
of untamed — one might say "pre-feminized"– women in local-color literature, such as Gertrude in Alexandre Weill's story, Hogg's Jenny Armstrong,
Galt's Betty Pawkie, or several of Scott's characters. Eventually (one might
say, unfortunately), after spending time in a town, Fadette adjusts her
manners and dress sufficiently to be accepted as within the norm. She also
inherits a huge sum of money from her grandmother, thus establishing her as
a marriageable bourgeoise, a conventional, if somewhat conformist, ending.

Les Maîtres sonneurs [The Master Pipers], Sand's final *roman champêtre*,
appeared in 1853. While writing it, Sand was reading the works of Sir
Walter Scott (Dickinson 118). Set in a woodland area, the novel is basically
a romance involving two couples: Étienne, the narrator, and Thérence, "a
wild child born and raised deep in the woods" ["une enfant sauvage, née et
élevée au fond des bois" (149)]; and that between Huriel, a mule-driver and
wood-cutter, and Brulette, who is illiterate but learning to read, despite the
narrator's warning her that to do so "you set your sights beyond your own
country and your friends!" ["vous mettez votre idée hors de votre pays et de
vos amis!" (103)]. Huriel's father, Bastien, is a master bagpiper, and there
is an association throughout the novel of music and the natural woodland
world — seen as a site of nonrational, enchanted, mystical happenings on
the fringes of civilization.

These woods-people are even more remote from modern civilization
than the peasants in Sand's previous novels. They are so immersed in their
own culture and forest world that they "had a kind of homesickness when
they had to live in the open" ["ils avaient comme le mal du pays quand il
leur fallait vivre en la plaine" (143)]. They seem indeed a part of the forest,
which itself is animated with living nonhuman presences. And they themselves have a pagan, animist view of the woods. Bastien, for example, "loved
the woods as if he had been a wolf or fox, even though he was among the
best of Christians" ["il aimait les bois comme s'il eût été loup ou renard,
encore qu'il fût le meilleur chrétien" (143)].

Huriel speaks of the guilt he feels in cutting down trees.

> You know . . . I love them, those beautiful old life-long companions who have told me so
> many things in the sounds of their leaves and the snapping of their branches! And . . . I
> thanked them by planting the axe in their heart and knocking them down at my feet like
> so many cadavers cut in pieces. Don't laugh at me, I never saw an old oak fall or even a
> young willow, without trembling with pity or fear, like an assassin of the works of God.

[Sais-tu que je les aime, ces beaux vieux compagnons de ma vie, qui m'ont raconté tant de choses dans les bruits de leur feuillages et les craquements de leurs branches! Et . . . je les ai remerciés en leur plantant la hache dans le cœur et en les couchant à mes pieds comme autant de cadavres mis en pièces. Ne ris pas de moi, je n'ai jamais vu tomber un vieux chêne, ou seulement un jeune saule, sans trembler de pitié ou de craint, comme un assassin des œuvres du bon Dieu.] (297)

Sand's continuing fascination with rural beliefs found expression in a nonfictional work, the *Légendes rustiques*, which appeared a few years later (1857). In it she collected and wrote down various myths and superstitions of her home region, Berry, which she says "seems to have preserved in its legends memories anterior to the cult of the Druids" ["semble avoir conservé dans ses légendes, des souvenirs antérieurs au culte des Druides" (5)]. (Much of the material gathered here was embodied fictionally in *Jeanne*.) The format Sand uses here is one picked up by American local-colorists, particularly Sarah Orne Jewett (whom Sand greatly influenced — see Epilogue), that of an outsider author encountering an indigenous storyteller who narrates the legend (set in direct quotes) to the author and who becomes a character in his own right. When she tries to get more specific details from him he demurs (33), and indeed sometimes, because he fears being mocked, she has to coax him to recount the story (42). Once again Sand concludes — what indeed could be considered the leitmotif of her works — that the peasant "has the extraordinarily poetic ability to personify the appearance of things and to capture their marvelous aspect" ["la faculté extraordinairement poétique de personnifier l'apparence des choses et d'en saisir le côté merveilleux" (69)]. In her *romans champêtres* Sand attempted to transmit and transcribe this enchanted world-view for the modern, alienated reader.

Writing at about the same time as Sand but stemming more directly from the German tradition, because of the translation of Gotthelf and Auerbach by Max Buchon, and projecting to be more realistic than Sand, was the circle of writers who gathered at the Brasserie Andler in Paris around the painter Gustav Courbet, but who wrote about their (and his) native region, Franche-Comté. The principal writers in this group were Francis Wey, Champfleury, and Buchon — all of whom were influenced by Courbet's paintings of peasant life, while he in turn was influenced by them. Particularly important were Courbet's three great paintings done between October 1849 and the summer of 1850 — "the great trilogy of Realism" (Clark 51): *Les Casseurs de pierres* [The Stonecutters], *Un Enterrement à Ornans* [A Burial at Ornans], and *Les Paysans de Flagey* [The Peasants of Flagey].

Wey's *Le Bouquet de cerises: Roman rustique*, the first of this school's works to appear, published in *Le National* in January 1850, is directly based on *Les Casseurs de pierres*, whereas Courbet is said to have read parts of Champfleury's novel *Les Oies de Noël* (1850) while working on *Les Casseurs* and *Un Enterrement*, which he painted in Ornans (his hometown) in Franche-Comté. In a 1851 review of Courbet's *Paysans de Flagey*, Max Buchon listed as literary "companion pieces" to Courbet's realist trilogy the following local-color canon: Sand's *Petite Fadette* and *François le champi*, Alexandre Weill's *Nouvelles alsaciennes*, along with the Wey and Champfleury novels noted above (Clark 183 n.90).

Le Bouquet de cerises [The Bunch of Cherries], like other works of this school, is much more politically charged than are Sand's works. As T. J. Clark notes, they "tried to invent a kind of political pastoral . . . in which the reader could sense the invasion of the rustic idyll by usury, class conflict, and expropriation" (116). Wey's novel depicts the economic ruination of a peasant family due to capitalist machinations by the propertied classes. Still the work is not didactic and by virtue of its realistic depiction of local habitation remains well within the confines of the local-color tradition.

Set in the "wild country of the Jura" ["dans les sauvages contrées du Jura" (2)] in Franche-Comté (11), the novel charts the misfortunes of a tenant family who are evicted from their home and farm because the owner, in financial difficulty, wants to sell it in order to increase his daughter's dowry (22). Wey opens the novel using a technique similar to that used by Harriet Beecher Stowe in *Uncle Tom's Cabin*, which begins with a sympathetic picture of a happy (in her case, slave) family whose lives are about to be changed by the proprietors in the "big house" who control their lives and make financial decisions regardless of their effect on their tenants/slaves. (*Uncle Tom's Cabin* appeared in French translation shortly after Wey's novel was published.)

The father in Wey's novel, who incidentally is also named Thomas, is like most peasants a traditionalist who resists modern education methods saying imitation — whereby *mētis* is transmitted from generation to generation — provides the best pedagogy. You put a child "in the field . . . he sees what his elder siblings are doing and copies them . . . In this way he learns very quickly . . . Excellent method, inspired by nature," much better than rote learning in the schools ["aux champs . . .: il voyait faire ses ainés et les imitent . . . De cette façon, il s'instruisait très-vite . . . Méthode excellente, inspirée de la nature" (16)].

A parallel plot concerns his daughter's fiancé, Jean Grusse, who lives with his 70-year-old mother, another rural wise woman. Jean is lured into letting smugglers use his land by a local eccentric, Fanfinet, who argues casuistically that smuggling is okay for poor people to use because they're screwed by the laws. "Here we have misery; there [in Paris] it means nothing, and that's where they make the laws . . . And isn't it excusable if people so mistreated indemnify themselves, as they can" ["Ici c'est la misère; là-bas, ce n'est rien, et c'est là-bas qu'on fabrique les lois . . . n'est-il pas pardon-nable à des gens si malmenés de s'indemnifiser comme ils peuvent" (79)]. He concludes with a political critique: "Twenty million souls live in dire straits in order to enrich four fat manufacturers" ["vingt million d'âmes sont à la gêne pour enrichir quatre gros fabricants" (81)]. Jean, who agrees to the smuggling deal to save his own land, is arrested, a blow that kills his mother, and he, though acquitted, is ruined, joining the recently evicted Thomas (whose family has been reduced to begging) as a stonecutter. Wey's descriptions of the two in this capacity derive directly from Courbet's paint-ing, *Les Casseurs de pierres*, indeed precisely detail the painting's subjects.

> The one, bent over by age, was a very thin old man, crouching over a pile of stones . . . Standing, behind his companion, the young man [Jean Grusse] energetically car-ries against his stomach a basket of crushed stones. [L'un, courbé par le faix des ans, était un vieillard très-maigre: accroupi sur un tas de pierres . . . Debout, derrière son compagnon, le jeune homme porte avec énergie contre son ventre, un panier de pierres brisées.] (148–9)

The novel ends happily, however; when the new owner of Thomas's old farmstead can't find anyone to run it, Thomas is rehired, along with Jean who marries the daughter.

Champfleury's *Les Oies de Noël* [The Christmas Geese], first published in Proudhon's socialist journal *Voix du Peuple* in 1850, similarly depicts bank-rupted peasants and foreclosed farms with Blaizot, a local moneylender, castigated as the evil usurer responsible. Blaizot gets his just retribution, however, when at a Christmas dinner — attended by his bureaucratic "convives" — "solicitors, attorneys, and bailiffs" ["des notaires, des avoués, des huissiers" (148)], he dies after eating the holiday goose. Interestingly, after dinner he has nightmares of being attacked by geese, "more than three hundred inside me, they are eating me from within" ["plus de trois cent dans moi; elles me mangent dedans" (196)], after which he dies. A local bard celebrates by composing a song, which concludes, "The greedy usurer/Justly punished by God" ["L'usurier avaricieux/Justement puni par Dieu" (203)]. With Blaizot removed, debtors are released from prison.

Though his own fictions appeared a few years after Wey's and Champfleury's, Max Buchon was probably the most influential member of the group. He was strongly influenced by Hebel, whose poetry he first translated in 1846, followed by a more complete edition that included a selection of his own poetic "Scènes champêtres," in 1853, at the same time as which he translated, as noted, works by Auerbach and Gotthelf. George Sand reviewed the Hebel translation in 1857, praising Buchon's own poetry for its "limpid" quality (a characterization that could justly be

applied to her own work), commenting in the same review on his translation of Auerbach's *Scènes villageoises de la Forêt Noire* (Zellweger 154, 162).
Apparently, Buchon had asked Sand to write a preface to the Auerbach
collection but this never materialized (Zellweger 159). (One critic, Robert
Minder, proposes a direct Hebel influence on Sand, suggesting that Sand's
prefaces to *La Petite Fadette* "could have been signed by Hebel" ["könnten
von Hebel unterzeichnet sein" (112)]). Champfleury noted that Hebel and
Auerbach had "a great influence on the new literary school" — meaning
the Courbet circle ["une grande influence sur la nouvelle école littéraire"
(Zellweger 151)].

Like most French writers Buchon was deeply affected by the 1848
Revolution and particularly the 1851 coup d'état, after which he went into
exile in Switzerland (he had been arrested but acquitted in 1849), which is
where he did his translation and wrote his own novels. The first of these, *Le
Matachin*, appeared in Champfleury's journal *La Revue des deux mondes*
in June 1854, and the second, *Le Gouffre gourmand*, in the same journal
in October 1854. The two were published together as *En Province: Scènes
Franc-Comtoises* in 1857. In his Preface to the book edition Buchon noted
that he hoped these "contes" would help "people to know our region,
already popularized in art by the paintings of my friend Courbet" ["à faire
connaître par le monde notre pays, déjà popularisé en peinture par les tableaux de mon ami Courbet" (10)]. He further notes how he was influenced
to write regional fiction by his encounter some 15 years previously with the
works of Hebel, Auerbach, and Gotthelf (11). Elsewhere, he acknowledged,
"reading Gotthelf was very useful to me" ["la lecture de Gotthelf m'a beau-
coup servi" (Zellweger 201)].

The title, *Le Matachin*, is the name of a poor section of Salins, which
is set "just at the base of the western slope of the great chain of the Jura"
["situé à la base même du versant occidentale de la grande chaîne du Jura"
(32)]. The plot is not unlike that seen in Sand's works (and Sand was clearly
another influence), that of two simple country romances — the peasant
Manuel's successful courtship of Fifine, at whose engagement her widowed
father proposes to his widowed mother. But the work includes more explicit
laments about peasant oppression and capitalist exploitation than Sand's or
indeed those of the German predecessors. "Alas, how many deprivations are
required in the country to make one millionaire in the city!" ["Hélas! combien d'économies . . . ne faut-il pas, à la campagne, pour faire à la ville un
millionnaire!" (60)]. And the author deplores the exploitation of the region's
woodlands by the central government: "no town . . . hasn't been radically
stripped by the state of its forest privileges" ["aucune commune . . . n'a été
. . . radicalement dépouillée par l'Etat de ses avantages forestiers" (32)].

And, as in many other local-color works, animals play roles as central characters. Indeed, concern about the treatment of animals becomes a central issue in this novel. Manuel works in logging with his two oxen, to one of which, Dsaillet, he is especially attached. When Manuel dares to begin courting Fifine, Dsaillet chastizes him. "Giving him a sly look, he seemed to say, 'Take us as an example, my dear. Resign yourself to the life you are assigned'" ["Dsaillet le regardait . . . d'un air narquois qui semblait lui dire: . . . 'Prends example sur nous, mon cher. Resigne-toi à la vie qui t'est faite'" (84)]. Manuel's mother, Jeanne-Antoine, is similarly attached to her cow, La Bouquette, "a superb creature" ["une superbe bête" (145)]. In a lengthy disquisition the author laments that people don't care enough for their oxen, who are admirable creatures (87–90).

In a grisly ending Manuel has to sell Dsaillet and shortly thereafter Fifine is shocked to see the animal's head on a local butcher's wall, realizing that the soup she's just prepared probably has meat from him in it. Even so, Manuel and her father insist on eating the soup but throw it up soon afterwards. Fifine laughs, "Poor Dsaillet . . . thus are you avenged" ["Pauvre Dsaillet . . . te voilà vengé" (171)].

Le Gouffre gourmand [The Greedy Abyss], the other work in *En Province* is a cross-class romance that — although replete with local details (it is set in a town near Besançon) — is really more of a melodrama, involving a dramatic elopement to Switzerland, than a *roman champêtre* and therefore need not concern us further.

In addition to Sand, the Courbet circle, and the Occitane school (which I treat below) there were other isolated examples of French regional writers that should be mentioned. In the preceding chapter we discussed the works of the Alsatian Alexandre Weill, which were first published in German. Weill, however, moved to Paris, became connected with the Courbet group (note that Buchon included his works as companion pieces to Courbet's paintings), and translated three of his stories into French — "Selmel," "Frohni," and "Gertrude et Udile" — in 1853 as *Histoires de Village*.

Weill undoubtedly had a direct influence on August Widal (1825–75), who published *Scènes de la vie juive en Alsace* [Scenes of Jewish Life in Alsace] in 1857–58 in the *Revue des deux mondes* under the pen name Daniel Stauben. In his Preface to the book publication in 1860, Stauben says, however, that his primary influence was George Sand, in particular *La Mare au diable* and *François le champi*. "We marveled at . . . this series of little masterpieces. These stories so simple, these tableaux so fresh . . . these popular traditions recounted so graciously . . . all that vividly impressed us," evoking "a crowd of memories . . . [of] a world at once analogous and different" ["Nous fûmes émerveillé à la lecture de cette série de petits chefs-d'œuvre. Ces récits si simples, ces tableaux si frais, . . . ces traditions populaires si gracieusement racontées . . . tout cela nous avait vivement impressionné" "une foule de reminiscences . . . un monde à la fois analogue et différent" (ii)]. "Le Berry, I told myself, isn't the only region of France where there live people with a distinctive character, ancient customs, a picturesque idiom." The same could be said of "the Jews of our hamlets in Alsace" ["Le Berry, me dis-je alors, n'est pas la seule contrée de la France où vivent des populations au caractère tranché, aux coutumes antiques, à l'idiome pittoresque" . . . "les Juifs de nos hameaux de l'Alsace" (iii)]. Not surprisingly, perhaps, Stauben also translated Leopold Kompert's works into French as *Scènes du Ghetto* (1859), *Les Juifs de la Bohème* (1860), and *Nouvelles juives* (1873).

Stauben laments that the traditional Jewish world, which he is attempting to capture, is fast disappearing because of "*progress*, aided by the railroad — in a few years, there will remain no vestiges of these primitive manners" ["le progrès et les chemins-de-fer aidant — quelques années encore, et il ne restera plus vestige de ces mœurs primitives" (v)].

Scènes de la vie juive en Alsace is structured as a *Heimkehr*. The Parisian narrator returns after a long absence to the village of Bollwiller near Mulhouse in Alsace. In this Jewish enclave the people speak in "an incorrect but precise and quaint Jewish-Alsatian lingo" ["incorrect mais fin et pittoresque jargon judaïco-alsacien" (14)] that is based on "a German-Jewish dialect" ["un patois allemand-juif" (26)] — i.e., Yiddish — of which the terms used are explained or translated (along with a few Hebrew words) in notes.

The work is accurately described as "scenes," because it consists of a series of vignettes or stories rather than a unified novel like Sand's. Many of the stories are told by the traditional village raconteur, Samuel, a counterpart to Sand's *chanvreur*. He tells "ordinary stories, extraordinary stories, legends, adventures, magical stories," things that "Parisians, who believe little or not at all in the supernatural," would not appreciate ["Vous autres Parisiens, vous croyez peu or point aux chose surnaturelles" (16)]. Some of these stories concern *Machschovim*, a "Hebrew word for *witch*" ["mot Hebreu, signifiant *sorcier*" (24 n.1)], *Sclédem* ["*demons*" (24 n.2)], the *Mohlkalb*, the village monster, the *Dorftier* ["village beast" (18 n.1)]. Stauben also describes various Jewish traditions, lamenting how "for us transplanted Alsatian Jews, the religion and customs of the ancestors are too quickly, alas, being reduced to memories" ["Pour nous autres israélites alsaciens transplantés, la religion et les coutumes des ancêtres sont trop vite, hélas, réduites à l'état de souvenirs" (96)].

Weill also probably had an influence on two other Alsatian writers, Émile Erckmann (1822–99) and Alexandre Chatrian (1826–90), who wrote numerous peasant novels as a team under the name Erckmann-Chatrian. One example is *Histoire d'un homme du peuple* [The Story of a Man of the

People] (1865), which details the life of an orphan, Jean-Pierre Clavel, who is informally adopted by a Madame Balais, a fruit-seller. Clavel becomes an apprentice carpenter but falls in love with a wealthy girl, prohibited him because of class; in despair he goes to Paris where he loses himself in the revolutionary street demonstrations of the 1848 uprising. In Paris he experiences intense homesickness for his home region, "le mal du pays": "I felt myself pining away. Night and day I only saw again Saverne, the coast, the woods and pines, the river, the evening shadows; I smelled the scent of the forests" ["Je me sentais dépérir. La nuit et le jour je ne revoyais que Saverne, la côte, les bois et les sapins, la rivière, les ombres de soir; je sentais l'odeur des forêts" (80)]. He even visits the Jardin des Plantes to see some greenery: "at least there it wasn't just stones, at least the plants were alive" ["Au moins là tout n'était pas des pierres, au moins ces plantes vivaient" (81)]. And he visits the zoo to see live animals but deplores their deprived conditions:

> a hawk in the mountains when he passes from rock to rock, letting out his wild cry . . . an ox who strains at the plough, or a shepherd dog who gathers the flock, seemed to me a thousand times more beautiful than these decrepit eagles, hyenas, and lions. [un épervier dans la montagne, quand il passe d'un roche à l'autre en jetant son cri sauvage . . . un bœuf qui fume à la charrue, ou un chien de berger qui rassemble le troupeau, me parassaient mille fois plus beau que ces aigles, ces hyènes et ces lions décrépits.] (82)

The political message in this work takes the shape of a demand for worker rights. Madame deplores the effect of wealth (in lamenting the class divide that blocks her son's amour): "Oh, wretched money, when you come in one door, happiness goes out the other" ["Ah! gueux d'argent, quand tu viens par la porte, le bonheur s'en va par l'autre" (41)]. And Clavel comes to resent how he's been bamboozled by religion to feel responsible for his miserable condition instead of learning that he'd been wrongfully deprived of his rights: "It is clear that they want to stupefy us all by making us think that we're responsible for Adam's eating some apples, instead of telling us about our rights" ["Il est clair qu'on veut tous nous abrutir, en nous faisant croire que nous sommes responsable de ce qu'Adam a mangé des pommes, au lieu de nous parler de nos droits" (80)]. In the work of Erckmann-Chatrian we thus see a merging of the political and the local-color novel, where the peasant comes to a political analysis of the reasons for his oppression. This branch of the French tradition culminated in the novels of Eugène Le Roy, *Le Moulin du Frau* (1891) and *Jacquou le croquant* (1899).

Writing about an entirely different region of France, Brittany (Bretagne), in a kind of school of his own was Émile Souvestre (1806–54). His first work, *Contes et nouvelles* (1832), while set in Brittany, has little local detail and thus cannot be considered part of the local-color tradition. His *Les Derniers*

Bretons (1835–37) is a collection of nonfictional ethnographic essays. His fictional *Le Foyer breton: Contes et récits populaires* (1844), which we focus on here, is, however, of considerable interest as a noteworthy example of the local-color genre. In his Introduction Souvestre mentions as influences the Scots James Hogg (*Le Calendrier du berger*) and Sir Walter Scott (12 n.1), noting that it is only in "popular traditions" that one can find "the intimate life of a nation," "its life in the home" ["la vie intime d'une nation," "sa vie du foyer" (8)], unlike in history books where one finds only "its official life" ["sa vie officielle" (8)].

Le Foyer breton is divided into four "foyers" or "hearths" set in different parts of Brittany, linked only by an outsider narrator who visits each of them in turn. Each "foyer" functions like the Irish *ceili* or Sand's *veillée* as a group gathers (around a hearth) to tell stories, which are recounted as the narrative.

The first "foyer", "Pays de Tréguier. La Ferme des Nids," is set on the Breton farm of Antonn Gorou where members of his family — his wife Glanda, daughter Margaridd, son Cleménez — along with an idiot shepherd Lawik, a tutor Kloarek, a teacher Guiller, and a beggar gather as a tale-telling circle. (All the names are characteristically Bretonese.) The tales they tell are ancient medieval romances, miracle fables, saints' legends (material that, in fact, one might have found in the writings of an earlier Breton writer, Marie de France).

The second "foyer" takes place in Léon where the narrator encounters (in 1831) two locals, one of whom is a "véritable Armoricain" (95) — another term for Breton — who tells about the "lavendières de nuit" ["night laundresses"] (103), mysterious nocturnal women akin to *fades* (these women are indeed alluded to in Sand's novel *Jeanne*). The narrative of the second local, "La Groac'h de l'Île du Lok" concerns an old woman, a "druidesse" (105 n.1) who has "powers over the elements" ["puissances sur les éléments" (105 n.1)], with the ability to turn humans into animals (she has turned several husbands into fish). Two other tales are included in this section.

The third setting, "Troisième Foyer: Pays de Cornouailles. l'Île de Saint-Nicolas," opens with the narrator arriving in a coastal Breton village seeking a boat. A widow and her son take him in theirs, but a storm forces them to take refuge on an island where he hears four magical stories of supernatural happenings from others sheltering there.

The final "foyer" is in Vannes where the narrator tells us there are fewer "traditions populaires" than elsewhere in Brittany because of "the invasion of the French language" ["l'envahissement de la langue française" (203)], displacing the native Breton dialect. However, during a storm the narrator finds shelter with a family who speak only Breton and don't understand standard French. That evening they tell tales "en Breton" (219) (which are, of course, translated by the author for the French-speaking reader). One of these, the "Récit du boucher: Les Pierres de Plouhinec" ["The Butcher's Tale: The Stones of Plouhinec" (268)], is of particular interest, as it records the clash between pagan beliefs and Christianity. It opens on Christmas Eve, a night when legend holds that animals are given speech in recompense for having been in attendance at the birth of Jesus. (Jeremias Gotthelf also had a story about the speaking animals on Christmas Eve — "Merkwürdige Reden gehört zu Krebsligen zwischen zwölf und ein Uhr in der Heiligen Nacht" [1846].) A tramp sleeping in a stable hears a donkey and a cow reveal that "the stones in the heath at Plouhinec are going to drink at the river . . . and while they're gone the treasures that they hide will be accessible" ["les pierres de la bruyère de Plouhinec vont boire à la rivière . . . et que, pendant ce temps, les trésors qu'elles cachent restent à découvert" (271)]. One needs certain herbs to avoid being crushed when the stones return to their places, and they also will require the death of a Christian. Hearing this, Bernèz, a Christian worker who needs money in order to marry Rozenn, goes with the tramp and gathers the gold. The tramp plans to sacrifice Bernèz to the returning stones but a stone on which Bernèz had carved a cross protects the Christian and crushes the tramp. The story (like many in this collection) shows Christian magic overpowering pagan.

One other early, though less significant, French local-colorist was Rudolphe Töpffer whose *Nouvelles genevoises* (1839) was set in Suisse Romande in and around Geneva. These stories, construed as memoirs of the author's youth, are mainly travelogues recounting journeys into the surrounding mountains. Details of local color, including information on the inhabitants' dialects and customs, are provided but there is little plot or thematic development.

Even Victor Hugo ventured into the local-color genre with his *Travailleurs de la mer* (1866), which he wrote in and around the Isle of Guernsey where he was in exile during the period of the Second Empire. The novel is about the failed romance of a fisherman, Gilliatt, a kind of maverick who is seen by locals to have magical powers. The work includes many details about local vegetation, history, and customs.

But the most important vein in the French local-color movement (along with Sand and the Courbet circle) was "l'École Occitane" (1860–90), which included the novels of Ferdinand Fabre and Léon Cladel, whose works are set in the southern region of France, Languedoc. Both were greatly influenced by Sand (Fabre said "he learned the art in her school" ["qu'il a appris l'art à son école" (Vernois 55)]), and both seem also to have absorbed the political perspective of the Courbet circle. Cladel in fact frequented the brasserie where the Courbet writers gathered and discussed with them Proudhon's socialist theories, according to Paul Vernois (80). Both attempted to inject a greater realism into the local-color genre but their characters retain the sense of innocent (and perhaps unrealistic) integrity of Sand's.

The first of the Occitane *romans champêtres* to appear was Fabre's *Les Courbezon*, which was written between 1857 and 1861, and published in *La Revue contemporaine* in 1861 and in book form in 1862. The novel concerns the struggles of l'abbé Courbezon to keep his parish afloat financially during the post-revolutionary period. It was envisaged by Fabre as part of a series, "Scènes de la vie cléricale," and it dwells at length on the intra-clerical political conflicts of the time. Thus, although it includes extensive ethnographic details of local color, it has less to do with rural peasant culture than with the ins and outs of institutional clerical struggles.

Fabre's next novel, *Le Chevrier* [The Goatherd] (1867), however, deals centrally with a peasant and his rustic world and thus is more within the mainstream of the *roman champêtre* than its predecessor. As with Sand's work, a frame narrative is established wherein the peasant Érembert, now an old man, recounts his story to a Parisian author, who vows to "retrace faithfully the story which the peasant of Larzac gave me" ["retracer fidèle-ment, le récit que me fit le paysan de Larzac" (8)]. The peasant, for his part, explains, "your father . . . tells me that you live in Paris so as to tell stories there in printed books" ["votre père . . . me dit que vous viviez à Paris pour y raconter des histoires en des livres imprimés" (5)], that "you make your living from writing stories down to amuse those Parisians in Paris" ["vous faites métier de coucher par écrit des histoires pour amuser ces Parisiens à Paris" (9)] — projecting a certain self-irony on the part of the author. Érembert's story is essentially a tragic romance — he loves a woman who loves someone else, after whose death she commits suicide, leaving her son to Érembert to raise; however, at least equally important is Érembert's relationship with his goats, particularly the lead goat, Scripant, "my best friend" ["mon meilleur ami" (257)]. He praises him as

the most handsome, strong, valiant of nature's creatures that one had ever known in the Hautes Cévennes [mountains]. Scripant had intelligence and knowledge to more than match the schoolmaster at Navacelle. [le plus beau, le plus fort, le plus vaillant aux entrprises de la nature qu'on eût jamais connu aux Cévennes-Hautes. Scipant avait de l'esprit et de la connaissance à en revendre au maître de l'école de Navacelle.] (70)

Based on Scripant, Érembert concludes that "animals love better, regret more, take greater offense than we do, because, when they love, it's forever" ["bêtes aiment mieux, regrettent mieux, s'estomaquent mieux que nous tous, car, aimant, c'est pour toujours" (111)] — a sad comment perhaps on his failed human relations. Érembert even wonders if fallen humans were once innocent animals: "Ah, monsieur, how beautiful animals are. It has often occurred to me that before being hard, querulous, wicked men, we were perhaps gentle, affectionate, peaceful animals" ["Ah, monsieur, que c'est donc beau les bêtes. Il m'est souvent fois venu l'idée qu'avant d'être hommes durs, querelleurs, méchants, avions-nous été peut-être animaux doux, affectueux, paisibles" (16)].

Érembert also loves the natural environment: "Monsieur, I was born in the country, and I take pleasure in the trees, the beautiful plants, and even the rocks of our Larzac . . . how much sweeter than humans are all these things and all these creatures!" ["Monsieur, je suis né à la campagne, et je prends plaisir aux arbres, aux belles herbes et mêmement aux rochers de notre Larzac . . . combien toutes ces choses et toutes ces êtres son plus doux que les humains!" (58)].

When he fears being shipped off to Africa in the army, having volunteered to substitute for his rival — the ultimate sacrifice for his beloved — Érembert realizes how deeply he loves his native region, feeling a kind of "mal du pays" avant la lettre. "Ah, monsieur, how beautiful one's native country and what a great number of ties one finds attach one's soul and body there . . . And so I feared never seeing them again once over there" ["Ah, monsieur, que c'est beau le pays natal, et quelle quantité de liens de l'âme et le corps s'y trouvent attachés . . . Eh bien, je craignais de ne plus les revoir par là-bas." (305)].

Léon Cladel's *Le Bouscassié* (1967) — a dialect term meaning "woodcutter who lives in the woods" ["bûcheron habitant les bois" (7)] — brings to culmination, and one might say perfection, several strands of the *roman champêtre* tradition: the growth and development of a Rousseauian wild child, the cross-class romance, the sensitivity to and compassion for animals, an animist view of nature, and a corresponding love and appreciation of the home region. As in Fabre's work, local dialect terms are occasionally included and explained but the main text — as with all the other local-colorists — remains in standard French. The novel is set in and around Quercy in the Languedoc region.

Guillaume Inot, an abandoned wild child, who is nursed by a dog ("une chienne allaitant" (10)], grows up mainly among animals whose behavior in the early years he takes as model.

> Paddling in the pond with the ducks and geese, crawling under the pensive oxen before the manger, hanging around the dog who had nursed him, sometimes walking on all fours like his wetnurse, and sometimes on two in the manner of poultry, he conducted himself in imitation of his companions whom he had taken for models. [Barbotant dans la mare avec les canards et les oies, rampant sous les bœufs pensifs devant la crèche, fréquentant la chienne qui l'avait allaité, tantôt marchant à quatre pattes comme sa mère la nourrice, et tantôt sur deux avec des allures de volaille, il se dirigeait à l'instar de ses compagnons qu'il avail pris pour modèles.] (12)

He understands animal language and sees more than most humans what is going on in the animals' world.

> Initiated from his earliest years into their exchanges and speaking their language he undoubtedly understood amazingly what the animals said . . . "Deaf as you are," he said one day to some diggers who asked him why he was sad and groaning, "don't you hear over there . . . that ewe who is crying and calling back her lamb whom they have taken or killed?" [Initié, dès son plus bas âge, à leur commerce et parlant à leur langage, il comprenait sans doute à merveille ce que disaient les animaux . . . "Sourds que vous êtes, dit-il un jour à des terrassiers qui lui demandaient pourquoi il était chagrin et gémissait, n'entendez-vous pas là-bas . . . cette brebis qui bêle et réclame son agneau qu'on lui a pris ou tué"?] (26)

There are several other instances where Guillaume shows compassion for and/or saves animals from harm. In a lengthy scene he cares for a dying mule and insists on giving the animal a decent burial when the owner wants to dismember the body to sell the skin (27–34). Later, at some risk to himself, he intervenes in a cruel sport where rats are being set on fire (133–5). And while consulting a fortune-teller/witch about how to avoid the military draft, he refuses to permit as part of the procedure a ritual decapitation of a bird (256).

Like Huriel in Sand's *Les Maîtres sonneurs*, Guillaume has a sense of the aliveness of the forest: "the trees were his brothers. The Trees! What compassion, what terror he felt when they fell under his axe . . . The trees spoke, he said, they complained about the one who was harming them" ["les arbres étaient ses frères. Les arbres! Il éprouvait on ne sait quelle compassion, on ne sait quelle terreur, quend ils tombaient sous sa hache . . . Les arbres parlaient, disait-il, ils se plaignaient de ce qui leur faisait du mal" (22)].

At the same time he resents the government's decision to cut down an entire section of the forest — "planned mutilation" ["mutilé à dessein" (332)] where "the woodmen [were] charged by the municipal authority with wiping out a corner of his beloved forest" ["bûcherons chargés par l'authorité municipale d'abolir un coin de sa forêt cherie" (320)]. Seeing the "mutilated trunks," he seems to hear an "almost human lamentation . . . a long cry of agony" ["les troncs mutilés . . . [une] lamentation presque humaine . . . [une] longe plainte d'agonie" (320)].

Guillaume experiences the forest in maternal terms, recalling the pre-oedipal, presymbolic character of the rural landscape in Sand's *Jeanne*. "His native forest! His mother . . . 'Mother, mother, I don't want to leave you, I want to live with you'" ["Sa forêt natale! sa mère . . . 'Mère, mère, je ne veux pas te quitter, je veux vivre auprès de toi'" (320)]. In the forest he senses the "universal soul" and understood "that mysterious language spoken by the seas, the mountains, the woods" ["l'âme universelle" "cette mystérieuse langue que parlent les mers, les monts, les bois" (319)].

Like Érembert in *Le Chevrier*, Guillaume becomes particularly appreciative of his native region when faced with the military draft — a signal institution of modernity that pulled people out of their native regions. "The [mountain] heights in the colors of ochre and ultramarine . . . Alas! I cannot describe the sublime beauty . . . The immense plains of Languedoc" ["les hauteurs d'ocre et d'outremer . . . hélas! Je ne peux rendre la sublime beauté . . . Les plaines immenses de Languedoc" (192)]. "And they would condemn me to never again see that!" ["Et l'on me condamnerait à ne jamais plus voir cela!" (194)].

The novel ends more or less happily. Guillaume cuts off a finger to avoid the draft, making himself one of the "mutilés," and parental obstacles to his courtship of Janille, a village girl, give way, so the two wed and set up their household in the woods.

With the exception perhaps of Eugène Le Roy's more politically driven local-color novels of the 1890s, Cladel's *Le Bouscassié* represents the high-water mark of the French *roman champêtre*, which, along with several of Sand's novels — *Jeanne*, *La Petite Fadette*, *La Mare au diable* — found its finest expression therein.

The French local-colorists, the writers of *romans champêtres*, therefore presented not so much a resistance to or even a critique of the growing hegemony of modernity — though examples of both in their novels have been pointed out — as proposed an alternative vision, a counter-world, one untouched by capitalism and industrialism, bourgeois property concerns, scientific rationalism, even liberal individualistic humanism. It is, rather, a communal, animistic realm where "thine and mine" are minimized and where humans, animals, and the natural world live in relatively ecological harmony. In some works — Sand's especially, but also *Le Bouscassié* — that world is maternal, pre-oedipal — governed by local emotional knowledge and where people speak not just a nonstandard regional dialect but a nonhuman language or dialect through which they communicate with all life-forms.

NOTE

1 Sources on French translations include Rafroidi; Zellweger; *Maria Edgeworth in France and Switzerland*, ed. Colvin, 289–90; "Bibliography of Scottish Literature in Translation," available online at <www.nls.uk/catalogues/resources/boslit/index> (accessed 4 December 2007); WorldCat (online).

A Sketch of the Local-Color
Movement in Other Countries

While the origin and early development of the local-color movement occurred mainly in the countries treated in this study — Ireland, Scotland, Germany, and France — the tradition also emerged and flourished in other countries of Europe, as well as in the Americas. In some cases the genre seems to have arisen spontaneously; more often it was stimulated by the influence of the core European writers — Scott, Edgeworth, Auerbach, and Sand.

The first Scandinavian provincial novel — *Hemmet* [The Home] by Swedish writer Fredrika Bremer (1801–65) — appeared as early as 1839, with her *Grannarna* [The Neighbors] following in 1842. Björnstjerne Björnson (1832–1910) of Norway published several peasant novels, including *Synnöve Solbakken* (1857), *Arne* (1858), and others.

The Spanish local-color school, the *novela costumbrista*, was inaugurated by Fernán Caballero (1796–1877) (pen name of Cecilia Böhl de Faber). Her novel *La Gaviota* [The Seagull], set in Andalusia, first appeared in 1849, followed by *Clemencia* (1852), *La familia de Alvareda* (1856), and others. Another important Spanish writer in the provincial tradition was José Maria de Pereda (1833–1906), with *Escenas montañesas* (1864), *Tipos y paisajes* (1871), *Sotileza* (1883), and others.

In Italy the movement, labeled *verismo*, retained many local-color elements but bordered on naturalism in its grim realism. Giovanni Verga (1840–1922), who depicted the hardscrabble lives of Sicilian peasants in a series of works, is perhaps the best-known representative of this school. "Nedda" (1874), a story about a Sicilian peasant girl, is considered his first significant work in the genre, followed by *Primavera* (1877), *Vita dei campi* (1880), *I Malavoglia* (1881), and *Novelle rusticane* (1883). His best-known work is "La cavalleria rusticana," a story in the latter collection. Another important Italian local-colorist was the prolific Matilde Sarao (1856–1927) whose *Leggende Napolitane* (1881) was set in Naples. Her best-known work is *Il paese di Cuccagna* (1890).

The Russian regionalist movement was heavily influenced by the works of George Sand, as reflected in the term *zhorzhzandism* [George Sandism] used to designate it. Ivan Turgenev (1818–83) was a great admirer of hers, as well as of Auerbach (whom he visited in Germany) and of Maria Edgeworth whose influence he acknowledged. His novel A *Sportsman's Sketches* (1847) was said to be written in imitation of Sand's *romans champêtres*. Leo Tolstoy was also a Sand and Auerbach enthusiast.

Latin America had its *novela de la tierra* (see Jordan); Quebec its *roman de la terre* (see Söderlind). In his study of Latin American *regionalismo* David M. Jordan sees the genre emerging as part of the "postcolonial condition" (4) with writers registering a "'metaphysical clash' within the colonial culture, a binary opposition" (132 n.3). "Many of the authors . . . were active outside their literary careers in struggles against the hegemony of centralized political structures" (10).

In his Preface to *Sonhos d'ouro* (1872) the Brazilian writer José de Alencar wrote:

> When the light of civilization, which suddenly alters the local colour, has not spread rapidly, there can still be found its original purity, without adulteration, the simple life of our country — traditions, customs, languages — all with a totally Brazilian character.

(quoted by Jordan 17)

His purpose was to prove to "an audience conversant with European culture" that Brazilian culture "is *every bit as good as* the culture from which it was born" (quoted by Jordan 18) — a purpose very similar to that announced by Maria Edgeworth and Sir Walter Scott.

The local-color movement also arose in the United States. As elsewhere, its emergence appears to have been partly spontaneous and partly due to the influence of the European local-color writers — the latter an aspect of American literary history grossly underestimated by Americanist critics.

Nineteenth-century American literary regionalism may be and has been divided into two camps: one, the "Old Southwest Humor" school consisting of mostly male authors, who used dialect and eccentric locals for humorous ends, expressed a kind of crude slapstick humor, and often featured trickster or prankster rogue characters. Included in this school — which culminated in later writers such as Bret Harte, Hamlin Garland, and Mark Twain — were Thomas Bangs Thorpe, George Washington Harris, and Augustus Baldwin Longstreet (on this school, see Cox). Their works were generally set in what is today the southeast of the country in the antebellum period. Despite having the trappings of other local-color works — the frame setting with an educated outsider as narrator/author, the use of regional dialect and manners, and the often expressed desire on the part of the author to preserve these against homogenizing trends — the "Old Southwest" works differ from the European local-color writings in that regional culture is not presented seriously or indeed sympathetically (a point made by Fetterley and Pryse 1992, xv, xvii–xviii).

The real heirs of the European local-color tradition in the United States were the women writers of the New England local-color school: Harriet Beecher Stowe (1811–96), Rose Terry Cooke (1827–92), Sarah Orne Jewett (1849–1909), and Mary E. Wilkins Freeman (1852–1930) — the other major branch of nineteenth-century American provincial writing (see Donovan, *New England Local Color Literature*, for an overview of their work). In their writing we find rural and village settings not unlike those described by their European predecessors: a precapitalist world of use-value production and *mētis*, still largely untouched — though threatened — by modernist homogenization and standardization. It is a world the writers are themselves emotionally attached to, take seriously for the most part — though at times critically — and whose history and customs they seek to record and preserve. As in the European works we find numerous eccentric, unassimilated personages treated respectfully or with sympathetic humor and a preponderance of strong women characters: Polly Mariner, for example, in several Cooke stories, Grandmother Badger in Stowe's *Oldtown Folks*, Mrs. Todd in Jewett's *Country of the Pointed Firs*, Mother in Freeman's story "The Revolt of 'Mother,'" and many others. As in Gotthelf's and Sand's works, the world depicted by the New England local-colorists is a matriarchal realm — the world of Demeter.[1] The American writers also were scrupulous to capture local dialects and often used the frame format developed by the Europeans of an educated outsider transmitting indigenous oral culture and history and committing it to print.

The tradition they forged was bequeathed to numerous other writers — mostly women — in other regions of the country, including Mary Noailles Murfree (Tennessee), Grace King (Louisiana, Creole culture), Alice Dunbar-Nelson (Louisiana, Creole and African-American cultures), Edward Eggleston (Indiana), Charles Chesnutt (the South, African-American culture), Sui Sin Far (the West Coast, Chinese-American culture), Zitkala-Ša (the West, Native American culture), and many others. (See Foote; Campbell; Fetterley and Pryse, *Writing out of Place*, for further discussion of these writers.)

Laurence Buell notes that American women writers seem to have been less "troubled about extricating themselves from the shadow cast by Europe than were their male counterparts" (436 n.1). By "male counterparts" Buell is here referring to the major writers of the so-called "American Renaissance" (Whitman, Emerson, Melville, Thoreau), who were concerned about ending, as Emerson famously put it in "The American Scholar" (1837), "our day of dependence" on European culture.

Perhaps because of the still strong sway this idea has in American Studies, scholars have long neglected the continuing and powerful influence European works had on American writers (especially, apparently, women writers) through the nineteenth century (and indeed later). Such was certainly the case with the European local-color writings, most of which were readily available in English translations and American editions soon after their original publication.

The most popular of the Europeans were Berthold Auerbach and George Sand, along with, of course, Sir Walter Scott and Maria Edgeworth. Auerbach's *Schwarzwälder Dorfgeschichten* appeared in English translation as early as 1846 as *Village Tales from the Black Forest* (translation by Meta Taylor). A later translation by Charles Goepp was published in Philadelphia in 1858 as *The Germans at Home: Berthold Auerbach's Village Stories of the Black Forest*, a title shortened for a 1869 New York publication as *Black Forest Village Stories*, which ran through six subsequent editions. Another edition, *German Tales*, was published by Roberts Brothers in Boston in 1869. Reviews of Auerbach appeared in major U. S. journals beginning in the late 1840s, and a survey article, "Berthold Auerbach," by T. S. Perry appeared in the *Atlantic Monthly* in 1874. The lead story in *Schwarzwälder Dorfgeschichten*, "Der Tolpatch," was translated as "Young Aloys; or, the Gawk from America" and published in *Lippincott's Magazine* in 1877. One of the earliest New England local-colorists, Eliza Buckminster Lee, translated an Auerbach novella, "Barfuessele," as *The Barefooted Maiden*, published in 1862. (Lee's own *Sketch of a New-England Village in the Last Century* appeared in 1838.) In fact, as one critic notes, Auerbach's "popularity [in the U. S.] reached phenomenal heights, judging by the numerous translations and editions and the widespread attention given to him in journals" (Puknat 975). One of the leading New England local-colorists, Mary E. Wilkins Freeman, is known to have read Auerbach's stories in her youth (Foster 33).

Jeremias Gotthelf's works appear to have been less well known. His *Leiden und Freuden eines Schulmeisters* was the first of his works to receive an English translation, appearing in London in 1864 as *Joys and Sorrows of a Schoolmaster*. *Geld und Geist* was published as *Wealth and Welfare* in London and New York in 1866. Adalbert Stifter's stories appeared in English translation in the 1850s and 1860s. "The Condor" appeared, for example, in a 1850 issue of *Democratic Review*. Alexandre Weill's stories were published as *Village Tales from Alsatia* in London in 1848. The works by the Eastern European Jewish writers also were translated and published in the U. S. Karl Emil Franzos's *The Jews of Barnow* appeared in New York in 1883, and a selection of Leopold Kompert's stories was published as *Christian & Leah & Other Ghetto Stories*, also in New York, in 1895. Even

Zschokke's *Das Goldmacher-Dorf* appeared in New York in 1846 as *The Goldmaker's Village*.

Of course, the works of the Celtic writers were readily available in the U. S. soon after their original publication — including all of Scott's novels, which, as elsewhere, were hugely popular and influential. Elizabeth Hamilton's *Cottagers of Glenburnie* was available in the U. S. as early as 1808, published in New York. Maria Edgeworth's *Castle Rackrent* was published in a Boston edition in 1814; *The Absentee* in 1812, *Ennui* in 1810; and a complete edition of her *Tales and Novels* (18 vols.) appeared in 1832–34 in New York. By 1808, two years after its original publication, Lady Morgan's *The Wild Irish Girl* had gone through six U. S. editions. James Hogg's *Winter Evening Tales* were also very popular; the first U. S. edition, which was published in Philadelphia in 1836, went through ten subsequent editions. Galt's *Annals of the Parish* appeared in 1820 (Philadelphia); *The Ayrshire Legatees* in 1823, and *The Provost* in 1822. Interestingly, John Galt also wrote novels set in North America. *Laurie Todd* (1830) is about Canadian settlers in New York; *Bogle Corbet; or the Emigrants* (1831) followed (see Shain).

George Sand's works were also translated for American readers soon after their French publication. One of her translators was Annie Adams Fields (Gollin 37). As the wife of Boston publisher James T. Fields and, after his death, partner of Sarah Orne Jewett, Annie Fields was really the effective hub of the New England local-color school (see Donovan, *New England Local Color Literature*, Chapter 3). *La Mare au diable* appeared in 1847 (New York) as *The Devil's Pool. La Petite Fadette* was published as *Fadette: A Domestic Story* in 1851 and shortly thereafter under the title *Fanchon, the Cricket*, which went through several editions. *François le champi* appeared as *Francis the Waif* in 1889, and *The Miller of Angibault* was published in Boston in 1863. *Mauprat* was also published in Boston in 1870 and *My Sister Jeannie* (*Jeanne*) in 1874. A six-volume English translation of Sand's œuvre published to that date was available as *The Works* as early as 1847 (London publication).

Sand's work also received numerous reviews in American journals. A lengthy (unsigned) article, "George Sand," appeared in the November 1861 issue of the *Atlantic Monthly*, and in 1876 at the time of her death Thomas Sergeant Perry published another discussion of her work, "George Sand," in the *Atlantic Monthly*, in which he expressed high praise for her *romans champêtres*. Of the character Jeanne he wrote, "it would be hard to find in contemporary fiction a figure of greater poetic worth" (450). A more negative view was expressed in Caroline Kirkland's "George Sand and the Journeyman Joiner" (*Union Magazine*, November 1847), but it focused mainly on Sand's unconventional life-style, her support of divorce, and critique of marriage (issues seen only incidentally in her *romans champêtres*). Kirkland's *A New Home — Who'll Follow?* (1838) was itself a variant of the local-color novel, providing a humorous critique of life and manners on the Michigan frontier. Her primary model was, however, the Englishwoman Mary Russell Mitford's nonfiction series of "village sketches," *Our Village* (1824–32), themselves cast under the influence of Maria Edgeworth.

The works of the other French provincial writers do not seem to have ever been translated into English. In the case of the Occitane school in particular, this seems an unfortunate loss for the American reader.[2]

While Harriet Beecher Stowe is, of course, best remembered for *Uncle Tom's Cabin* (first published serially 1851–52), she was also one of the leading figures in the New England local-color school; indeed, she inaugurated the genre with her story "A New England Sketch" (later retitled "Uncle Lot"), which appeared in *Western Monthly* in 1834 (discussed in Chapter One). That story and several others were collected as *The Mayflower; or, Sketches of Scenes and Characters among the Descendants of the Pilgrims*, published by Harper in New York in 1843. Her subsequent local-color novels included *The Minister's Wooing* (first published serially in the 1858 volume of the *Atlantic Monthly*, followed by book publication in 1859); *The Pearl of Orr's Island: A Story of the Coast of Maine*, 1862; and *Oldtown Folks*, 1869.

Probably the greatest literary influence on Stowe was Sir Walter Scott. Numerous critics have pointed out the extent of that influence (Kirkham 76; Westbrook 24–5). Reading *Uncle Tom's Cabin*, for example, in tandem with a Scott novel one cannot but be struck by the narrative techniques Stowe picked up from her Scottish predecessor. That influence should not be surprising. While Stowe was growing up, Scott's "Waverley novels were in every house" (Brooks 56). Reading Scott's novels aloud became "a Beecher family institution"; a game was played to see "who could recall the most of incident and passage from Scott's novels" (Hedrick 20). At the time she began writing *Uncle Tom's Cabin* in the fall of 1850, Stowe had "a stack of Walter Scott's novels on her bedside table" (Wilson 243) and was systematically re-reading them in order of publication.

Scott's influence may also be seen in her local-color work. Indeed, it may well be his example that led her to write about her native region; noting Scott's "reproductions of Scottish dialect, scenery, life, and, above all, character" led her to realize that "analogous material was available in New England" (Westbrook 24). Where Stowe came "nearest to Scott," Perry Westbrook claims, was "in her burning pride of locality" (24). Fittingly, on a trip to Scotland after the publication of *Uncle Tom's Cabin*, Stowe paid a visit to Scott's grave.

In an interesting article included in *Transatlantic Stowe* (2006) Monika Elbert draws comparisons between *The Pearl of Orr's Island* and *The Bride of Lammermoor*, arguing that "Scott's legacy to Stowe appears in her transformation of the New England landscape into a supernatural world in which the boundaries between magic and nature become indistinct" (46). Stowe's novel is "indebted to Scott for the merging of pagan with spiritual elements" (61).

Maria Edgeworth was another important influence. Her work was also read to Stowe as a child, and it may well be, as Joan Hedrick suggests, that Edgeworth provided her with a model for the use of dialect (210–11). Certainly Edgeworth's antipretentious satirical humor, seen in *Castle Rackrent* and elsewhere, is one that echoes through all of Stowe's work as well. In another article in *Transatlantic Stowe*, Clíona Ó Gallchoir argues for the influence of the "Irish National Tale," especially developed by Edgeworth and Lady Morgan, on *Uncle Tom's Cabin* (24–45).

Stowe may also have been influenced by George Sand, though her attitude toward the French author was ambivalent. Scandalized at first, like Caroline Kirkland, by Sand's love life and her endorsement of "free divorce and free love" (Hedrick 373), Stowe nevertheless seemed to change her opinion after Sand's rapturous review of *Uncle Tom's Cabin* appeared in *La Presse* in 1852. (The French translation, *Le Père Tom; ou, Vie des nègres en Amérique*, appeared almost immediately after the U. S. publication. The French title was soon thereafter changed to *La Case de l'oncle Tom*.) Indeed, in her Introduction to a later edition of *Uncle Tom's Cabin*, Stowe included Sand's review in its entirety, calling Sand "one of the greatest powers in the literary world of France" (Stowe, "Author's Introduction," lxxv). "Eventually," in any event, Stowe "read everything that George Sand wrote" (Hedrick 266).

Stowe herself had a considerable impact on European writers. After the phenomenal success of *Uncle Tom's Cabin*, which was eventually translated into nearly 60 languages, with nearly 60 editions in French alone and over 80 in German, Stowe's local-color novels were readily translated. *The Mayflower* appeared in France in 1853 as *Nouvelles americaines*, followed by several subsequent editions, and in Germany the same year as *Die Maiblume: Bilder und Charaktere*. *The Minister's Wooing* received a French translation in 1860 and a German one in 1859; *The Pearl of Orr's Island*, two French translations, 1862; and *Oldtown Folks*, a German one in 1870.

La Perle de l'île d'Orr likely influenced Victor Hugo in his *Les Travailleurs de la mer*, which has many of the same elements as the Stowe novel. Interestingly, Hugo's novel was translated into English by Annie Adams Fields, published as *Toilers of the Sea* by Harper in New York in 1866, a copy of which was owned by Sarah Orne Jewett.

Stowe's European influence also extended to Berthold Auerbach. *Uncle Tom's Cabin*, which was translated as *Onkel Toms Hütte*, inspired him to write a novel about slavery, *Das Landhaus am Rhein* (1869). The novel concerns a German former slave-trader who tries to hide his past and whose children try to come to terms with their father's evil legacy. In the process the son reads *Onkel Toms Hütte* and is brought to tears. Various characters resemble those in Stowe's novel, as do the philosophical debates about slavery (see Maclean, 62–8, for a full discussion).

Sarah Orne Jewett, widely considered the greatest of the New England local-color writers, was also heavily influenced by the European counterparts, particularly by George Sand, although, like most American women writers of the day, she also undoubtedly read and learned from Maria Edgeworth, Sir Walter Scott, and possibly Berthold Auerbach. Her celebrated comment in her Preface to the second (1893) edition of *Deephaven* (a remark she attributes to Plato) that "the best thing that can be done for the people of a state is to make them acquainted with one another" (Jewett, Preface 3) is a curious echo of a discussion in Maria Edgeworth's "Essay on Irish Bulls" in which a character expresses a hope that the Irish, Scotch, and English may become "better acquainted with one another" through the *Act of Union* (146). And, in a 1895 interview Jewett stated, "The busier I get, the more time I take to read the 'Waverley' novels" (Jewett, Interview 284).

But it was the Sand influence that was probably the greatest. A portrait of the French writer hung in Jewett's home, and she once said she was going to learn French in order to read Sand in the original (Fields, ed., *Letters* 38). (Curiously, Jewett doesn't seem to have been put off by Sand's flamboyant romantic liaisons, as Kirkland and Stowe evidently were.)

In her 1869 diary Jewett mentions reading *Fanchon the Cricket*, which was a translation of *La Petite Fadette*, a work that seems to have deeply affected her, as traces of it may be seen in Jewett's own writings. In particular, the tomboyish life-style of Nan Prince in Jewett's novel *A Country Doctor* (1884) very much resembles that of Fadette. Like her French counterpart Nan runs freely through the fields and grows up untrammeled by civilized restraints. Particularly interesting is the fact that both authors raise the question of gender identity with their respective characters (recall that Fadette is accused of being a *mâlot*; i.e., too "mannish"). Similar concerns are raised about Nan Prince, though the author deflects them by protesting that Nan "showed no sign of being . . . mannish" (Jewett, *Country Doctor* 160), even though she was inclined from an early age toward masculine pursuits and activities (for a further discussion see Donovan "Nan Prince"). Jewett's Nan, however, unlike Fadette, never conforms to traditionally female roles but becomes a doctor, then an almost entirely masculine profession.

Traces of Sand's novel *Jeanne* may also be seen in Jewett's work — in Sylvie, the young girl in "A White Heron" (1886), who rejects the male ornithologist-hunter to protect her woodland companion, the heron; in the shepherdess Esther in "A Dunnet Shepherdess" (1899) and "William's Wedding" (1910); even in Joanna, the solitary hermit in *The Country of the Pointed Firs*. One might also see aspects of Sand's Bricoline, the mad-woman in *Le Meunier d'Angibault*, in Joanna, who likewise was crushed by the loss of her beloved, curses God in rage, but instead of becoming violent toward others engages in lifelong self-flagellation in exile on her island retreat. Jewett also adopted the narrative technique used by Sand and other European local-colorists, that of the educated outsider narrator encountering a native storyteller who then relates the embedded tale.

Perhaps the most powerful evidence of the Sand influence lies in Jewett's inclusion of a passage from Sand's *Légendes rustiques* in her Preface to the second edition of her first novel *Deephaven* (1877).

> In rustic neighborhoods [Jewett wrote] there will always be those whom George Sand had in mind when she wrote her delightful preface for "Légendes Rustiques": "Le paysan est donc, si l'on peut ainsi dire, le seul historien qui nous reste des temps antehistorique. Honneur et profit intellectuel à qui se consacrent à la recherche de ses traditions merveilleuses de chaque hameau qui rassemblées ou groupées, comparées entre elle et minutieusement disséquées, jetteraient peut-être de grands lueurs sur la nuit profonde des âges primitifs."

> (Jewett, Preface 5)

The French passage (which Jewett did not translate) reads:

> The peasant thus, if one may put it this way, is the only historian remaining from prehistoric times. Honor and intellectual reward [are due] to those who consecrate themselves to searching out these marvelous traditions from every hamlet which, collectively grouped together, compared with one another, minutely dissected, may perhaps throw much light on the deep night of primitive ages.

In her Preface Jewett notes how "tradition and time-honored custom" in the New England of her day were being "swept away together by the irresistible current" of modernity (4). And like her European predecessors she said she was motivated to write her local-color works out of a desire to counter stereotypical and mistaken views of the country people of her region, "the caricatured Yankee, striped trousers, bell-crowned hat, and all" (3).

Beginning in Ireland with Maria Edgeworth's *Castle Rackrent*, continuing in Scotland, Germany, and France, spreading eventually throughout the Western world, writers — themselves for the most part of the educated elite — likewise sought to rescue country people from ridicule, caricature, and stereotype, and to preserve ancient customs and traditions that were threatened with erasure and assimilation by the forces of modernity. In the case of the Irish and Scottish writers it was a matter of valorizing an oppressed ethnic Celtic culture against Anglo domination, denigration, and repression. The German writers — many of whom were Jewish — were also concerned to preserve the uniqueness of regional ethnic culture, including that in Jewish enclaves, against assimilation into dominant empires. In France, similarly, writers evinced a concern to preserve the ancient native cultures and traditions of Franche-Comté, Berry, Alsace, Bretagne, and Languedoc. And in the United States, where the genre flourished after the Civil War, regionalist writers likewise resisted the call for national homogenization and standardization. All these writers show a respect for nonconformity, eccentricity, and diversity, and treat their irregular, unassimilated characters sympathetically.

They also treat their characters' premodern culture with appreciation, considering that it may offer positive alternatives to modern institutions and ideologies. The world they describe is a precapitalist, self-sustaining economy of use-value production governed for the most part by a kinship ethic of communal care and loyalty. Included as part of the kinship network were animals, to whom people were as attached as to other humans. The species boundary was much less well defined than in the Cartesian ideology of modernity where animals are often objectified, cast in opposition to human subjects. Gender boundaries were also less rigid in the premodern world depicted in these works. We have seen numerous examples of powerful women who behave forcefully in "mannish" ways or engage ably in masculine activities, and there seems as well to be more of a tolerance for same-sex liaisons as being within the norm, as yet unstigmatized as "deviant" by modernist pseudosciences like sexology.

Modern medicine and science are treated skeptically in the premodern societies depicted in local-color literature. Many characters are adept in herbal medicine, a mostly matrilineal tradition, and many resist agricultural "improvements," such as the Highland Clearances, which not only destroyed traditional practices (though the methods they introduced may have been more efficient and therefore more profitable) but also displaced thousands of destitute peasants, depriving them of their traditional livelihood.

There is also the fear that modern technologies, in failing to respect local knowledge and wisdom, will override and suppress them. For each locale is seen to have its own bioregional knowledge — its *mētis* — which is handed down from parent to child orally and practically. Unlike the broad universalizing sweep of Enlightenment theoretical knowledges, these local knowledges may be workable only in the micro-places in which they emerged and evolved. But, as they are not exchangeable according to universally fixed standards, they are not workable in a global exchange economy and thus are not viable in the modern world.

The premodern world described in local-color literature is an oral culture, and the language spoken is a locally specific, proudly different, dialect. Stories, wisdom, and knowledge are passed around communally and handed down generationally. Most of the characters are illiterate; their thought processes are nonlinear, situational, and "poetic" — as George Sand tried to explain of her peasant Patience in *Mauprat*.

We found likewise in these works a widespread belief in the nonrational — a feeling that much lay beyond the ken of modern science and rationalism. Throughout European peasant culture there remained a pagan belief in invisible beings — fairies, the "good people," *fades* — whom one must take care not to offend, who influence events for good or ill. Moreover, many characters hold a basically animistic approach to nature, a sense that the natural world is infused with a living spirit, that there are no natural *objects*, all are subjects — and worthy of respect. It is not just animals who are thus perceived to be subjects but also trees, insects, even rock formations. It is a world enchanted with living spirits.

Finally, the local-color writers valorized *"Heimatlichkeit,"* the sense of being rooted in one's own particular locale, and fearing and resisting forces and powers that threatened to erase its unique qualities and character.

In this study I have hoped to shed some light on this lost literary tradition, to bring it back into view, and thereby aid in the resurrection of what Foucault called the "subjugated knowledges" of the premodern universe. Like the writers here considered, I believe that many of these offer positive alternatives to the institutions and ideologies of modernity that now rule our lives.

NOTES

1 In *After the Fall: The Demeter-Persephone Myth in Wharton, Cather, and Glasgow* I discuss how that world was falling apart in the early twentieth century.
2 Sources on translations include Hathaway; Waidson, "Jeremias Gotthelf's Reception"; Parks and Temple; *The National Union Catalog, Pre-1956 Imprints*; WorldCat (online).

Works Cited and Other Relevant Titles

Aldrich, Ruth I. *John Galt.* Boston, MA: Twayne, 1978.

Anderson, Benedict. *Imagined Communities: Reflections on the Origin and Spread of Nationalism.* London: Verso, 1983.

Anderson, Carol, and Aileen M. Riddell. "The Other Great Unknowns: Women Fiction Writers of the Early Nineteenth Century." In *A History of Scottish Women's Writing,* ed. Douglas Gifford and Dorothy McMillan, 179–95. Edinburgh: Edinburgh University Press, 1997.

Aristotle. *Poetics [De Poetica].* In *The Basic Works of Aristotle,* ed. Richard McKeon, 1455–87. New York: Random House, 1941.

Ashcroft, Bill, Gareth Griffiths, and Helen Tiffin. *The Empire Writes Back: Theory and Practice in Post-Colonial Literatures.* London and New York: Routledge, 1989.

Auerbach, Berthold. *Samtliche Schwarzwälder Dorfgeschichten.* 10 vols. Vols. 1–2. Stuttgart, DE: F. G. Cotta'schen, 1884.

Bakhtin, M. M. *The Dialogic Imagination: Four Essays,* ed. Michael Holquist; trans. Caryl Emerson. Austin, TX: University of Texas Press, 1981.

Banim, John. *The Nowlans.* 1826. In *Tales by the O'Hara Family.* Vols. 1–2. Belfast: Appletree Press, 1992.

[———, and Michael]. *Crohoore of the Bill-Hook.* In *Tales of the O'Hara Family.* Vols. 1–2. London: W. Simpkin & R. Marshall, 1825.

Baur, Uwe. *Dorfgeschichte: Zur Entstehung und gesellschaftlichen Funktion einer literarischen Gattung im Vormärz.* Munich: William Fink, 1978.

Bellamy, Liz. "Regionalism and Nationalism: Maria Edgeworth, Walter Scott and the Definition of Britishness." In *The Regional Novel in Britain and Ireland, 1800–1990,* ed. K. D. M. Snell, 54–77. Cambridge: Cambridge University Press, 1998.

Berman, Marshall. *All That Is Solid Melts into Air: The Experience of Modernity.* New York: Simon & Schuster, 1982.

Bloch, Ernst. *Literary Essays,* ed. Werner Hamacher and David E. Wellbery; trans. Andrew Joron, et al. Stanford, CA: Stanford University Press, 1998.

Boisdeffre, Pierre de. Introduction to *La Petite Fadette* by George Sand, vii–xxiv. Paris: Livre de Poche, 1973.

Bourdieu, Pierre. *Ce que parler veut dire: L'Économie des échanges linguistiques.* Paris: Fayard, 1982.

Bowron, Jr., Bernard R. "Realism in America." *Comparative Literature* 3, no. 3 (1951):268–85.

Brooks, Van Wyck. *The Flowering of New England, 1815–65.* Garden City, NY: Garden City, 1946.

Brunton, Mary. *Discipline.* 1814. London: Pandora, 1986.

———. *Self-Control.* 1810–11. London: Pandora, 1986.

Buchon, Max. *Le Gouffre gourmand.* In *En Province: Scènes Franc-Comtoises,* 175–300. Paris: Michel Lévy, 1858.

———. *Le Matachin.* In *En Province: Scènes Franc-Comtoises,* 1–171. Paris: Michel Lévy, 1858.

Buell, Lawrence. "American Literary Emergence as a Postcolonial Phenomenon." *American Literary History* 4, no. 3 (Fall 1992):411–42.

Burke, Edmund. *Reflections on the Revolution in France.* 1790. Harmondsworth, UK: Penguin, 1968.

Butler, Marilyn. *Maria Edgeworth: A Literary Biography*. Oxford: Clarendon, 1972.

———. Introduction to *Castle Rackrent and Ennui*. London: Penguin, 1992.

Campbell, Donna. "Realism and Regionalism." In *A Companion to the Regional Literatures of America*, ed. Charles L. Crow, 92–110. Malden, MA: Blackwell, 2003.

Carleton, William. *Traits and Stories of the Irish Peasantry*. 1843. 2 vols. Savage, MD: Barnes & Noble, 1990.

Cary, Richard. *Sarah Orne Jewett Letters*. Waterville, ME: Colby College Press, 1967.

Certeau, Michel de, *et al. Une Politique de la langue: La Révolution française et les patois: l'enquête de Grégoire*. Paris: Gallimard, 1975.

Champfleury, M. *Les Oies de Noël*. Paris: Hachette, 1853.

Cladel, Léon. *Le Bouscassié*. 1867. Paris: Alphonse Lemerre, 1869.

Clarke, T. J. *Image of the People: Gustave Courbet and the Second French Republic 1848–1851*. London: Thames & Hudson, 1973.

Colvin, Christina, ed. *Maria Edgeworth in France and Switzerland: Selections from the Edgeworth Family Letters*. New York: Oxford University Press, 1979.

Cooke, Rose Terry. "Miss Lucinda." In *"How Celia Changed Her Mind" and Other Stories*, ed. Elizabeth Ammons, 151–81. New Brunswick, NJ: Rutgers University Press, 1986.

Cox, Rosemary D. "The Old Southwest: Humor, Tall Tales, and the Grotesque." In *A Companion to the Regional Literatures of America*, ed. Charles L. Crow, 247–65. Malden, MA: Blackwell, 2003.

Craig, Cairns. "Scotland and the Regional Novel." In *The Regional Novel in Britain and Ireland, 1800–1990*, ed. K. D. M. Snell, 221–56. Cambridge: Cambridge University Press, 1998.

Craig, David. *Scottish Literature and the Scottish People, 1680–1830*. London: Chatto & Windus, 1961.

Cutler, Evelyn Starr. "Representations of Maine Coast Dialect in the Work of Sarah Orne Jewett." Ph.D. dissertation, New York University, 1976.

Davys, Mary. *The Fugitive*. London: G. Sawbridge, 1705.

———. *The Works of Mrs. Davys*. 2 vols. London: H. Woodfall, 1725.

Deane, Seamus. *Strange Country: Modernity and Nationhood in Irish Writing since 1790*. Oxford: Oxford University Press, 1997.

Deleuze, Gilles, and Félix Guattari. *Kafka: Pour une littérature mineure*. Paris: Editions de Minuit, 1975.

Dickinson, Donna. *George Sand: A Brave Man — the Most Womanly Woman*. Oxford: Berg, 1988.

Dike, Donald A. "Notes on Local Color and Its Relation to Realism." *College English* 14, no. 2 (1952):81–8.

Doerr, Karin. "The Specter of Anti-Semitism in and around Annette von Droste-Hülshoff's *Judenbuche*." *German Studies Review* 17 (1994):447–71.

Dominick, Raymond H. *The Environmental Movement in Germany: Prophets and Pioneers 1871–1921*. Bloomington, IN: Indiana University Press, 1992.

Donovan, Josephine. *After the Fall: The Demeter-Persephone Myth in Wharton, Cather, and Glasgow*. University Park, PA: Pennsylvania State University Press, 1989.

———. "Breaking the Sentence: Local-Color Literature and Subjugated Knowledges." In *The (Other) American Traditions*, ed. Joyce W. Warren, 226–43. New Brunswick, NJ: Rutgers University Press, 1993.

———. "Nan Prince and the Golden Apples." *Colby Library Quarterly* 22, no. 1 (March 1986):17–27.

———. *New England Local Color Literature: A Women's Tradition*. New York: Ungar, 1983.

Dreyfus, Herbert L., and Paul Rabinow. *Michel Foucault: Beyond Structuralism and Hermeneutics*. Chicago, IL: University of Chicago Press, 1982.

Droste-Hülshoff, Annette von. *Die Judenbuche: Ein Sittengemälde aus dem gebirgigten Westphalen*, ed. Heinz Rölleke. Bad Homburg, DE: Gehlen, 1970.

———. "Bilder aus Westphalen." 1842. In *Gesammelte Werke*, 4 vols in 1. 4:175–220 Vaduz: Liechtenstein, 1948.

Duncan, Ian. Introduction to *Winter Evening Tales: Collected among the Cottagers in the South of Scotland*, by James Hogg, xi–xxvi. Edinburgh: Edinburgh University Press, 2002.

Eagleton, Terry. *Heathcliff and the Great Hunger: Studies in Irish Culture.* London: Verso, 1995.

———, et al. *Nationalism, Colonialism and Literature.* Minneapolis, MN: University of Minnesota Press, 1990.

Ebner-Eschenbach, Marie von. *Dorf- und Schlossgeschichten.* Berlin: Paetel, 1905.

———. "Die Unverstandene auf dem Dorfe." 1883. In *Dorf- und Schlossgeschichten*, 175–306. Berlin: Paetel, 1905.

Edgeworth, Maria. *The Absentee.* 1812. London: Penguin, 1999.

———. *Castle Rackrent.* 1800. New York: Norton, 1965.

———. *Ennui.* 1809. In *Castle Rackrent and Ennui.* London: Penguin, 1992.

———. "Essay on Irish Bulls." 1802. In *Tales and Novels.* 9 vols. 1:93–203. New York: Harper, 1835.

———. *Harrington.* 1817. In *Tales and Novels.* Vols. 17–18. New York: Harper, 1836.

———. *Ormond.* 1817. London: Penguin, 2000.

Elbert, Monika. "Nature, Magic, and History in Stowe and Scott." In *Transatlantic Stowe: Harriet Beecher Stowe and European Culture*, ed. Denise Kohn, et al., 46–64. Iowa City, IA: University of Iowa Press, 2006.

Erckmann, [Émile]-Chatrian, [Alexandre]. *Histoire d'un homme du peuple.* 1865. Oxford: Clarendon, 1915.

Ewell, Barbara, and Pam Menke, eds. *Southern Local Color: Stories of Region, Race and Gender.* Athens, GA: University of Georgia Press, 2002.

Fabre, Ferdinand. *Les Courbezon.* 1862. Geneva: Slatkine Reprints, 1980.

———. *Le Chevrier.* 1867. Paris: Bibliothèque-Charpentier, 1913.

Faderman, Lillian. "The Morbidification of Love between Women by Nineteenth-Century Sexologists." *Journal of Homosexuality* 4 (1978):73–90.

Farías, Victor. *Heidegger and Nazism.* Philadelphia, PA: Temple University Press, 1989.

Ferrier, Susan. *Marriage: A Novel.* 1818. London: Oxford University Press, 1971.

Ferris, Ina. *The Romantic National Tale and the Question of Ireland.* Cambridge: Cambridge University Press, 2002.

Fetterley, Judith, and Marjorie Pryse, eds. *American Women Regionalists, 1850–1910.* New York: Norton, 1992.

———. *Writing out of Place: Regionalism, Women, and American Literary Culture.* Urbana, IL: University of Illinois Press, 2003.

Fields, Annie, ed. *Letters of Sarah Orne Jewett.* Boston, MA: Houghton Mifflin, 1911.

Flanagan, Thomas. *The Irish Novelists, 1800–1850.* New York: Columbia University Press, 1959.

Foote, Stephanie. "The Cultural Work of American Regionalism." In *A Companion to the Regional Literatures of America*, ed. Charles L. Crow, 25–41. Malden, MA: Blackwell, 2003.

Foster, Edward. *Mary E. Wilkins Freeman.* New York: Hendricks House, 1956.

Foucault, Michel. *Histoire de la sexualité.* Vol. 1, *La Volonté de savoir.* Paris: Gallimard, 1976.

———. *Power/Knowledge: Selected Interviews and Other Writings*, ed. Colin Gordon. New York: Pantheon, 1980.

Franzos, Karl Emil. *Die Juden von Barnow: Geschichten.* 1876. 6th ed. Berlin: Concordia Deutsche Verlags-Inhalt, 1899.

[Freeman], Mary E. Wilkins. *A Humble Romance and Other Stories.* 1887. New York: Garrett, 1969.

———. *A New England Nun and Other Stories.* New York: Harper, 1891.

Galt, John. *Annals of the Parish: Or the Chronicle of Dalmailing during the Ministry of the Rev. Micah Balwhidder Written by Himself.* 1821. London: Oxford University Press, 1967.

———. *The Ayshire Legatees.* 1820–21. In *The Works of John Galt*, ed. D. S. Meldrum and William Roughead. 10 vols. 2:69–280. Edinburgh: John Grant, 1936.

———. *The Provost.* 1822. In *The Works of John Galt*, ed. D. S. Meldrum and William Roughead. 10 vols. Vol. 10. Edinburgh: John Grant, 1936.

Gandhi, Leela. *Postcolonial Theory: A Critical Introduction.* New York: Columbia University Press, 1998.

Gaston, Roger. *Maîtres du roman de terroir*. Paris: Editions André Silvaire, 1959.

Goldsmith, Oliver. *The Vicar of Wakefield*. 1766. Rahway, NJ: Merson, n.d.

Gollin, Rita K. *Annie Adams Fields: Woman of Letters*. Amherst, MA: University of Massachusetts Press, 2002.

Gotthelf, Jeremias. "Der Besenbinder von Rychiswyl." In *Kleinere Erzählungen*. 2 vols. 2:95–122. Erlenbach-Zurich, CH: Eugen Rentsch, 1966.

———. "Das Erdbeeri-Mareili." 1851. In *Kleinere Erzählungen*. 2 vols. 2:5–51. Erlenbach-Zurich, CH: Eugen Rentsch, 1966.

———. *Geld und Geist oder die Versöhnung*. 1844. Erlenbach-Zurich, CH: Eugen Rentsch, 1964.

———. "Marei, die Kuderspinnerin, und ihr Tröster." 1840. In *Sämtliche Werke*, vols 22–4 (in 1 vol.), 181–95. Erlenbach-Zurich, CH: Eugen Rentsch, 1921.

———. "Merkwürdige Reden gehört zu Krebsligen zwischen zwölf und ein Uhr in der Heiligen Nacht." In *Sämtliche Werke*, vol. 18. Erlenbach-Zurich, CH: Eugen Rentsch, 1921.

———. *Wie Anne Bäbi Jowäger haushaltet und wie es ihm mit dem Doktern geht*. 1843–44. Erlenbach-Zurich, CH: Eugen Rentsch, 1963.

———. "Wie fünf Mädchen im Branntwein jämmerlich umkommen: Eine merkwürdige Geschichte." 1838. In *Kleinere Erzählungen*. 2 vols. 2:609–91. Erlenbach-Zurich, CH: Eugen Rentsch, 1966.

———. *Zeitgeist und Berner Geist*. 1852. Erlenbach-Zurich, Switzerland: Eugen Rentsch, 1966.

Grant, Anne MacVicar. *Essays on the Superstitions of the Highlanders of Scotland*. 2 vols. 1811. N.p.: Norwood, 1975.

Gray, Richard T. "Red Herrings and Blue Smocks: Ecological Destruction, Commercialism, and Anti-Semitism in Annette von Droste-Hülshoff's *Die Judenbuche*." *German Studies Review* 26, no. 3 (2003):515–41.

Hall, S. C. *Sketches of Irish Character*. 1829. 3rd ed. London: Chatto & Windus, [1854].

Hamilton, Elizabeth. *The Cottagers of Glenburnie: A Tale for the Farmer's Fire-Side*. New York: E. Sargeant, 1808.

Harding, Sandra. *The Science Question in Feminism*. Ithaca, NY: Cornell University Press, 1986.

Hathaway, Lillie V. *German Literature of the Mid-Nineteenth Century in England and America as Reflected in the Journals 1840–1914*. Boston, MA: Chapman & Grimes, 1935.

Hebel, Johann Peter. *Erzählungen und Briefe*, ed. Helmuth Rabanus. Recklinghausen, Germany: Bitter, 1950.

———. "Der grosse Sanhedrin zu Paris." In *Poetische Werke*, 108–12. Munich: 1961. Available online at: <http://www.zeno.org/Literatur/M/Hebel,+Johann+Peter/Prosa>. Accessed 4 April 2009.

Hedrick, Joan D. *Harriet Beecher Stowe: A Life*. New York: Oxford University Press, 1994.

Heidegger, Martin. "Hölderlin and the Essence of Poetry." In *European Literary Theory and Practice*, ed. Vernon W. Gras. New York: Delta, 1973.

Hein, Jürgen. *Dorfgeschichte*. Stuttgart: J. B. Metzlersche, 1976.

Helfer, Martha B. "'Wer wagt es, eitlen Blutes Drang zu messen?': Reading Blood in Annette von Droste-Hülshoff's *Die Judenbuche*." *German Quarterly* 71, no. 3 (Summer 1998):228–53.

Hennig, John. "Goethe and the Edgeworths." *Modern Language Quarterly* 15, no. 4 (December 1954):366–71.

———. "Studien zur deutschsprachigen Irlandkunde im 19. Jahrhundert." *Deutsche Vierteljahrsschrift für Literaturwissenschaft und Geistesgeschichte* 47 (1973):167–79.

Hildrith, Margaret Holbrook. *Harriet Beecher Stowe: A Bibliography*. Hamden, CT: Archon, 1976.

Hogg, James. *Winter Evening Tales: Collected among the Cottagers in the South of Scotland*. 1820. Edinburgh: Edinburgh University Press, 2002.

———. "Further Anecdotes of the Shepherd's Dog." *Blackwood's Edinburgh Magazine* 2 (March 1818):621–6.

Horkheimer, Max, and Theodor Adorno. *Dialectic of Enlightenment*. 1944. New York: Continuum, 1988.

Hovenkamp, J. W. *Mérimée et la couleur locale: Contribution à l'étude de la couleur locale*. Paris: Societé d'Edition "Les Belles Lettres", 1928.

Hugo, Victor. *Toilers of the Sea*. New York: Harper, 1866.

———. *Travailleurs de la Mer*. 2 vols. Paris: Nelson, 1866.

Immermann, [Karl LeBrecht]. *Münchhausen: Eine Geschichte in Arabesken*. 1837–38. In *Werke*, ed. Benno von Wiese. 5 vols. Vol. 3. Frankfurt, Germany: Athenäum, 1972.

Jewett, Sarah Orne. "An Autumn Holiday." In *Country By-Ways*, 139–62. Boston, MA: Houghton Mifflin, 1881.

———. *A Country Doctor*. Boston, MA: Houghton Mifflin, 1884.

———. *Country By-Ways*. Boston, MA: Houghton Mifflin, 1881.

———. *The Country of the Pointed Firs*. Boston, MA: Houghton Mifflin, 1896.

———. "The Courting of Sister Wisby." In *The King of Folly Island and Other People*, 50–80. Boston, MA: Houghton Mifflin, 1888.

———. "The Flight of Betsey Lane." In *The Country of the Pointed Firs and Other Stories*, ed. Willa Cather, 172–93. Garden City, NY: Doubleday, 1956.

———. Interview (Anon). *Philadelphia Press*, 18 August 1895. In *The Country of the Pointed Firs and the Dunnet Landing Stories*, ed. Deborah Carlin, 280–6. Peterborough, Ontario, CA: Broadview, 2009.

———. "Miss Debby's Neighbors." In *The Mate of the Daylight, and Friends Ashore*, 190–209. Boston, MA: Houghton Mifflin, 1884.

———. Preface to *Deephaven*, 2nd ed. 1893. South Berwick, ME: Old Berwick Historical Society, 1993.

———. "River Driftwood." In *Country By-Ways*, 1–33. Boston, MA: Houghton Mifflin, 1881.

———. "A White Heron." In *The Country of the Pointed Firs and Other Stories*, ed. Willa Cather, 161–71. Garden City, NY: Doubleday, 1956.

[Johnstone, Christian Isobel.] *Clan-Albin: A National Tale*. 4 vols in 1. Philadelphia, PA: Edward Earle, 1815.

Jordan, David M. *New World Regionalism: Literature in the Americas*. Toronto: University of Toronto Press, 1994.

Juker, Bee. *Wörterbuch zu den Werken von Jeremias Gotthelf*. Erlenbach-Zurich, CH: Eugen Rentsch, 1972.

Kahn, Lothar. *Between Two Worlds: A Cultural History of German-Jewish Writers*. Ames, IA: Iowa State University Press, 1993.

Kamerbeek, Jr., Jan. *Tenants et aboutissants de la notion 'couleur locale'*. Utrecht, NL: Instituut Algemene Literatuurwetenschap, 1962.

Keller, Gottfried. "Das Verlorene Lachen." In *Die Leute von Seldwyla*. In *Kellers Werke*, ed. Hans Richter. Vol. 2, 226–321. Berlin und Weimar: Aufbau-Verlag, 1966.

Kirkham, E. Bruce. *The Building of "Uncle Tom's Cabin."* Knoxville, TN: University of Tennessee Press, 1977.

[Kirkland, Caroline]. *A New Home — Who'll Follow? Or, Glimpses of Western Life*. 1839. New York: Garrett, 1969.

Kohn, Denise, *et al.*, eds. *Transatlantic Stowe: Harriet Beecher Stowe and European Culture*. Iowa City, IA: University of Iowa Press, 2006.

Kompert, Leopold. "Der Dorfgeher." 1851. In *Der Dorfgeher: Geschichten aus dem Ghetto*, ed. Florian Krobb, 45–90. Göttingen, DE: Wallstein, 1997.

Leadbeater, Mary. *The Annals of Ballitore*. In *The Leadbeater Papers*. 2 Vols. 1862. London: Routledge/Thoemmes, 1998.

———. *Cottage Dialogues among the Irish Peasantry*. Philadelphia: Johnson & Warner, 1811.

Lears, Jackson. *No Place of Grace: Antimodernism and the Transformation of American Culture, 1880–1920*. New York: Pantheon, 1981.

[Lee, Eliza Buckminster]. *Sketches of a New England Village in the Last Century*. Boston, MA: James Monroe, 1838.

Le Roy, Eugène. *Le Moulin du Frau*. 1891. Paris: E. Fasquelle, 1905.

———. *Jacquou le croquant*. 1895. Bordeaux: Editions Sud Ouest, 1997.

Lewis, C. S. *English Literature in the Sixteenth Century Excluding Drama*. Oxford: Clarendon, 1954.

Lloyd, David. *Nationalism and Minor Literature: James Clarence Mangan and the Emergence of Irish Cultural Nationalism*. Berkeley, CA: University of California Press, 1987.

Lukács, Georg. *The Historical Novel*, trans. Hannah and Stanley Mitchell. Harmondsworth, UK: Penguin, 1969.

MacCarthy, B. G. "Irish Regional Novelists of the Early Nineteenth Century." *Dublin Magazine* 21, no. 1 (January–March 1946):26–32.

———. "Irish Regional Novelists of the Early Nineteenth Century." *Dublin Magazine* 21, no. 2 (July–September 1946):28–37.

MacDonald, Edgar E., ed. *The Education of the Heart: The Correspondence of Rachel Mordecai Lazarus and Maria Edgeworth*. Chapel Hill, NC: University of North Carolina Press, 1977.

MacLachlan, Robin W. "Scott and Hogg: Friendship and Literary Influence." In *Scott and His Influence*, ed. J. H. Alexander and David Hewitt, 331–40. Aberdeen, UK: Association for Scottish Literary Studies, 1983.

Maclean, Grace Edith. *"Uncle Tom's Cabin" in Germany*. New York: D. Appleton, 1910.

Magnusson, Magnus. *Scotland: The Story of a Nation*. New York: Grove, 2000.

Martino, Alberto. *Die Deutsche Leihbibliothek: Geschichte einer literarischen Institution (1756–1914)*. Wiesbaden, DE: Otto Harrassowitz, 1990.

Marx, Karl, and Friedrich Engels. *Manifesto of the Communist Party*. New York: International, 1948.

Mayer, Sylvia. *Naturethik und Neuengland-Regionalliteratur: Harriet Beecher Stowe, Rose Terry Cooke, Sarah Orne Jewett, Mary E. Wilkins Freeman*. Heidelberg, DE: Universitätsverlag Winter, 2004.

McInnis, Edward. "Zschokke's *Das Goldmacherdorf* and the Development of the *Dorfgeschichte* in the 1840s." *Orbis Litterarum* 50, no. 3 (1995):129–41.

———. "Realism, History and the Nation: The Reception of the 'Waverley' Novels in Germany in the 19th Century." *New German Studies* 16, no. 1 (1990–91):39–51.

McMahon, Helen. *Criticism of Fiction: A Study of Trends in the Atlantic Monthly 1857–1898*. New York: AMS, 1973.

McNeil, Kenneth. *Scotland, Britain, Empire: Writing the Highlands, 1760–1860*. Columbus, OH: Ohio State University Press, 2007.

Mecklenburg, Norbert. *Erzählte Provinz: Regionalismus und Moderne im Roman*. Königstein, DE: Athanäum, 1982.

Metz, Joseph. "Austrian Inner Colonialism and the Visibility of Difference in Stifter's *Die Narrenburg*." *PMLA* 121, no. 5 (October 2006):1475–92.

Minder, Robert. "Johann Peter Hebel und die französische Heimatliteratur." In *Dichter in der Gesellschaft: Erfahrungen mit deutscher und französischer Literatur*, 108–39. Frankfurt: Insel, 1966.

Mitford, Mary Russell. *Our Village: Sketches of Rural Character and Scenery*. 5 vols. London: G. & W. B. Whittaker, 1824–32.

[Moir, D. M.] *The Life of Mansie Waugh, Tailor in Dalkeith, Written by Himself*. Edinburgh and London: William Blackwood, [1828].

Morgan, Lady [Sydney Owenson]. *Florence Macarthy: An Irish Tale*. 4 vols. 1818. New York: Garland, 1979.

———. *O'Donnel: A National Tale*. London: H. Colburn, 1814.

———. *The O'Briens and the O'Flahertys: A National Tale*. 1827. New York: Garland, 1979.

———. *Patriotic Sketches of Ireland*. Baltimore, MD: Geo. Dobbin & Murphy; Callender & Wills, 1809.

———. *The Wild Irish Girl*. 1806. London: Pandora: 1986.

———. "Woman and Her Master." In *Unsung Champions of Women*, ed. Mary Cohart, 151–64. Albuquerque, NM: University of New Mexico Press, 1975.

Nettels, Elsa. *Language, Race, and Social Class in Howells' America*. Lexington, KY: University Press of Kentucky, 1988.

Ó Gallchoir, Clíona. "Uncle Tom's Cabin and the Irish National Tale." In *Transatlantic Stowe: Harriet Beecher Stowe and European Culture*, ed. Denise Kohn, *et al.*, 24–45. Iowa City, IA: University of Iowa Press, 2006.

O'Neill, Patrick. "Image and Reception: The German Fortunes of Maria Edgeworth, Lady Morgan, Thomas Moore, and Charles Maturin." *Canadian Journal of Irish Studies* 6, no. 1 (1980):36–49.

Ong, Walter J. *Orality and Literacy.* London: Routledge, 1988.

Parks, George B., and Ruth Z. Temple. *The Literature of the World in English Translation: A Bibliography.* Vol. 3, *The Romance Literatures.* Pt. 2, *French Literature.* New York: Ungar, 1970.

Parsons, Coleman O. *Witchcraft and Demonology in Scott's Fiction, with Chapters on the Supernatural in Scottish Literature.* Edinburgh: Oliver & Boyd, 1964.

Perry, Thomas Sergeant. "Berthold Auerbach." *Atlantic Monthly* 34, no. 204 (October 1874):433–40.

———. "George Sand." *Atlantic Monthly* 38, no. 228 (October 1876):441–51.

[Pestalozzi, Johann Heinrich]. *Lienhard und Gertrud.* Zurich: n.p., 1781.

Potet, Michel. "Couleur locale: Thème et version." *Revue de littérature comparée* 49 (1975):5–18.

Puknat, Siegfried B. "Auerbach and Channing." *PMLA* 72, no. 5 (December 1957):962–76.

Rafroidi, Patrick. *Irish Literature in English: The Romantic Period (1789–1850).* Atlantic Highlands, NJ: Humanities Press, 1980.

Rank, Josef. *Aus dem Böhmerwalde und volkskundliche Beiträge aus Ranks übrigen Werken,* ed. Karl Wagner. Prague: J. G. Calve, 1917.

Reed, James. *Sir Walter Scott: Landscape and Locality.* London: Athlone, 1980.

Renza, Louis A. *"A White Heron" and the Question of Minor Literature.* Madison, WI: University of Wisconsin Press, 1984.

Richter, Bodo L. O. "Genesis and Fortunes of the Term 'Couleur Locale': A Review Guide." *Comparative Literature Studies* 3 (1966):299–308.

Robertson, Ritchie. *The "Jewish Question" in German Literature, 1749–1939: Emancipation and Its Discontents.* New York: Oxford University Press, 1999.

Rogers, Nancy E. "Sand's Peasant Heroines: from Victim to Entrepreneur, from 'Connaissance' to 'Idée,' from *Jeanne* to *Nanon.*" *Nineteenth-Century French Studies* 24 (Spring–Summer 1996):347–60.

Rütte, Albert von. *Erklärung der schwierigen dialektischen Ausdrücke in Jeremias Gotthelfs gesammelten Schriften.* Berlin: Julius Springer,1858.

Sagarra, Eda, and Ulrike Tanzer. "Die Rezeption irischer Autorinnen in Deutschland 1815–1848." In *Beiträge zur Rezeption der britischen und irischen Literatur des 19. Jahrhunderts im deutschsprachigen Raum,* 79–91. Amsterdam, NL, and Atlanta, GA: Rodopi, 2000.

Said, Edward W. *Culture and Imperialism.* New York: Knopf, 1993.

———. "Yeats and Decolonization." In *Nationalism, Colonialism and Literature,* ed. Terry Eagleton, *et al.,* 67–95. Minneapolis, MN: University of Minnesota Press, 1990.

Sand, George. "Au Village." In *Dernières Pages,* 277–83. Paris: Michel Lévy, 1877.

———. *François le champi.* 1850. Paris: Nelson/Calmann Lévy, 1928.

———. *Jeanne.* 1844. 2 vols in 1. Brussels: Meline, Caus & Co., 1844.

———. *Légendes rustiques.* 1857. Paris: Édition Libres-Hallier, 1980.

———. *Les Maîtres sonneurs.* 1853. Paris: Calmann-Lévy, 1928.

———. *La Mare au diable.* 1846. Paris: Nelson/Calmann Lévy, 1931.

———. *Mauprat.* 1837. Paris: Nelson/Calmann Lévy, 1930.

———. *Le Meunier d'Angibault.* 1845. Paris: Calmann Lévy, 1888. Available online at: <http://newfirstsearch.oclc.org> 9 October 2007. Accessed 20 June 2009.

———. *La Petite Fadette.* 1849. Paris: Livre de Poche, 1973.

Schutz, Alexander Herman. *The Peasant Vocabulary in the Works of George Sand. University of Missouri Studies,* 2, no. 1 (1 January 1927):114.

Scott, James C. *Seeing Like a State: How Certain Schemes to Improve the Human Condition Have Failed.* New Haven, CT: Yale University Press, 1998.

Scott, Walter. *The Antiquary.* 1816. London: Penguin, 1998.

———. *The Bride of Lammermoor.* 1819. Oxford: Oxford University Press, 1998.

———. *Guy Mannering; Or, the Astrologer.* 1815. London: Penguin, 2003.

———. *Rob Roy.* 1817. New York: Signet, 1995.

———. *Waverley; Or, 'Tis Sixty Years Since.* 1814. London: Penguin, 1972.

Sebald, W. G. "Westwärts-Ostwärts: Aporien deutschsprachiger Ghettogeschichten." *Literatur und Kritik*. No. 233–4 (1989):161–77.

Shain, Charles E. "John Galt's America." *American Quarterly* 8 (1956):254–63.

Sloan, Barry. *The Pioneers of Anglo-Irish Fiction, 1800–1850*. Gerrards Cross, Buckinghamshire, UK: Colin Smythe, 1986.

Smith-Rosenberg, Carroll. *Disorderly Conduct: Visions of Gender in Victorian America*. New York: Knopf, 1985.

Snell, K. D. M., ed. *The Regional Novel in Britain and Ireland, 1800–1900*. Cambridge: Cambridge University Press, 1998.

Söderlind, Sylvia. *Margin/Alias: Language and Colonization in Canadian and Québécois Fiction*. Toronto: University of Toronto Press, 1991.

Souvestre, Émile. *Contes et nouvelles*. 1832. Paris: Michel Lévy, 1877.

———. *Le Foyer breton: Contes et récits populaires*. 1844. Paris: Nelson, n.d.

Stauben, Daniel. *Scènes de la vie juive en Alsace*. Paris: Michel Lévy, 1860.

Stifter, Adalbert. "Der Condor." 1840. In *Gesammelte Werke*. Vol. 1, *Studien*, 9–36. Wiesbaden, DE: Insel-Verlag, 1959.

———. *Gesammelte Werke*. Wiesbaden, Germany: Insel-Verlag, 1959.

———. *Das Haidedorf*. 1840. In *Gesammelte Werke*. Vol. 1, *Studien*, 169–204. Wiesbaden, DE: Insel-Verlag, 1959.

———. *Die Mappe meines Urgrossvaters*. 1841. In *Gesammelte Werke*. Vol. 1, *Studien*, 441–674. Wiesbaden, DE: Insel-Verlag, 1959.

Stowe, Harriet Beecher. "The Author's Introduction." *The Writings of Harriet Beecher Stowe*. Vol. 1, liii–xc. 1896. New York: AMS, 1967.

———. *The Mayflower; Or, Sketches of Scenes and Characters among the Descendants of the Pilgrims*. New York: Harper, 1843.

———. *The Minister's Wooing*. 1859. Ridgewood, NJ: Gregg, 1968.

———. "A New England Sketch." 1834. In (under the title "Uncle Lot") *Regional Sketches: New England and Florida*, ed. John R. Adams, 31–55. New Haven, CT: College and University Press, 1972.

———. *Oldtown Folks*. 1869. Boston, MA: Houghton Mifflin, 1894.

———. *The Pearl of Orr's Island: A Story of the Coast of Maine*. 1862. Boston, MA: Houghton Mifflin, 1896.

———. "Sir Walter Scott and His Dogs." *Our Young Folks* (November 1865):722–9.

———. *Uncle Tom's Cabin; Or, Life among the Lowly*. 1852. New York: Penguin, 1981.

Thompson, John B. *Studies in the Theory of Ideology*. Berkeley, CA: University of California Press, 1984.

Töpffer, [Rudolphe]. *Nouvelles genevoises*. 1839. 2 vols in 1. Brussels: Alphonse Lebègue, 1853.

Van Tieghem, Paul. "Le Roman rustique (Suisse-Allemagne-France-Angleterre): 1840–1860." *Revue des cours et conférences*, 2nd ser. No. 9 (30 March 1932):695–706; (15 April 1932):1–19; (15 May 1932):264–75.

Vernois, Paul. *Le Roman rustique de George Sand à Ramuz: Ses Tendences et son évolution (1860–1925)*. Paris: A. G. Nizet, 1962.

Waidson, H. W. *Jeremias Gotthelf: An Introduction to the Swiss Novelist*. Westport, CT: Greenwood, 1978.

———. "Jeremias Gotthelf's Reception in Britain and America." *Modern Language Review* 43 (1948):223–38.

Warfel, Harry R., and G. Harrison Orians, eds. *American Local-Color Stories*. New York: American Book Co., 1941.

Weber, Betty Nance. "Droste's *Judenbuche*: Westphalia in International Context." *Germanic Review* 50 (1976):200–12.

Weill, Alexandre. *Sittengemälde aus dem elsässischen Volksleben*. 2 vols. in 1. Stuttgart: Franckh'sche, 1847.

———. *Histoires de village*. Paris: Dentu, 1853.

Westbrook, Perry D. *Acres of Flint: Writers of Rural New England, 1870–1900*, rev. ed. Washington, DC: Scarecrow, 1981.

Wey, Francis. *Le Bouquet de cerises: Roman rustique*. Paris: D. Giraud & J. Dagneau, 1852.

[Whitty, Michael]. *Tales of Irish Life, Illustrative of the Manners, Customs, and Condition of the People*. 2 vols. London: J. Robins, 1824.

Wilson, Forrest. *Crusader in Crinoline: The Life of Harriet Beecher Stowe*. Philadelphia, PA: Lippincott, 1941.

Wollstonecraft, Mary. *A Vindication of the Rights of Woman*. 1792. Harmondsworth, UK: Penguin, 1975.

Yeats, W. B., comp. *Representative Irish Tales*. 1891. Gerrards Cross, Buckinghamshire, UK: Colin Smythe, 1979.

Zellweger, Rudolf. *Les Débuts du roman rustique: Suisse, Allemagne, France, 1836–1856*. Paris: Librairie E. Droz, 1941.

Zimmerman, Michael E. *Heidegger's Confrontation with Modernity: Technology, Politics and Art*. Bloomington, IN: Indiana University Press, 1990.

Zschokke, Johann Heinrich Daniel. *Das Goldmacher-Dorf*. In *Deutsche National-Litteratur*, ed. Joseph Kürschner. Vol. 2, *Erzählende Prosa der klassischen Periode*, ed. Felix Bobertag, 239–351. Berlin and Suttgart: W. Spemann, [1873?].

Index